THE THRIVING LAWYER

The Thriving Lawyer: A Multidimensional Model of Well-Being for a Sustainable Legal Profession is based on an innovative model, grounded in science. This book serves as a resource for promoting well-being and culture-change in the legal community by educating about pertinent issues impacting lawyers, and how to address them. It is a roadmap, highlighting the many overarching and interconnected aspects of well-being, and enabling readers to identify and target the issues most relevant to their unique situations.

Along with practical strategies, the book provides a big-picture framework, illustrating how the many intersecting individual and organizational factors which influence well-being are all related, yet separate and distinct. The framework provides a foundation for creating change, and where you focus first will depend on the needs, the situation, and any unique challenges faced by you or your organization.

The Thriving Lawyer explains why, in addition to self-care, change is needed on the organizational level in terms of workplace culture and policies, as well as normalizing self-care and eradicating stigma. This book is intended to benefit individual lawyers, their organizations, and the professionals who support them, by educating, motivating, and promoting self-care and healthy work environments.

Traci Cipriano, JD, PhD, is a clinical psychologist and formerly practicing attorney who has been utilizing her education, training, research, and experience to address and promote well-being and culture-change within the legal community since 2005. In recognition of her contributions to lawyer well-being, she was named a *2022 Connecticut Legal Awards Game Changer Honoree*. Dr Cipriano is in independent practice and is also an Assistant Clinical Professor in the Yale School of Medicine, Department of Psychiatry, Law and Psychiatry Division, and a former Consulting Clinical Supervisor in the Yale Psychology Department. She has held leadership and governance positions in the American Psychological Association, the Connecticut Psychological Association, and the Connecticut Bar Association. She was the recipient of the *2015 Distinguished Contribution to the Practice of Psychology Award* from the Connecticut Psychological Association. www.thethrivinglawyerbook.com

"Through accurate insights and analysis that demonstrate an intimate understanding of the challenges so many committed attorneys face, *The Thriving Lawyer* offers a helpful roadmap for critical individual and institutional change needed to improve lawyer well-being. This book is a must-read for both attorneys and HR professionals across all legal organizations."

—**Claire Coleman**, *State of Connecticut Consumer Counsel; former Biglaw firm associate, non-profit and government attorney*

"The interest in wellness and self-care has gained unprecedented momentum among professionals in general, and lawyers in particular. The available resources, however, tend to be repetitive and non-directive. With this book, Dr Cipriano has filled a critical void through a scientifically based model of wellness as a way of life, the basis for decision-making, and the guide for actions. She has seamlessly integrated philosophy, psychological research, and pragmatic interventions within a persuasive narrative about making a commitment to well-being. Although this book will be of interest to any professional, Dr Cipriano incorporates her education and experience as an attorney to address the unique challenges in the practice of law. Practicing attorneys, law students and law schools, and mental health professionals who advise and counsel the legal community will gain insights and strategies for promoting genuine well-being.

Dr Cipriano introduces a model of well-being that goes far beyond usual stand-alone recommendations for specific behaviors. After reading her book, I realized that I cannot attain well-being through any routine of meditation and yoga or any other add-on activity. True wellness is a state of being that affects all life domains; true wellness encompasses all aspects of professional and personal life.

Dr Cipriano does not stop with her unique theoretical model of well-being; she incorporates in an informative, compelling narrative, pathways for translating the concept of well-being into pragmatic actions. Lawyers, law students and law schools, and those who give counsel and treatment to the legal community will find this book a valued and lasting resource."

—**Madelon V. Baranoski**, *PhD, Yale School of Medicine*

THE THRIVING LAWYER

A MULTIDIMENSIONAL MODEL OF WELL-BEING FOR A SUSTAINABLE LEGAL PROFESSION

TRACI CIPRIANO

informa law
from Routledge

Designed cover image: Skylight Collective, Portland, Oregon, USA

First published 2024
by Informa Law from Routledge
4 Park Square, Milton Park, Abingdon, Oxon OX14 4RN

and by Informa Law from Routledge
605 Third Avenue, New York, NY 10158

Informa Law from Routledge is an imprint of the Taylor & Francis Group, an informa business

British Library Cataloguing-in-Publication Data
A catalogue record for this book is available from the British Library

Library of Congress Cataloging-in-Publication Data
Names: Cipriano, Traci, author.
Title: The thriving lawyer: a multidimensional model of well-being for
a sustainable legal profession/Traci Cipriano.
Description: Abingdon, Oxon [UK]; New York, NY: Routledge, 2023. |
Includes bibliographical references and index. | Summary: – Provided by publisher.
Identifiers: LCCN 2023001011 (print) | LCCN 2023001012 (ebook) |
ISBN 9781032258942 (hardback) | ISBN 9781032258959 (paperback) |
ISBN 9781003285519 (ebook)
Subjects: LCSH: Practice of law. | Lawyers. | Happiness.
Classification: LCC K120 .C57 2023 (print) | LCC K120 (ebook) |
DDC 340.023–dc23/eng/20230403
LC record available at https://lccn.loc.gov/2023001011
LC ebook record available at https://lccn.loc.gov/2023001012

ISBN: 978-1-032-25894-2 (hbk)
ISBN: 978-1-032-25895-9 (pbk)
ISBN: 978-1-003-28551-9 (ebk)

DOI: 10.4324/9781003285519

Typeset in Times New Roman
by Deanta Global Publishing Services, Chennai, India

To my daughters, Audrey and Olivia:
May their lives reflect a full honeycomb of well-being.

CONTENTS

CONTENTS

10 Creating Change   173

LIST OF ILLUSTRATIONS

FIGURES

TABLE

LIST OF BOXES

PREFACE

Many aspiring lawyers are drawn to the law by their desire to bring order to the chaos of humanity. The law is a noble profession, comprising individuals who strive for justice and fairness. Lawyers are essential to the function of society, but the profession can be taxing on mind, body, and spirit. I had the privilege of being a practicing lawyer and have much admiration for the profession. I was also fortunate in that I was able to return to graduate school to obtain my doctorate in clinical psychology. What I learned as a doctoral student provided me with a framework for understanding the burdens of the law which can detract from a sense of professional satisfaction, passion for one's work, as well as physical, mental, and emotional vitality. Recognizing the importance of sustainability of the profession and continuing to attract—and retain—top talent, this book aims to help you and your organization promote well-being at both the individual and organizational levels.

When discussing the challenges of promoting well-being in the legal community, I have shared a story from graduate school:

> While interviewing with a prominent psychologist, I was asked about my dissertation research. I began to enthusiastically share details about my then-cutting-edge study, which involved looking at relationships among work–life balance, perfectionism and optimism, and physical and mental health outcomes in attorneys. Before long, he interrupted me, holding up his hand, and said, "Hold on. Who the hell cares about attorneys?"

Initially, I was shocked. But once I had a chance to reflect on his comment, I realized that his sentiments were probably more universal than I would have liked to acknowledge. Lawyers are viewed by many as a privileged class, whose rewards are substantial enough to balance any adversity the profession creates.

This exchange brought forth the realization that few people, if any, outside the legal community were paying much attention to lawyer struggles. It is up to the profession itself to acknowledge and unequivocally address some of the unhealthy aspects of legal culture. Recognizing that the legal profession is a challenging one, what can be done to evolve, adapt, and make the most of the situation, as well as promote a thriving profession?

ACKNOWLEDGEMENTS

This book has been years in the making, the idea developing over time with my increasing appreciation for the many factors involved in promoting lawyer well-being. That appreciation developed thanks to many individuals, beginning with my primary dissertation advisor, the late George J. Allen, who was generous with his time and mentorship, as well as dissertation mentor Janet Barnes-Farrell, who welcomed me into her lab to learn more about work–family conflict. I am grateful to the Connecticut Bar Association Young Lawyers Section, and then-Chair Daniel Schwartz, for providing me with a platform to introduce my research and collect data. I am also grateful to Stacy Smith Walsh for her tremendous enthusiasm and support during that time with data collection, and going forward. There have been many other people along the way who have in one way or another supported my learning, growth, and development in this area, in particular Madelon Baranoski, Karen DeMeola, Beth Griffin, Michael Marciano, and Amy Lin Meyerson, as well as others who have supported my work and shared their thoughts, experiences and insights as legal professionals, for which I am very grateful. Thank you to my editor, Guy Loft, for his unwavering faith in this project. I also must thank my dedicated reviewers, Madelon Baranoski, Melanie Capobianco, and Greer Spatz, for their time and feedback. I am ever grateful to my family and friends who are always there to cheer, listen, and bring some levity. Much gratitude to my brother, David Cipriano, for his cover design. And a special thank you to my husband, Michael Cummings, for his unending support and encouragement.

Permission granted from Glasbergen Cartoon Service for use of Randy Glasbergen's apropos "Stress is for wimps!" cartoon.

CHAPTER 1

Introduction to Lawyer Well-Being and a Guide to Reading This Book

Lawyer well-being is a hot topic, and you are likely flooded with information about many different strategies and approaches. But how do you make sense of all that information? And is there more to it? *The Thriving Lawyer: A Multidimensional Model of Well-Being for a Sustainable Legal Profession* is based on an innovative and comprehensive model which illustrates the intersection of individual and organizational factors related to well-being, providing a guiding framework for readers by pulling together these important elements in one place. Each chapter stands alone and can be read as time and interest permit. This book does not need to be read cover-to-cover in one sitting, though you certainly can do so.

Why read a book about lawyer well-being? Lawyers ensure all aspects of society—business, government, non-profit, personal—are functioning in accordance with a set of predefined values related to fairness and efficiency. Lawyers protect us from injustice and preserve our rights and freedoms. At the same time, the profession is struggling like never before. Research and surveys related to lawyer stress, depression, substance use, healthcare utilization, and suicide all suggest that law is a particularly stressful profession, and lawyer stress often arises as a result of the nature of the work, especially in combination with common lawyer traits.

As of 2022, a multitude of surveys have been conducted in the legal community, including in the US, Canada, the UK, Australia, and Singapore, and by the International Bar Association. These surveys confirm what we have long suspected: The legal profession is universally a high-pressure profession dominated by competitive perfectionists, with little room for error, low psychological safety, and high rates of burnout, depression, anxiety, and substance misuse.

Advances in technology, once revered as products which would make our lives easier, particularly smartphones and mobile devices, have further blurred the line between work and home life. This lack of separation of professional and personal roles has limited attorney "downtime," while at the same time arguably exacerbating the negative effects of certain pre-existing personal traits and professional stressors, with an overall negative

 DOI: 10.4324/9781003285519-1

impact on lawyer well-being. It is incumbent on the legal profession to acknowledge there is a problem, own it, and begin to address it. Change is slow and imperfect, and yet it must begin somewhere. At the very least this change needs to begin at the top, with leaders in the law, law firms, and law schools.

There are myriad occupational risk factors faced by lawyers, such as time pressures, billing pressures, rainmaking pressures, the adversarial nature of profession, and technology. Lawyers are particularly susceptible to the disadvantages of modern technology—always accessible by phone, email, or text, 24/7, 365. Common pressures, such as multiple competing deadlines, time management and organizational difficulties, unreasonable opposing counsel, office politics, and personal crises over time can lead to chronic stress. In addition, depending on practice area or pro bono work, lawyers often experience compassion fatigue, burnout, and vicarious trauma.

If there is a sincere desire to improve lawyer well-being, the focus needs to be on prevention and on promoting wellness before someone reaches a crisis point, begins abusing alcohol or drugs, or even contemplates suicide; or before work suffers because thinking is not as quick, clear, and sharp; before physical illness takes its toll; or before relationships with colleagues, significant others, friends, and children deteriorate. Stress is toxic, and it permeates all aspects of our lives and our work. It is easy for conscientious, competitive, hard-driving individuals to take for granted our minds, our bodies, and our relationships; but if we do not tend to them, they will suffer, along with our work quality and productivity.

All lawyers, if they have not done so already, need to begin to think about how they deal with the stress of the profession and what strategy or strategies help to reduce their stress and improve their individual well-being. We are not going to eliminate the stress of the legal profession (nor do we want to, as some degree of stress is adaptive, see Chapter 3, Attention to Overall Physical and Mental Health), though changes in organizational culture can be made to mitigate it. It is no longer adequate to expect individual lawyers to figure everything out on their own, even after attending a few workshops. And realistically speaking, it isn't possible or adaptive for individual lawyers to change their approach to self-care, managing competing work and home life demands, and relating to others in the workplace, when the overall culture does not support them in doing so. Broad cultural change within the legal community is needed, and it is essential that this change come from the top down, promoted and role-modeled by senior lawyers, not just human resources staff.

If you are an organizational leader, I ask you to begin the dialogue, or continue it, and if you are early or mid-career, I ask you to suggest such a conversation to your leaders. If you do not know where to begin, start with this book.

What Can You Expect from This Book?

The goal of this book is to promote well-being and culture-change in the legal community by educating about some of the most pertinent issues impacting well-being on individual and organizational levels, and how to begin to address them. This book is intended to benefit individual lawyers, their organizations, and professionals who support them, by educating, motivating, and promoting self-care and healthy work environments. Consider it a roadmap, highlighting the many overarching and interconnected aspects, and enabling readers to identify and target the issues most relevant to their unique situations.

With this goal in mind, the book is written to be user-friendly and easy to read, allowing you to focus on those chapters most relevant at any particular moment. The content is based on psychological science, as well as my education, training, and experiences as both a psychologist and a formerly practicing lawyer. While each chapter will include a bibliography at the end, the goal is to provide you with an easy reading experience, and not distract you with references, footnotes, or endnotes. Throughout the book I have inserted anonymous quotes, from lawyers with whom I have crossed paths, related to the topic within each chapter.

BOX 1.1 FUN FACT

The societal need for, and value of, lawyers has been officially recognized in the US since the late 1700s, when America's first law schools, the Litchfield Law School in Connecticut and William & Mary Law School in Virginia, were established. Law schools had been in existence centuries earlier in Europe and elsewhere outside of the US. It is worth noting that the issue of which law school was in fact first in the US is not without controversy, but historical sources suggest the Litchfield Law School was the first applied/apprenticeship teaching institution whereas William & Mary Law School was the first academic/professorial program.

As a result of the historically limited interest in lawyer well-being, funding for quality research projects addressing the lawyer experience and how to best promote healthy, productive attorneys and workplaces has also historically been minimal. Therefore, the research basis of the many aspects of well-being as defined in *The Thriving Lawyer: A Multidimensional Model of Well-Being for a Sustainable Legal Profession* often reflects the application of research conducted in the general population to the legal community, in addition to limited lawyer-specific research.

Lawyer Well-Being Needs to Begin in Law School

Let's start at the beginning. Lawyer well-being begins in law school. In addition to indoctrination with foundational caselaw and instruction on how to read and interpret it, first year law students are also taught how to "think like a lawyer"—rational, practical, without emotions that cloud judgment. Law students quickly learn that emotions are "bad"; they represent weakness and negatively influence judgment and competence. By implication, emotions are to be avoided or suppressed. This learning, when combined with the hard-driving, time-urgent, perfectionistic, and competitive traits found in many law students, can be a recipe for un-wellness. While first year students, also known as 1Ls in the US and Canada, are learning to think like lawyers, they also need to be educated on the importance of maintaining healthy self-care habits and have adequate on-campus resources to promote well-being. Fortunately, a good number of law schools now recognize this need, offering resources and programming, but the same top-down principles apply.

In addition, many law students arrive at law school with honorable goals of promoting social justice and equity, preserving the environment and the habitability of Earth, and slowing climate change, or simply empowering the underdog, whomever that may be. Very quickly however, in the hierarchical law school environment, students are lured toward opportunities which embody status and power. In addition, burgeoning law school debt may disproportionately influence career decisions based on economics rather than passions. As a result, many young lawyers find themselves seeking prestige, clout, and financial gain in corporate law jobs working most hours of the day and week, ignoring idealistic longings, and suppressing or self-medicating any emotions or feelings of dissatisfaction.

What Is Health, and Does It Depend on Whom You Ask?

The World Health Organization (WHO) defines "health" as "a state of complete physical, mental and social well-being and not merely the absence of disease or infirmity." David Misselbrook, GP, Dean Emeritus of the Royal Society of Medicine, wrote about the conceptualization of health in the medical profession in 2014:

> Could health be a more positive concept? Can we go beyond facts and admit values into our concept of health? Dietrich Bonhoeffer defined health as "the strength to be." Bonhoeffer was saying that health is the ability to pursue our life story without insurmountable obstruction from illness. Unless I am an Olympic skier I can be healthy even after the loss of a leg. If I am Olympic skier I can regain health—I can still flourish—by seeking the courage to rewrite my life script. Thus health can be seen as the ability to flourish without being unduly impeded by illness or disability or, if necessary, by overcoming illness or disability.

Misselbrook raises important questions about how we view health and whether we can take a more positive, glass-half-full approach to viewing individual circumstances. I would argue the same applies to lawyers, their own individual well-being, and law firm culture.

What Is Thriving?

The WHO defines "mental health" as "a state of well-being in which an individual realizes his or her own abilities, can cope with the normal stresses of life, can work productively and is able to make a contribution to his or her community." This definition evokes the notion of flourishing, which, according to Professor Corey Keyes, in turn reflects the presence of "positive feelings and positive function in life." Moreover, the US Surgeon General defines "mental health" as "a state of successful performance of mental function, resulting in productive activities, fulfilling relationships with other people, and the ability to adapt to change and to cope with adversity." In other words, thriving.

Where to Go from Here?

The legal profession will always involve competing pressures and responsibilities, adversity, and insufficient time. There will always be mental health, substance use, and physical health issues to be dealt with. These challenges must be acknowledged and appreciated before they can be addressed. But instead of focusing only on the negative, what is wrong with the profession, or what is wrong with individual lawyers, let's focus on the issue through a more positive lens—What can we do to improve individual and organizational health and well-being? What can we do to make the most of the situation? How can we evolve and adapt to difficult challenges? And ultimately, what can we do to promote flourishing, as individuals and organizations?

Well-being does not just happen! Well-being is a deliberate *Way of Being*. It is intentional, involving commitment, diligence, and hard work—at least at the beginning, until the framework of well-being permeates our life. It requires planning, strategy, and follow through. When we think about the self-care aspect of well-being, and within that, the expertise aspect of self-care, adopting a new personal exercise, diet, sleep, or meditation regimen requires commitment and practice. Similarly, organizations can work toward effectuating positive culture-change through commitment and practice by proactively promoting and role-modeling a healthy work environment, as well as supporting employee self-care and well-being. *The Thriving Lawyer: A Multidimensional Model of Well-Being for a Sustainable Legal Profession* addresses the multitude of individual, contextual, and organizational factors influencing well-being, thriving, and productivity. It is up to you whether to make a change that propels your behavior in a positive direction. You decide.

Bibliography

1966 Debate over the first law school in America, *scholarship repository*. William & Mary Law School. https://scholarship.law.wm.edu/lawschooldebate1966/

Beck, C. J. A., Sales, B. D., & Benjamin, G. A. H. (1995). Lawyer distress: Alcohol-related problems and other psychological concerns among a sample of practicing lawyers. *Journal of Law and Health, 10*(1), 1–60.

Bergin, A. J., & Jimmieson, N. L. (2014). Australian lawyer well-being: Workplace demands, resources and the impact of time-billing targets. *Psychiatry, Psychology and Law, 21*(3), 427–441. https://doi.org/10.1080/13218719.2013.822783

Cadieux, N., Cadieux, J., Gouin, M.-M., Fournier, P.-L., Caya, O., Gingues, M., Pomerleau, M.-L., Morin, E., Camille, A. B., & Gahunzire, J. (2022). *Research report (preliminary version): Towards a healthy and sustainable practice of law in Canada. National study on the psychological health determinants of legal professionals in Canada, Phase I (2020–2022)*. Université de Sherbrooke, Business School, 379 pages.

Cadieux, N., Cadieux, J., Youssef, N., Gingues, M., & Godbout, S.-M. (2020). *Research report: A study of the determinants of mental health in the workplace among Quebec lawyers, phase II—2017–2019*. Research Report, Université de Sherbrooke, Business School, 177 pages.

Canadian Bar Association/Ipsos Reid. (2012). *Survey of lawyers on wellness issues, legal profession assistance conference*. Canadian Bar Association.

Chlap, N., & Brown, R. (2022). Relationships between workplace characteristics, psychological stress, affective distress, burnout and empathy in lawyers. *International Journal of the Legal Profession*. https://doi.org/10.1080/09695958.2022.2032082

Collier, R. (2016). Wellbeing in the legal profession: Reflections on recent developments (or, what do we talk about, when we talk about wellbeing). *International Journal of the Legal Profession, 23*(1), 41–60.

Gabriel, H. D. (1989). America's oldest law school. *Journal of Legal Education, 39*(2), 269–274. www.jstor.org/stable/42893038

Geok-choo, L., Yiu-chung, K., & Kwok-bun, C. (2008). Work stress and coping amongst lawyers in Singapore. *Asian Journal of Social Science, 36*(5), 703–744.

International Bar Association Presidential Task Force on Mental Wellbeing in the Legal Profession. (2021). *Mental wellbeing in the legal profession: A global study*, International Bar Association. www.ibanet.org/document?id=IBA-report-Mental-Wellbeing-in-the-Legal-Profession-A-Global-Study

James, C. (2008). Lawyers' wellbeing and professional legal education. *Law Teacher, 42*(1), 85–98.

Keyes, C. L. M. (2002). The mental health continuum: From languishing to flourishing in life. *Journal of Health and Social Behavior, 43*(2), 207–222. https://doi.org/10.2307/3090197

Litchfield Law School History. *The Ledger.* Historical Society. https://ledger.litchfi
eldhistoricalsociety.org/ledger/studies/history_school

Misselbrook, D. (2014). W is for wellbeing and the WHO definition of health. *The British Journal of General Practice : The Journal of the Royal College of General Practitioners, 64*(628), 582. https://doi.org/10.3399/bjgp14X682381

National Task Force on Lawyer Well-Being. (2017). *The path to lawyer wellbeing: Practical recommendations to positive change.* American Bar Association. www.americanbar.org/content/dam/aba/images/abanews/ThePathToLawyerWell
BeingReportRevFINAL.pdf

Nickum, M., & Desrumaux, P. (2022). Burnout among lawyers: Effects of workload, latitude and mediation via engagement and over-engagement. *Psychiatry, Psychology and Law.* https://doi.org/10.1080/13218719.2022.2035840

Positive. (2015). *Wellbeing at the Bar: A Resilience Framework Assessment (RFA),* The Bar Council. www.barcouncil.org.uk/resource/wellbeing-at-the-bar-report.
html

Tapping Reeve House and Litchfield Law School. Litchfield Historical Society. www.
litchfieldhistoricalsociety.org/museums/tapping-reeve-house-and-law-school/

Tapping Reeve and the Litchfield Law School. Connecticut Judicial Branch. www.jud.
ct.gov/lawlib/history/tappingreeve.htm

United States Surgeon General. (1999). *Mental health: A report of the surgeon general.* Department of Health and Human Services, Center for Mental Health Services, National Institute of Mental Health, US Public Health Service, p. 4. https://profiles.nlm.nih.gov/spotlight/nn/catalog/nlm:nlmuid-101584932X120-
doc; see reference info: https://profiles.nlm.nih.gov/spotlight/nn/catalog?utf8=
%E2%9C%93&exhibit_id=nn&search_field=all_fields&q=Mental+Health%3A
+A+Report+of+the+Surgeon+General+%28ISBN+0-16-050300-0%29+)

World Health Organization, Constitution, 1948. www.who.int/about/governance/
constitution

World Health Organization Fact Sheets. (2018, March 30). *Mental Health: Strengthening our response.* www.who.int/news-room/fact-sheets/detail/mental-
health-strengthening-our-response

CHAPTER 2

Introducing the Multidimensional Model of Lawyer Well-Being, aka, The Honeycomb Model of Well-Being—A Way of Being

When we think about well-being, often the first thing that comes to mind is practicing self-care.

Self-care is essential, but it is one small piece of the puzzle. There are many factors, internal and external, individual and organizational, impacting our well-being. It can be helpful to conceptualize well-being broadly, encompassing many facets.

To begin with, we can organize the many factors into three overarching general categories incorporating: 1) individual factors; 2) life-context factors; and 3) work-related factors. The composition and influence of each of these three broad categories vary by person and their circumstances. We practice self-care to help us prevent, manage, and mitigate the effects of stress and distress in each of these three general areas arising from our 1) individual thoughts, feelings, behaviors, and our physical health; 2) external pressures related to our life in general; and 3) workplace culture and legal practice-related pressures.

The Honeycomb Model of Well-Being, addressed later in this chapter, is a more specific model arising out of these three domains, reflecting individual and contextual factors within each domain, including actions that involve thinking, behavior, and relating at the personal, social, and organizational levels.

What Does Well-Being Mean to You?

Before you can take steps toward improving or enhancing well-being, you need to understand what well-being means to you, and what your goals are for achieving it. Does well-being mean practicing self-care? Optimal physical health? Optimal psychological health? Stress-free living? Freedom from addictions? Maintaining positive and supportive relationships? Something else?

On the individual level, we have our personal traits and how we relate to the world, including self-care, as well as our mental and physical health

DOI: 10.4324/9781003285519-2   8

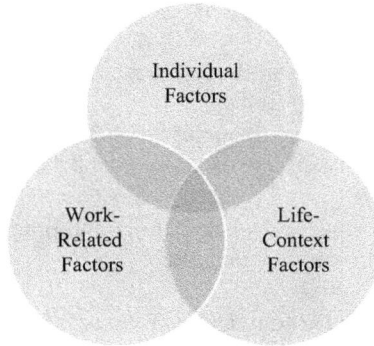

Figure 2.1 Intersection of Individual, Life-Context, and Work-Related Factors in Well-Being

status, which can serve to mitigate or aggravate stress and distress. Some of these aspects are reflected in the questions below:

- How do you manage stress?
- Do you engage in self-care strategies?
- Are you generally a positive, optimistic person?
- Do you view the world through a negative, skeptical, or cynical lens?
- Do you tend toward perfectionistic thinking?
- Are you flexible or rigid in your thinking and behavior?
- Do you appreciate the difference between being assertive versus being aggressive?
- Are you competitive or collaborative?
- Are you dealing with an acute or long-term mental illness?
- Are you dealing with unresolved personal trauma?
- Are you dealing with an acute or long-term life-threatening physical illness?

When we think about life-context factors, there are many, some of which include:

- Are you single or in a romantic relationship? What is the quality of that relationship?
- Do you live alone or with a partner and/or children or other relatives?
- Do you have school-aged children?
- Do you have elder-care responsibilities?
- What kind of social support do you have? Have you maintained healthy relationships with friends? Are there colleagues at work whom you trust and can consult for advice or ask for assistance?

- Is someone in your family living with an acute or long-term mental illness?
- Is someone in your family experiencing an acute or long-term life-threatening physical illness?
- Are you experiencing financial difficulties?
- Do you participate in non-work-related hobbies or interests?

When thinking about your workplace culture and practice-related stressors, some of the many factors at play include:

- Practice area and accompanying pressures and rhythms of work (the stressors and pressures involved in social justice or social order-related advocacy versus the transactional nature of corporate law are quite different).
- Type of organization (corporate, education, government, law firm, not-for-profit).
- Size of organization.
- Written and unwritten organizational policies and expectations.
- The other people who work there.
- How people are treated.

Lawyer Well-Being: The Multidimensional Model

The Multi-Dimensional Model of Lawyer Well-Being, aka The Honeycomb Model of Well-Being, arose out of an effort to organize, conceptualize, and simplify the many aspects of lawyer well-being. It is a comprehensive model which illustrates the intersection of individual and organizational factors and was designed as a roadmap to well-being for the legal community. It takes a broader view of well-being, as well as the roles of leadership and workplace culture in promoting it.

The model also reflects an intentional *Way of Being* on both the individual and organizational levels. As a whole, the different components of the model address overall physical and psychological health, self-care, and how we relate to the world, as well as external influences and pressures. The various components of the model (see Figure 2.2) will each be considered in more detail in separate chapters.

Before you can address well-being and engage in prevention (or intervention) strategies, you must first understand the big picture, the context of both the individual and the organization, and the many factors which influence individual well-being and organizational culture. The best interventions will be tailored to the specific person, culture, and circumstances, and involve repeated reinforcement.

What Is Well-Being?

A Way of Being

- Intentional

- Multidimensional

- Individual & Organizational

- Evidence-Based

- Individualized

- Always Evolving

Work Environment, Workload, & Unique Work Pressures

Self-Care Strategies & Routines

Attention to, and Overall, Physical and Mental Health

Meaning, Purpose, Passion

Work-Life Balance

Personal Relationships & Social Supports

Financial & Other Resources

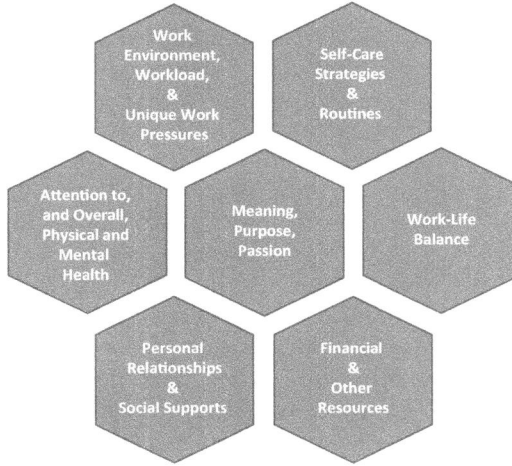

Figure 2.2 The Multidimensional Model of Lawyer Well-Being, aka, The Honeycomb Model of Well-Being—A Way of Being

Well-Being Is an Intentional Way of Being

A lifestyle or workplace culture of well-being requires commitment. Making a specific commitment increases our likelihood of follow-through. When we make a commitment, we are making a deliberate decision to do something (or even to do nothing), as opposed to seeing what happens. Often going with the flow can lead to inaction by default, although sometimes a decision not to act is intentional. In the case of well-being, individualized self-care strategies, leadership role-modeling, organizational policies, and robust employee benefits all involve proactive, deliberate decision-making toward promoting personal well-being and a healthy, productive workplace. When thought of in such global terms, we realize well-being is a way of being.

On the personal level, if you told me you want to ramp up your exercise regimen, the only time you can exercise regularly is at 5:30 am, and you will see how you feel when your alarm clock goes off tomorrow morning, we both know you will most likely hit the "snooze" button, or turn off the alarm, roll over, and sleep until the time you usually get out of bed. Leaving behavior change to happenstance tends not to be a successful strategy. On the other hand, if you tell me you are determined to exercise every morning and you have decided to get up each day at 5:30 am to go for a jog, when your alarm clock sounds at that early hour you will be much more likely to get out of bed and go for that jog. If you lay out your running gear the night before, and intentionally get to bed at a reasonable hour, this preparation will only enhance your commitment. And if you take it one step further and agree to meet a friend or "workout buddy" at 5:45 am, this commitment to another person is an external motivator which creates a higher level of account-ability and greatly increases the likelihood of your follow-through on the plan. These commitments and actions reflect a more intentional approach to behavior change.

At the organizational level, it is one thing to say you support well-being, and yet another to role model and instill policies that promote well-being, such as going offline while on vacation, as well as allowing flexible work arrangements, establishing electronic communication policies, and providing robust insurance coverage that includes comprehensive mental health bene-fits. There is a big difference between sending out a weekly e-newsletter with well-being tips versus having a managing partner take a true, offline vacation. There is a big difference between providing a workshop on the importance of sleep versus setting a firm-wide policy limiting workplace communications to certain hours. If the boss tells you vacations are important, but is con-stantly calling, emailing, and texting while on vacation, what message does this send? Moreover, lip-service or policies espousing the importance of psy-chological safety are meaningless if toxic leaders are not called out and their communication style addressed. The same goes for associate development, it is one thing to say it is important and another to provide regular mentorship and required educational experiences.

An example of a more intentional approach to addressing electronic com-munications and time management would involve creating an electronic communications policy specifying time frames, including times of day, weekends, etc., when lawyers and staff are not expected to respond to non-urgent communications, and defining what is considered "urgent" or an "emergency."

Well-Being Is Multidimensional

As a multidimensional construct, well-being involves many intercon-nected aspects, each of which also stands alone. The Honeycomb Model of Well-Being helps to conceptualize the big picture, and the varied elements involved, including attention to overall physical and mental health, self-care, a multitude of workplace issues, work–life balance, financial resources, per-sonal relationships and social supports, as well as meaning, purpose, and passion. Once you understand the big picture, you can then begin to focus on specific aspects, perhaps also at different times, depending on your needs and circumstances and those of your organization. The chapters in this book will address many of these aspects in more detail.

Well-Being Is Reflected on the Individual and Organizational Levels

Lawyers tend to be achievement-oriented professionals with strong perfectionist tendencies who believe hard work is the best route to success, with law school and legal practice reinforcing these values and beliefs. These values and beliefs underlie law firm policies and culture, influencing the work environment and individual well-being.

The Honeycomb Model reflects the significance of both individual and organizational factors which influence lawyer well-being, such as individual self-care strategies and organizational work environment and workload. In addition to acknowledging and addressing the separate individual and organizational aspects at play, it is also necessary to address the intersection of these factors, specifically the impact organizational culture and policies have on individual well-being. Some examples of organizational factors at play were highlighted in the section above on intentionality.

Self-Care By Itself Is Not Enough. Many law firms have gradually come to appreciate the importance of self-care in terms of health, well-being, and ultimately productivity and financial advantages. Meditation apps and workshops run rampant in the legal community. Nutrition programming and yoga classes abound. Yet, self-care is not enough. It is unrealistic to expect individual attorneys to attend a few self-care and stress management workshops, download a meditation app, and suddenly experience well-being; if a workplace is unhealthy or work responsibilities unreasonable, burnout is likely to occur.

The Impact of Organizational Factors on Individuals. Organizational factors, such as a toxic work environment, or an environment in which vacations are subtly frowned upon and personal time always involves an expectation of being on call 24/7, will wear out everyone, particularly the most diligent and conscientious attorneys and staff (in other words, the people you want to keep around), which ultimately works against the important end goals of productivity and employee retention.

Evidence-Based Approaches to Understanding and Promoting Well-Being

Research on promoting self-care and healthy work environments abounds. There is more than enough information to enable you to develop a well-being strategy or program guided by science, instead of folklore or common sense. This book is based on research related to individual and organizational factors impacting health and well-being, and how to manage them.

A potential additional reason why attorneys struggle with self-care relates to the constant bombardment in recent years of advertising related to products and services to promote well-being. While some of these are science-based, others may in fact be "woo-woo." It is difficult to know where to turn and where to invest your time and resources.

A psychologist colleague likes to explain folklore vs. science this way:

> Grandma always said chicken soup is good for a cold. It tastes good and feels good in our throats and stomachs, but for a long time we did not know why. Now we know through science that chicken soup truly is good for a cold; it helps clear nasal congestion and helps thin mucus so you can better cough it up, it can help boost hydration by replenishing electrolytes, and it may also have a mild anti-inflammatory effect that can help ease cold symptoms. But grandma also said to feed a cold and starve a fever. We now know through research that starving a fever is not the best thing to do when we are ill. We need nutrients to help fight infections.
>
> *(Baranoski, M.)*

You want to know your time and resources are being well-invested in strategies that have a basis in research.

An Individualized Approach to Well-Being Interventions

There are no one-size-fits-all solutions. The best approaches to promoting well-being will be ever-changing—individualized, tailored to the person, work environment, and other unique circumstances. For instance, if you do not like meditation, you need to find other ways to clear your mind, such as through exercise, listening to relaxing music, reading, creative pursuits, or another pleasurable activity. If your workflow has hills and valleys of workload and intensity, your needs will be different from those of an attorney, practice group, or law firm with a constant, never-ending moderate-to-high intensity stream of work. The litigation group and the mergers and acquisitions group within the same firm experience different workflow and time pressures. The best lawyer well-being programs, policies, or interventions are customized to address individual needs and contextual pressures.

Effective Well-Being Strategies Are Always Evolving

Once a program, policy, or intervention is established, it will be most effective in the long term if it is regularly revisited, re-evaluated, and revised, identifying and accounting for any changes in needs or circumstances, as well as any barriers to the well-being end-goal(s). Strategies and interventions will be adjusted over time as new information is acquired.

For instance, although a new electronic communication policy may have been adopted on paper, are law firm partners and leaders adhering to the policy when communicating with staff and associates? Has a new flexible work arrangement policy led to less physical office space, which then impacts the productivity of staff and attorneys who have come to realize they need the structure and routine of a physical workplace and heading to-and-from the office each day? The best approaches to promoting lawyer well-being are continuously evolving to meet changing individual and organizational needs over time.

If Well-Being Is So Important, Why Hasn't the Legal Community Embraced It More Before Now?

The legal profession has long been known for its lack of prioritization of self-care and well-being. Many lawyers hesitate to express mental health and self-care needs out of fear of being viewed as weak or incompetent. Low-level anxiety, depression, substance misuse, or unmitigated stress can then snowball into serious illness and difficulty functioning. Even when the situation becomes more dire, many lawyers continue to struggle to seek help and often do not get it until they reach a breaking point, with a mental health or physical health crisis, or more rarely, an intervention by a supervisor telling them they must take a break. Many reasons for a reluctance to address mental health needs are at play, including stigma, which will be addressed in Chapter 4, Self-Care Strategies and Overcoming Barriers to Healthy Routines.

But even in the absence of stigma, self-care is hard work, as is promoting a well-being culture. Promoting well-being and self-care requires a commitment to oneself, and because we are only accountable to ourselves, it is easier to let it slide. Along the same lines, our own self-care may be the only aspect of our lives over which we have complete control. As a result, it can be pushed aside, with commitments and responsibilities to others, such as our clients, and loved ones, taking precedence. This same dynamic can play out through inaction at the organizational leadership level; without a commitment, as well as adoption of policies and procedures for addressing continuous re-evaluation, a lack of accountability persists, and culture-change stagnates.

Bibliography

Baca-Motes, K., Brown, A., Gneezy, A., Keenan, E. A., & Nelson, L. D. (2013). Commitment and behavior change: Evidence from the field. *Journal of Consumer Research*, *39*(5), 1070–1084. https://doi.org/10.1086/667226

Church, A. H., & Dawson, L. M. (2018). Agile feedback drives accountability and sustained behavior change. *Strategic HR Review*, *17*(6), 295–302. https://doi.org/10.1108/SHR-07-2018-0063

Lokhorst, A. M., Werner, C., Staats, H., van Dijk, E., & Gale, J. L. (2013). Commitment and behavior change: A meta-analysis and critical review of commitment-making strategies in environmental research. *Environment and Behavior*, *45*(1), 3–34. https://doi-org.yale.idm.oclc.org/10.1177/0013916511411477

CHAPTER 3

Attention to Overall Physical and Mental Health

The Mind–Body Connection and Impact of Stress on Health and Performance

During a conversation about pressures within the legal profession, a mid-career lawyer recently said to me, "It's constant 'perma-stress,' without ever thinking about why I feel this way." This statement says it all. Lawyers as a group tend not to be introspective. We learn early on in law school that emotions and focusing on internal experience can make us appear weak and incompetent. Rampant mental health stigma further reinforces these views. Accordingly, many lawyers are not attuned to internal signs of distress—in the form of bodily signals, negative thinking, or negative emotions—and do not recognize when they are feeling stressed or otherwise out of sorts. This lack of self-reflection and attention goes along with the historical devaluation of well-being and self-care within the legal profession. The highly competitive nature of the profession promotes a laser-sharp focus on prevailing at all costs, including costs measured in terms of mental and physical health, happiness, and social connectedness. What is not known or acknowledged is that this intense professional drive, to the exclusion of self-care, also comes at additional costs to cognitive performance (problem-solving, memory, concentration), physical health, and mental health.

BOX 3.1 DID YOU KNOW?

"*Karoshi*," or "work to death" is a Japanese word dating back to the 1980s. The term reflects recognition of the physical and psychological health problems, and ultimately death, which can arise from working long hours, and the accompanying stress and fatigue.

When speaking with the lawyer quoted above, I followed up with some questions related to this person's perceptions of their experience and whether they tried to change anything, to which the lawyer responded, "We just do our jobs; we don't think about how miserable we are."

DOI: 10.4324/9781003285519-3   16

Attention to your overall mental and physical health is essential. Notably, recent research highlights the importance of being in tune with your internal experience, finding that people who reported stress levels consistent with their internal physiological stress markers (i.e., heart rate), also experienced better overall levels of well-being, as measured in terms of anxiety, depression, and coping strategies, and decreased inflammatory markers.

Your Brain and Health Are Your Greatest Assets. If protecting your health and well-being for the sake of a long and enjoyable life is not enough, consider this: Cognitive performance, mental health, and physical health are arguably the greatest worker assets in the legal profession. When we recognize this, it naturally follows that lawyers and their employers should be doing everything they can to protect, preserve, and replenish. Mental and physical health are equally important. Poor physical health can also lead to decreased energy and overall performance, not to mention disability or death.

The Mind–Body Connection

A large body of research reveals the strength of our mind–body connection. One area of research, psychoneuroimmunology looks at relationships among stress, mood, and immune function. Other areas look at the relationships among stress and risk for various diseases. In addition, cognitive behavioral theory explains how our thoughts and feelings influence our behaviors, which in turn reciprocally influence our thoughts and feelings, and all of which are further related to our physiological responses, and our overall physical and mental health. For more information on this relationship and how to intervene, see Chapter 4, Self-Care Strategies and Overcoming Barriers to Healthy Routines.

When we experience constant stress, the automatic physiological response over time leads to inflammation in our bodies and decreased immune

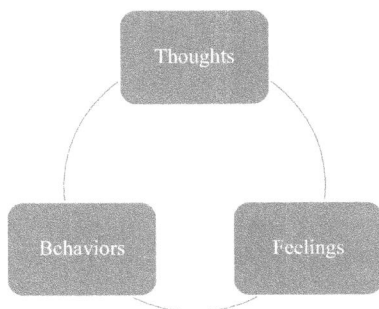

Figure 3.1 The Cycle of Influence Among Thoughts, Feelings, and Behaviors

function, both of which create a whole host of negative health risks. If left unchecked, costly chronic diseases can emerge.

What Is Stress?

Hans Selye, a pioneer in stress theory, wrote in 1973, "Everyone knows what stress is and nobody knows what it is." Nearly 40 years earlier, in 1936, Selye had described stress as reflecting a "non-specific" physiological response to "any demand for change," attention, or action, including an actual or perceived threat. Stress is a primitive, automatic, adaptive response. Walter Cannon first identified and labeled the acute stress response, our "fight-or-flight" response, in 1915.

Fight-or-Flight, an Immediate Stress Response

BOX 3.2 GENERAL ADAPTATION SYNDROME

In 1936, Hans Selye theorized the physiological stress response follows a predictable pattern, which he called the General Adaptation Syndrome. Selye described the stress response as involving three phases: 1) an *alarm reaction*, in which your sympathetic nervous system is suddenly activated by the detection of the stressor; 2) a *resistance phase*, during which you cope with the stressor, and your sympathetic nervous system remains aroused to provide energy and protection against illness; and, 3) *exhaustion*, the final stage, occurs when your body's energy is depleted. During this stage, resistance to illness is diminished, and energy levels are low.

The "fight-or-flight" response is triggered when we perceive a threat, such as an approaching wooly mammoth or an aggressive phone call from opposing counsel. The fight-or-flight response immediately kicks in before we are even consciously aware of the precipitating threat. This involves a complex system of physiological and neurobiological processes which mobilize our minds and bodies to respond to perceived threats. Our breathing becomes much more rapid and shallow, our heart rate and blood pressure increase, blood is shunted to muscles in our limbs and to our brain, our muscles become tense, and the hormones adrenaline and cortisol are released to promote glucose metabolism. This response provides us with a sudden burst of physical strength, energy, and mental clarity, enabling us to fight off the wooly mammoth (or opposing counsel), or run away. Similarly, this response is what enables us to jump out of the way of a speeding car that flies around the corner just as

Stress

Acute Stress – "Fight or Flight"

Chronic Stress – Endless Cycle

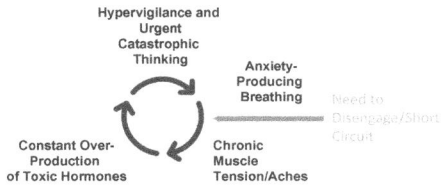

Hypervigilance and Urgent Catastrophic Thinking

Anxiety-Producing Breathing

Need to Disengage/Short Circuit

Constant Over-Production of Toxic Hormones

Chronic Muscle Tension/Aches

Sudden Burst of Energy, Strength, Mental Clarity

Physically, Mentally, Emotionally Draining

Figure 3.2 Acute vs. Chronic Stress

we are stepping off the curb to cross an intersection. We jump away before we even mentally process what is happening. Once the threat has passed, our parasympathetic nervous system kicks in, counteracting the physiological responses that had mobilized us to quickly respond. Our breathing slows and deepens, our heart rate and blood pressure return to normal, our muscles and brain relax, and the hormone release subsides. The fight-or-flight response is an adaptive brief response to an immediate threat.

Chronic Stress

Chronic stress, on the other hand, involves long-term activation of the stress response. While the acute "fight-or-flight" stress response is adaptive, problems can arise when this response is continuously activated by non-physical threats in your environment, such as when you are bombarded with never-ending work deadlines and emergencies, even after-hours.

Your body is in an endless cycle of muscle tension, shallow breathing, urgent and catastrophic thinking, and over production of toxic hormones.

The Impact of Unmanaged Chronic Stress on Physical Health

During a conversation with an associate at a large, big-city law firm who was contemplating their long-term career goals and the pros and cons of Big Law practice, this lawyer said to me, "When I think about it, I realize a lot of partners have died relatively young from heart attacks or strokes."

Ongoing perceived threats lead to constant activation of the acute stress response, which in turn can cause your health to deteriorate. While the acute stress response (minutes to hours) can enhance immune reactivity, chronic stress is associated with decreased immunity and susceptibility to a variety of health issues. When this chronic cycle happens, in response to continuous

19

perceived threats—such as in the form of never-ending deadlines, continuous client "emergencies," or a toxic work environment—your immune system becomes suppressed, increasing the risk of contracting viruses such as the common cold or flu. High percentages of the female and male lawyer participants, 46% and 33% respectively, in my 2007 dissertation research study reported being ill over the previous 30 days (e.g., cold, flu, strep throat, bronchitis, or pneumonia.

When you are under constant stress, the automatic physiological response leads to inflammation and decreased immune function, which creates a host of physical and mental health risks, new health problems, or exacerbation of existing issues. High levels of ongoing stress, combined with inadequate coping and self-care strategies, lead to poor physical health outcomes. Chronic stress and resulting inflammation have been shown to increase risk of cardiovascular events, stroke, musculoskeletal pain, increased respiratory issues, gastrointestinal problems, reproductive issues (fertility, desire, impotence), metabolic issues, and weight changes. If left unchecked, costly chronic diseases can emerge, including:

- Cardiovascular disease
- Diabetes
- Cancer
- Autoimmune syndromes, including arthritis
- Gastrointestinal disorders
- Obesity
- Insomnia
- Addictions
- Exacerbation of other serious physical or mental illnesses

The Impact of Unmanaged Chronic Stress on Cognitive Functioning and Mental Health

Chronic stress also negatively impacts our brain functioning and psychological health. Stress leads to narrower, more constricted thinking, thinking which is inflexible and does not leave room for creative problem-solving. Over time, persistent stress can lead to memory, problem-solving, and attention deficits, and is related to difficulties concentrating, making decisions, self-regulating, as well as poorer judgment. Constant strain can also lead to mental health issues such as depression, anxiety, and substance misuse, and at its nadir, suicide. Many lawyers have begun to share their personal experiences with anxiety and depression, in an effort to raise awareness, destigmatize mental health issues, and ideally create culture-change and expectations within the profession.

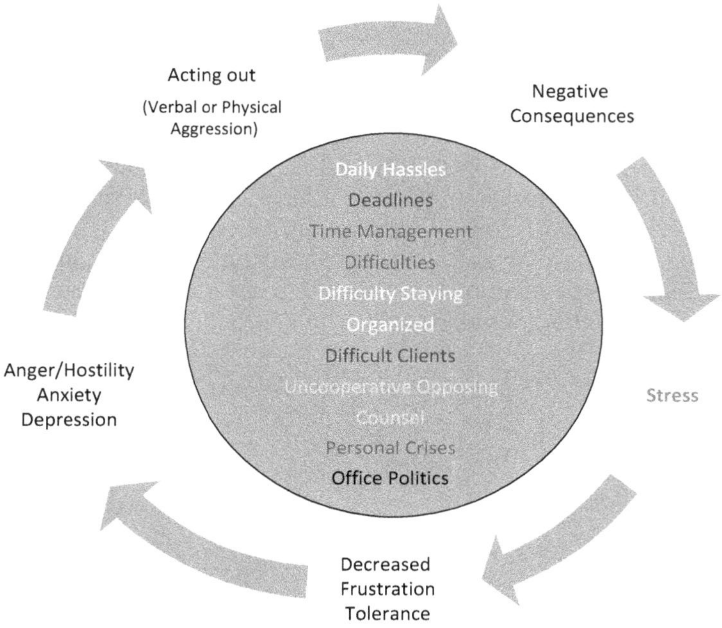
Acting out
(Verbal or Physical Aggression)
Negative Consequences
Daily Hassles
Deadlines
Time Management Difficulties
Difficulty Staying Organized
Difficult Clients
Uncooperative Opposing Counsel
Personal Crises
Office Politics
Stress
Decreased Frustration Tolerance
Anger/Hostility
Anxiety
Depression

Figure 3.3 The Impact of Unmanaged Stress—A Negative Cycle

The cycle of stress, beginning with a decreased ability to tolerate seemingly small stressors or hassles, if not addressed, can lead to anger and hostility and to acting out with verbal or physical aggression toward colleagues or loved ones. Such acting out often has negative consequences, which then leads to more stress in a never-ending vicious cycle.

Chronic stress leads to changes in the brain which can promote a constant state of vigilance, or constant scanning of one's environment for threats. Neutral or ambiguous information may be more likely to be perceived as threatening. As a result, work-related or life stress in combination with many lawyers' already cynical, skeptical, and sometimes aggressive tendencies can be an unpleasant recipe. Brain changes may have occurred prior to law school or legal practice due to adverse childhood events, in which case the stressors of law school and legal practice may trigger or exacerbate underlying issues of depression, anxiety, or suicidality. High-profile lawyer suicides have been publicized by the US media, and frequently cited US Centers for Disease Control and Prevention (CDC) data from the 2010s found that lawyers ranked fourth in suicide rates when compared to other professions—behind dentists, pharmacists, and physicians. In my 2007 study involving Connecticut, US, lawyers, 46% of women and 33% of men reported experiencing "a lot" or "extreme" levels of overall stress (notably almost mirroring the percentages reporting they were ill over the past 30 days). In the same study, 52% of the women and 36% of men reported "a lot" or "extreme" work stress.

While effective in the short term, continuous activation of the fight-or-flight response and its associated hormone release exerts an incredible toxic strain on the body, immune system, and brain. Lower-back or neck pain, headaches, frequent colds or viruses, difficulty concentrating, decreased problem-solving ability, poorer memory, increased weight (particularly in the abdomen), sleep problems, anxiety, and depression are all indirect symptoms of chronic stress. Stress also causes inflammation, and at its most sinister, it can indirectly increase risk for autoimmune diseases, cardiovascular diseases, and cancer.

BOX 3.3 THE IMPACT OF UNMANAGED STRESS

Brain Functioning

- Attention and concentration difficulties
- Decreased problem-solving ability
- Difficulty making decisions
- Memory deficits
- Self-regulation difficulties
- Poorer judgment

Mental Health and Related Challenges

- Depression
- Anxiety
- Sleep difficulties
- Substance misuse
- Suicidal ideation

Like batteries, our bodies are not designed to operate full throttle non-stop. Over time, alkaline or electric battery power wanes as energy is depleted. Without a pause and recharge, the battery eventually loses its energy. Similarly, over time under chronic stress, our bodies will lose energy and become less efficient and effective, mentally, physically, and emotionally. We need to rest our bodies and recharge. The American Psychological Association Center for Psychology and Health reported in 2014 that up to 70% of visits to primary care physicians are related to underlying issues of stress, depression, anxiety, and panic. Anxiety and depression can make existing physical health symptoms, such as pain, worse. Poor physical health can also lead to decreased energy and overall performance, not to mention disability or death.

An understanding of this mind–body relationship helps you to appreciate the importance of using self-care strategies to disengage or "short-circuit" the cycle of chronic stress. For more information on how to do this, see Chapter 4, Self-Care Strategies and Overcoming Barriers to Healthy Routines.

The Impact of Unmanaged Chronic Stress on Brain Structure—Stress and Depression Shrink Your Brain

As if all the above physical, cognitive, and mental health effects were not enough, researchers using MRI scans have found that stress and depression can shrink your brain, impacting brain areas related to self-control and emotions, as well as other important physiological processes. When someone is under chronic stress, grey matter in brain areas which influence performance and mental health shrinks. And this effect can happen fairly quickly.

> [E]ven the brains of subjects who had only recently experienced a stressful life event showed markedly lower gray matter in portions of the medial prefrontal cortex, an area of the brain that regulates not only emotions and self-control, but physiological functions such as blood pressure and glucose levels.
>
> (Yale News, *January 9, 2012)*

These findings help explain why people may struggle when dealing with an accumulation of stressors which also require mental energy to regulate responses and engage in self-control. A second study, published later that year, explained some of the mechanisms behind the shrinkage. Together these studies suggest explanations for poorer judgment and heightened negative emotions during times of intense stress. They also help explain the connection between stress and poor physical health outcomes involving cardiovascular events and metabolic issues.

Notably, meditation and Mindfulness-Based Stress Reduction can remediate these stress effects on brain volume and lead to increased gray matter density. Specifically, these strategies have been found to be associated with increases in grey matter volume in brain areas responsible for learning, memory, emotion regulation, and perspective taking. Antidepressant medications have also been found to be helpful in reversing these effects. For more on managing stress, see Chapter 4, Self-Care Strategies and Overcoming Barriers to Healthy Routines.

The Cost of Stress

Healthcare costs are a major employer expenditure. Additional hidden physical and mental health costs arise through decreased productivity. Annual medical and productivity costs related to stress-related physical and psychological health issues are astounding, never mind mortality risks. According to the US Centers for Disease Control and Prevention (CDC), 90% of the US annual healthcare expenditure ($2.8 trillion) is for chronic diseases,

Table 3.1 Medical and Productivity Costs of Health Risk Behaviors and Chronic Disease

Alcohol Misuse	1 in 10 deaths in working-age adults; $249 billion with $28 billion for healthcare (2019) and $2/5 dollars paid by the public (2010); $179 billion due to lower workplace productivity (2019)
Arthritis	2013 estimated costs in medical expenses and lost productivity were $303.5 billion
Cancer	600,000 deaths/year; costs estimated to reach $240 billion by 2030
Depression and Anxiety	$259 billion; depression—$210.5 billion, with 50% attributable to workplace/lost productivity costs (2010); anxiety—$48.72 billion (2013)
Depression and Anxiety (Global)	$1 trillion/year in lost productivity, global economic impact
Diabetes	2017 estimated costs in medical expenses and lost productivity were $327 billion
Heart Disease and Stroke	877,500+ deaths/year; $216 billion healthcare costs; $147 billion in lost productivity (2018)
Hostility	Higher cardiac-related hospitalization costs; greatly increased likelihood of death from cardiovascular incident; increased risk of stroke in middle-aged and older adults
Opioid Use Disorder and Fatal Overdose	$1,021 billion, with $471 billion for disorder and $550 billion for fatal overdose (2017)
Obesity	$260.6 billion/year in medical costs (2016)
Pain	$560–635 billion/year in healthcare ($261–300 billion) and lost productivity (days of work missed, hours of work lost, and less income) costs (2008)
Physical Inactivity	$117 billion/year (2006–2011)
Sleep Insufficiency (US)	Up to $411 billion due to lower productivity and higher mortality (2016)
Sleep Insufficiency (US, UK, Japan, Germany, Canada)	Up to $680 billion due to lower productivity and higher mortality (2017)
Tobacco Use	$300 billion/year, with $156 billion in lost productivity

including mental health conditions. When considering the high costs of an unhealthy workforce (see Table 3.1 above), preventive measures also make financial sense.

Insurance industry data suggests lawyer healthcare costs for depression are above the norm, and lawyers tend to be more likely to experience depression than the general population. It is also notable that back pain and musculoskeletal issues were the primary cost drivers, issues which are intertwined with stress and mood.

BOX 3.4 LAW FIRM INSURANCE DATA IS TELLING

A law firm industry analysis by a large insurer from the 2010s revealed back pain and musculoskeletal issues were the primary cost drivers while pregnancy and depression were the most prevalent diagnoses within law firms, with depression rates 12–13% higher than the norm.

Environmental and Individual Risk Factors for Lawyer Stress

Occupational Risk Factors

There are several occupational "risk factors" for stress in the legal profession. These include time pressures, billing pressures, rainmaking pressures, and the adversarial nature of the profession. In addition, technology which was conceived to make your life easier has actually made it much more difficult for lawyers to create boundaries between work and home life and to protect downtime for relaxation and self-care. Modern technology now makes it much easier for your work-life to merge with your home-life, as you are always accessible by phone, email, or text. In addition to these work-specific factors, personal traits, employer policies and expectations, level of supervisor support, and organizational culture can also exacerbate or buffer the effects of stress. For more on unique pressures in the legal profession and other workplace stressors, see Chapter 5, Understanding and Addressing Workplace Issues Which Impact Well-Being.

Personal Traits and Behaviors Can Increase Stress

Hostility. Hostility, a trait not uncommon in lawyers, is a behavior not an emotion. It reflects unaddressed underlying negative emotions, such as anger, sadness, or hopelessness, and has more to do with attorney behavior, perhaps in response to workplace challenges. Hostility has been found to be particularly insidious across studies. It involves a negative attitude, characterized by cynicism, skepticism, and the dislike, negative evaluation, or denigration of others, all of which can lead to aggressive behavior. Research further suggests stress exacerbates hostility, which can then further increase stress, perpetuating an unhealthy feedback loop.

In 1983, Barefoot and colleagues reported the results of a 25-year follow-up with physicians who completed a personality measure while in medical school. The data revealed that physicians who were on the higher end in

25

measured hostility were more likely to die of cardiovascular events in general. Most notably, *those who were higher in hostility were also more than six times more likely to have died by age 50 from all causes* (cardiovascular, cancer, accidents, suicide, gastrointestinal issues). Although this study looked at physicians, similar results have been found in other studies involving the general population. In addition, anecdotal reports from the legal community are consistent with this finding.

> Stress and hostility were familiar at the big-city law firm where the partnership-track associate quoted above worked, where partners were dying early from cardiovascular events. The associate was at a fork in the career road: While acknowledging that the lure of the economic benefits of partnership was strong, the associate was also questioning "At what cost?" The prospect of a potential shortened life-span was unappealing, even when considering the financial benefits of a Big Law career. If the likelihood of early death was high, was it worth it? The associate further questioned whether they would actually be able to enjoy the fruits of their labor.

Notably, hostility has also been found to be associated with heavy drinking, which may be a contributing factor to the association between hostility and early death.

Perfectionism. High levels of perfectionism can have serious mental health implications, including, burnout, anxiety, depression, and even suicide. Many lawyers have perfectionist tendencies, which are reinforced during competitive legal training and through adversarial work. The stakes are high, and any error can mean a big loss, in terms of life, liberty, justice, and finances. Perfectionist thinking is characterized by a fear of failure, and accompanying rigid, defensive, negative, all-or-nothing thinking. Such extreme rigidity not only leaves little room for creativity or collaborative work, but it also can lead to high levels of stress and distress when your expectations for yourself are not met, or you never feel as though you have done enough. When striving for perfection in competing and highly salient roles, unattainable ideals (e.g., "supermom" or "superparent," who is always the top performer at work, is always available to clients and colleagues, yet has a homecooked healthy dinner on the table by 5:00 pm every night, is readily available to their children at the drop of a hat, and attends every school and activity related event) and the inevitable inability to meet one's high expectations for oneself can lead to burnout, depression, anxiety, and unhealthy coping strategies.

High levels of negative perfectionism, in combination with high levels of work–family conflict, have been found to be related to high levels of overall distress, depression, and anxiety in lawyers. My dissertation research found that lawyers working primarily in independent practice in a range of law firm sizes in the Northeast state of Connecticut (which is nestled between New York and Massachusetts) who reported the highest levels of perfectionism and work–family conflict also reported distress levels greater than 89% of the

US population. Similarly, the percentile levels for reported depression and anxiety in these lawyers were in the mid- to upper-70s. Subsequent research has also found perfectionism predicts work–family conflict.

Optimism. Personal outlook comes into play here as well. Positive psychology research has shown us that the trait of optimism is related to beliefs that things will eventually work out, and a tendency toward viewing the world through a lens that sees the glass as half-full as opposed to half-empty. Optimistic people tend to view difficulties as temporary problems or challenges, rather than permanent failures without hope for change. Importantly, an optimistic outlook can be particularly beneficial when a situation is, or is believed to be, outside of one's control, or in times of uncertainty. See Chapter 4, Self-Care Strategies and Overcoming Barriers to Healthy Routines for more information on how thoughts, perceived control, and mindset are related to the stress experience and effectively managing it.

Stress Is Adaptive—Moderation Is Key

While a great deal of research has focused on the negative effects of stress, recent research has explored the benefits of stress. For instance, stress is associated with increased motivation. Stress is energizing. It boosts your immunity, creativity, and work quality. The Yerkes-Dodson Law, while controversial, is oft-cited by the well-being community. This "law" of stress is well-known for its bell-shaped curve visualization of optimum stress levels. It provides a handy explanation for the important role of stress in motivating us: Without any stress response, you lack motivation. As the stress response increases, so do your attention and interest, up to a certain point—this is the top of the bell-shaped curve, representing the experience of optimal arousal and performance. After that point, however, an unmanaged stress response can lead to the impaired performance mentioned earlier, as it becomes increasingly strong or overwhelming, and this is represented by the declining curve to the right of the Yerkes-Dodson peak.

Litigators will often report experiencing "butterflies" each time they enter the courtroom. These "butterflies," reflecting an adaptive stress response, signal that the work to be done is important and you want to do it well. If the day comes when you no longer experience "butterflies" before an important work event, you may want to ask yourself why—does this lack of stress response reflect a lack of personal investment in the work to be done, or burnout?

A Brief Note on Topics Covered Elsewhere: Burnout, Vicarious Trauma, Microaggressions, and Self-Care

The term "burnout" refers to the impact of ongoing, unrelenting workplace stressors on functioning. It is a non-clinical term reflecting tension experienced by a person arising out of their workload, work pressures, or work environment.

Vicarious trauma refers to the experience of anxiety and mood changes as a result of exposure to trauma through client stories and the nature of one's work.

Microaggressions are behaviors and interactions that reflect racist, sexist, homophobic, or other biases. They are subtle and often unintentional, but they are nonetheless psychologically hurtful, causing stress and distress.

Burnout, vicarious trauma, and microaggressions are all significant workplace issues which create stress and distress, impacting mental and physical health, well-being, and productivity.

For more on understanding and addressing these issues, see Chapter 5, Understanding and Addressing Workplace Issues Which Impact Well-Being, and Chapter 4, Self-Care Strategies and Overcoming Barriers to Healthy Routines.

Bibliography

Adelson, R. (2004, November). Hormones, stress and aggression–A vicious cycle. *Monitor on Psychology, 35*(10). www.apa.org/monitor/nov04/hormones

American Psychological Association, Center for Psychology and Health. (2014, January). *Briefing series on the role of psychology in healthcare: Primary care.* American Psychological Association. www.apa.org/health/briefs/primary-care.pdf, *citing* Hunter, C. L., Goodie, J. L., Oordt, M. S., & Dobmeyer, A. C. (2009). *Integrated behavioral health in primary care: Step-by-step guidance for assessment and intervention.* American Psychological Association.

Ansell, E. B., Rando, K., Tuit, K., Guarnaccia, J., & Sinha, R. (2012). Cumulative adversity and smaller gray matter volume in medial prefrontal, anterior cingulate, and insula regions. *Biological Psychiatry, 72*(1), 57–64. https://doi.org/10.1016/j.biopsych.2011.11.022

Barefoot, J. C., Dahlstrom, W. G., & Williams, R. B., Jr. (1983). Hostility, CHD incidence, and total mortality: a 25-year follow-up study of 255 physicians. *Psychosomatic medicine, 45*(1), 59–63. https://doi.org/10.1097/00006842-198303000-00008

Blount, A., Schoenbaum, M., Kathol, R., Rollman, B. L., Thomas, M., O'Donohue, W., & Peek, C. J. (2007). The economics of behavioral health services in medical settings: A summary of the evidence. *Professional Psychology: Research and Practice, 38*(3), 290–297. https://doi.org/10.1037/0735-7028.38.3.290

Bose, M., Oliván, B., & Laferrère, B. (2009). Stress and obesity: The role of the hypothalamic-pituitary-adrenal axis in metabolic disease. *Current Opinion in Endocrinology, Diabetes, and Obesity, 16*(5), 340–346. https://doi.org/10.1097/MED.0b013e32832fa137

Boyle, S.H., Mortensen, L., Grønbæk, M., & Barefoot, J.C. (2008). Hostility, drinking pattern and mortality. *Addiction, 103*, 54–59. https://doi.org/10.1111/j.1360-0443.2007.02024.x

Boyle, S. H., Williams, R. B., Mark, D. B., Brummett, B. H., Siegler, I. C., & Barefoot, J. C. (2005). Hostility, Age, and Mortality in a Sample of Cardiac Patients. *The American Journal of Cardiology*, *96*(1), 64–66. https://doi.org/10.1016/j.amjcard.2005.02.046.

Carlson, S. A., Fulton, J. E., Pratt, M., Yang, Z., & Adams, E. K. (2015). Inadequate physical activity and health care expenditures in the United States. *Progress in Cardiovascular Diseases*, *57*(4), 315–323. https://doi.org/10.1016/j.pcad.2014.08.002

Cawley, J., Biener, A., Meyerhoefer, C., Ding, Y., Zvenyach, T., Smolarz, B. G., & Ramasamy, A. (2021). Direct medical costs of obesity in the United States and the most populous states. *Journal of Managed Care and Specialty Pharmacy*, *27*(3), 354–366. https://doi.org/10.18553/jmcp.2021.20410

Chrousos, G. P., & World Congress on Stress. (1995). *Stress: Basic mechanisms and clinical implications*. New York Academy of Sciences.

Cipriano, T. A. (2007). Relationships among work–family interference, conflict, and health risk outcomes in attorneys: Moderation by dispositional optimism and perfectionism. Doctoral Dissertations, AAI3279270. https://opencommons.uconn.edu/dissertations/AAI3279270

Cohen, S., Janicki-Deverts, D., & Miller, G. E. (2007). Psychological stress and disease. *JAMA*, *298*(14), 1685–1687. https://doi.org/10.1001/jama.298.14.1685

Cummings, N. A., & VandenBos, G. R. (1981). The twenty years Kaiser-Permanente experience with psychotherapy and medical utilization: Implications for national health policy and national health insurance. *Health Policy Quarterly*, *1*(2), 159–175.

Davidson, K. W., Gidron, Y., Mostofsky, E., & Trudeau, K. J. (2007, August). Hospitalization cost offset of a hostility intervention for coronary heart disease patients. *Journal of Consulting and Clinical Psychology*, *75*(4), 657–662. https://doi.org/10.1037/0022-006X.75.4.657

Dhabhar, F. S. (2014). Effects of stress on immune function: The good, the bad, and the beautiful. *Immunologic Research*, *58*(2–3), 193–210. https://doi.org/10.1007/s12026-014-8517-0

Duffing, T.M., Greiner, S.G., Mathias, C.W., & Dougherty, D.M. (2014). Stress, substance abuse, and addiction. In: C. Pariante & M. Lapiz-Bluhm (Eds.), Behavioral neurobiology of stress-related disorders: Current topics in behavioral neurosciences (vol 18). Springer, Berlin, Heidelberg. https://doi-org.yale.idm.oclc.org/10.1007/7854_2014_276

Dunkley, D. M., Blankstein, K. R., Masheb, R. M., & Grilo, C. M. (2006). Personal standards and evaluative concerns dimensions of "clinical" perfectionism: A reply to Shafran et al. (2002, 2003) and Hewitt et al. (2003). *Behaviour Research and Therapy*, *44*(1), 63–84. https://doi.org/10.1016/j.brat.2004.12.004

Egido, J. A., Castillo, O., Roig, B., Sanz, I., Herrero, M. R., Garay, M. T., Garcia, A. M., Fuentes, M., & Fernandez, C. (2012). Is psycho-physical stress a risk factor for stroke? A case-control study. *Journal of Neurology, Neurosurgery, and Psychiatry*, *83*(11), 1104–1110. https://doi.org/10.1136/jnnp-2012-302420

Evans, S. (2020). BAME excess deaths: Chronic stress and constant hostility. *British Journal of General Practice: The Journal of the Royal College of General Practitioners*, *70*(697), 395. https://doi.org/10.3399/bjgp20X712145

Everson, S. A., Kauhanen, J., Kaplan, G. A., Goldberg, D. E., Julkunen, J., Tuomilehto, J., & Salonen, J. T. (1997, July 15). Hostility and increased risk of mortality and acute myocardial infarction: The mediating role of behavioral risk factors. *American Journal of Epidemiology, 146*(2), 142–152. https://doi.org/10.1093/oxfordjournals.aje.a009245

Fischer, S., Doerr, J. M., Strahler, J., Mewes, R., Thieme, K., & Nater, U. M. (2016). Stress exacerbates pain in the everyday lives of women with fibromyalgia syndrome–The role of cortisol and alpha-amylase. *Psychoneuroendocrinology, 63*, 68–77. https://doi.org/10.1016/j.psyneuen.2015.09.018

Flett, G. L., Madorsky, D., Hewitt, P. L., et al. (2022). Perfectionism cognitions, rumination, and psychological distress. *Journal of Rational-Emotive and Cognitive-Behavior Therapy, 20*, 33–47. https://doi-org.yale.idm.oclc.org/10.1023/A:1015128904007

Greenberg, P. E., Fournier, A., Sisitsky, T., Pike, C. T., & Kessler, R. C. (2015). The economic burden of adults with major depressive disorder in the United States (2005 and 2010). *Journal of Clinical Psychiatry, 76*(2), 155–162. https://doi.org/10.4088/JCP.14m09298

Groër, M., Meagher, M. W., & Kendall-Tackett, K. (2010). An overview of stress and immunity. In K. Kendall-Tackett (Ed.), *The psychoneuroimmunology of chronic disease: Exploring the links between inflammation, stress, and illness* (pp. 9–22). American Psychological Association. https://doi.org/10.1037/12065-001

Hafner, M., Stepanek, M., Taylor, J., Troxel, W. M., & van Stolk, C. (2017). Why sleep matters-the economic costs of insufficient sleep: A cross-country comparative analysis. *Rand Health Quarterly, 6*(4), 11.

Hathaway, B. (2012a, January 9). Even in the healthy, stress causes brain to shrink, Yale study shows. *Yale News.* https://news.yale.edu/2012/01/09/even-healthy-stress-causes-brain-shrink-yale-study-shows

Hathaway, B. (2012b, August 12). Yale team discovers how stress and depression can shrink the brain. *Yale News.* https://news.yale.edu/2012/08/12/yale-team-discovers-how-stress-and-depression-can-shrink-brain

Hewitt, P. L., & Flett, G. L. (1991). Perfectionism in the self and social contexts: Conceptualization, assessment, and association with psychopathology. *Journal of Personality and Social Psychology, 60*(3), 456–470. https://doi.org/10.1037/0022-3514.60.3.456

Hölzel, B. K., Carmody, J., Vangel, M., Congleton, C., Yerramsetti, S. M., Gard, T., & Lazar, S. W. (2011). Mindfulness practice leads to increases in regional brain gray matter density. *Psychiatry Research, 191*(1), 36–43. https://doi.org/10.1016/j.pscychresns.2010.08.006

Kanai, A. (2009). "Karoshi (work to death)" in Japan. *Journal of Business Ethics, 84*(S2), 209–216. https://doi.org/10.1007/s10551-008-9701-8

Krantz, D. S., & McCeney, M. K. (2002). Effects of psychological and social factors on organic disease: A critical assessment of research on coronary heart disease*. *Annual Review of Psychology, 53*, 341–369. http://bi.gale.com.yale.idm.oclc.org/global/article/GALE%7CA83789650?u=29002

Kroenke, K. (2003). Patients presenting with somatic complaints: Epidemiology, psychiatric comorbidity and management. *International Journal of Methods in Psychiatric Research, 12*(1), 34–43. https://doi.org/10.1002/mpr.140

Kroenke, K., Spitzer, R. L., Williams, J. B. W., Lowe, B., & Monahan, P. O. (2007). Anxiety disorders in primary care: Prevalence, impairment, comorbidity and detection. *Annals of Internal Medicine*, *146*(5), 317. https://doi.org/10.7326/0003-4819-146-5-200703060-00004

Kuo, L. E., Kitlinska, J. B., Tilan, J. U., Li, L., Baker, S. B., Johnson, M. D., Lee, E. W., Burnett, M. S., Fricke, S. T., Kvetnansky, R., Herzog, H., & Zukowska, Z. (2007). Neuropeptide Y acts directly in the periphery on fat tissue and mediates stress-induced obesity and metabolic syndrome. *Nature Medicine*, *13*(7), 803–811. https://doi.org/10.1038/nm1611

Leger, K. A., Gloger, E. M., Maras, J., & Marshburn, C. K. (2022). Discrimination and health: The mediating role of daily stress processes. *Health Psychology*, *41*(5), 332–342. https://doi.org/10.1037/hea0001173

Lou, F., Li, M., & Florence, C. (2021). State-level economic costs of opioid use disorder and fatal opioid overdose—United States, 2017. *MMWR Morbidity and Mortality Weekly Report*, *70*(15), 541–546. http://doi.org/10.15585/mmwr.mm7015a1

Löwe, B., Kroenke, K., Williams, J. B. W.,Mussell, M., Schellberg, D., & Spitzer, R. L. (2008). Depression, anxiety and somatization in primary care: Syndrome overlap and functional impairment. *General Hospital Psychiatry*, *3*(3), 191–199. https://doi.org/10.1016/j.genhosppsych.2008.01.001

McEwen, B. S. (2013). The brain on stress: Toward an integrative approach to brain, body, and behavior. *Perspectives on Psychological Science: A journal of the Association for Psychological Science*, *8*(6), 673–675. https://doi.org/10.1177/1745691613506907

National Academy of Sciences. (2011). *Relieving pain in America, a blueprint for transforming prevention, care, education and research*. Institute of Medicine Report from the Committee on Advancing Pain Research, Care, and Education. www.ncbi.nlm.nih.gov/books/NBK91497/pdf/Bookshelf_NBK91497.pdf

Nerurkar, A., Bitton, A., Davis, R. B., Phillips, R. S., & Yeh, G. (2013). When physicians counsel about stress: Results of a national study. *JAMA Internal Medicine*, *173*(1), 76–77. https://doi.org/10.1001/2013.jamainternmed.480

Novak, M., Björck, L., Giang, K. W., Heden-Ståhl, C., Wilhelmsen, L., & Rosengren, A. (2013). Perceived stress and incidence of type 2 diabetes: A 35-year follow-up study of middle-aged Swedish men. *Diabetic Medicine: A Journal of the British Diabetic Association*, *30*(1), e8–e16. https://doi.org/10.1111/dme.12037

Pittenger, C., & Duman, R. (2008). Stress, depression, and neuroplasticity: A convergence of mechanisms. *Neuropsychopharmacology*, *33*(1), 88–109. https://doi.org/10.1038/sj.npp.1301574

RAND Corporation. "Lack of sleep costing US economy up to $411 billion per year." News Release, November 30, 2016. https://www.rand.org/news/press/2016/11/30.html

Schneiderman, N., Ironson, G., & Siegel, S. D. (2005). Stress and health: Psychological, behavioral, and biological determinants. *Annual Review of Clinical Psychology*, *1*, 607–628. https://doi.org/10.1146/annurev.clinpsy.1.102803.144141

Shirneshan, E. (2013). Cost of illness study of anxiety disorders for the ambulatory adult population of the United States. Theses and Dissertations (ETD). Paper 370. http://doi.org/10.21007/ etd.cghs.2013.0289

Sommerfeldt, S. L., Schaefer, S. M., Brauer, M., Ryff, C. D., & Davidson, R. J. (2019). Individual differences in the association between subjective stress and heart rate are related to psychological and physical well-being. *Psychological Science, 30*(7), 1016–1029. https://doi.org/10.1177/0956797619849555

Steptoe, A., & Kivimäki, M. (2012). Stress and cardiovascular disease. *Nature Reviews Cardiology, 9*(6), 360–370. https://doi.org/10.1038/nrcardio.2012.45

Toivanen, S. (2012). Social determinants of stroke as related to stress at work among working women: A literature review. *Stroke Research and Treatment, 2012*, 873678. https://doi.org/10.1155/2012/873678

Torino, G. (2017, November 10). How racism and microaggressions lead to worse health. *Center for Health Journalism.* https://centerforhealthjournalism.org/2017/11/08/how-racism-and-microaggressions-lead-worse-health

US Centers for Disease Control and Prevention, Alcohol and Public Health. *The cost of excessive alcohol use: A drain on the American economy.* www.cdc.gov/alcohol/onlinemedia/infographics/cost-excessive-alcohol-use.html

US Centers for Disease Control and Prevention, National Center for Chronic Disease Prevention and Health Promotion (NCCDPHP). www.cdc.gov/chronicdisease/about/costs/

US National Institutes of Health, National Institute on Drug Abuse Archives. *Costs of substance use.* https://archives.drugabuse.gov/trends-statistics/costs-substance-abuse#supplemental-references-for-economic-costs

Walker, J. G., Littlejohn, G. O., McMurray, N. E., & Cutolo, M. (1999). Stress system response and rheumatoid arthritis: A multilevel approach. *Rheumatology, 38*(11), 1050–1057. https://doi.org/10.1093/rheumatology/38.11.1050

World Health Organization. (2022). *Mental health at work: Policy brief.* www.ilo.org/wcmsp5/groups/public/---ed_protect/---protrav/---safework/documents/publication/wcms_856976.pdf

CHAPTER 4

Self-Care Strategies and Overcoming
Barriers to Healthy Routines

Self-care is a responsibility, not a luxury. Self-care reflects those healthy behaviors you engage in to keep your mind and body running smoothly. It means different things to different people, and where you focus your energy will depend on your individual needs and circumstances.

Self-care is no less important than work, family, or our household responsibilities. Nonetheless, many people treat self-care as an extravagance, as something they need to earn, or something they will indulge in occasionally. Today, the importance of promoting well-being in the legal community is more appreciated, but this was not always the case. As a colleague in the state bar association once said to me, "In the 1990s, lawyer well-being meant getting together for a few drinks at happy hour after work." Self-care has traditionally been viewed as an excess that perhaps one will get to eventually. Maybe tomorrow, maybe this weekend, maybe next week, next month, next year…

Despite recent heightened awareness in the legal profession about the importance of self-care, many lawyers still do not know how to nurture themselves, or at least do not give themselves permission to set aside time for what is perceived as self-indulgence. As an achievement-oriented group, hard work is considered the best route to success. Law school and legal practice further reinforce a staunch work ethic, and de-emphasize the importance of, and focus on, internal experiences and self-care. During law school, budding attorneys quickly learn to avoid, suppress, or ignore emotions, as well as the physical sensations which indicate stress. This chronic avoidance can lead to unhealthy coping strategies, such as self-medication with alcohol or drugs. Early idealistic views can quickly become trampled by the realities of law practice and the accompanying stressors, which can further exacerbate distress.

Self-care is often neglected when we are tired, stressed, or feeling pressed for time. When we are busy or feeling overwhelmed, self-care tends to be the first thing we let slide. Why do we neglect our self-care at the times when it is most important? Quite possibly because our own self-care is one of the only things over which we have complete control. We think we can put it off and

33   DOI: 10.4324/9781003285519-4

"Stress management is for wimps!"

Figure 4.1 Stress Management Is for Wimps (Randy Glasbergen, 2004)

"get to it later," although later may never happen. It may also feel selfish or impractical to focus on yourself in the face of major work or family stressors.

Self-care is not a temporary band-aid, applied solely during times of stress. While most needed during challenging times, self-care strategies and routines build resiliency, grounding us against unexpected turns of events, sudden demands, and downturns. Self-care builds a foundation for stability, endurance, and perseverance. Self-care is preventive, helping you deal with day-to-day hassles and inoculating you against overwhelm during those times when you hit a bump in the road. It helps you manage conflicts and pressures in relation to self, personal life, and work. Self-care does not remove all chance of symptoms, but it does help reduce the severity of stress and distress in daily life and when facing major workplace challenges or life events.

This is why it is so important to establish a self-care routine before you need it, when you have the energy to learn a new skill and the time to develop a new routine through repeated behaviors. Just as you practiced oral arguments and trial strategy in law school before setting foot in a courtroom, practiced an instrument before getting on stage, or practiced a sport before jumping into a game or meet, self-care strategies need to be practiced in advance of times of stress, so they become an automatic process, like driving home from work each day or brushing your teeth.

Finally, setting realistic expectations is important for any new undertaking. When embarking on a new project, including prioritizing self-care, your

34

likelihood for success will be influenced by the expectations you set for yourself. Realistic expectations and goals are things which are attainable, as opposed to setting the bar so high you also set yourself up for failure. When establishing goals for yourself, keep in mind that although achieving success, no matter how small, is a powerful motivator, failure can have the opposite effect. It helps to practice self-compassion, and compassion for others, and remember that self-care helps protect us from adversity, but it does not necessarily completely eliminate distress.

Part I: Overcoming Barriers and Recognizing the Importance of Self-Care

Barriers to Self-Care in the Legal Community

Mental Health Stigma and the Fallacy That Only
Wimps Need to Practice Self-Care

For a long time, issues related to self-care and well-being were not topics for consideration or discussion, lest one be considered "soft," "weak" and maybe even a little "woo-woo" or flakey. Besides, who has time for self-care?

When presenting to lawyers and legal professionals on the importance of self-care, I often begin with the cartoon earlier in this chapter (Figure 4.1), depicting a character holding a person-sized coffee cup and declaring to a colleague "Stress management is for wimps!" (Randy Glasbergen, 2004). This slide invariably brings chuckles. While the slide is amusing, I also point out the fact that it is amusing because there is more than a kernel of truth to it in the legal community.

Based on my experiences as a law student and practicing lawyer, and later working with lawyers as a psychologist and coach, I came to realize stress is considered a badge of honor for many in the legal profession. The thinking behind the bias goes something like this: *If you are stressed, you must be busy (and important)! And if you waste billable hours with yoga, meditation, or exercise, you must be a wimp, or at least not that busy or important.* And yet, as legal practice becomes increasingly complicated by modern technology, lawyers need to practice self-care in order for it to be sustainable.

Mental health stigma in the legal profession is broad in scope, seemingly encompassing any emotional expression that could be construed as vulnerable, such as symptoms of anxiety, depression, or overwhelming stress. The origins of this stigma are likely a combination of the personal traits of those who self-select into the profession, the emphasis on and framing of emotions as representing irrationality during the first year of law school, as well as the history of character and fitness questions on state bar examinations.

Over time, the meaning of the word "stigma" has shifted away from the literal reference to a mark, spot, scar, or branding, to reflect a shameful trait, such as mental illness. Erving Goffman wrote that stigma is "an attribute that is deeply discrediting" which diminishes a person "from a whole and usual person to a tainted, discounted one." Ahmedani defined stigma as "stereotypes or negative views attributed to a person or groups of people when their characteristics or behaviors are viewed as different from or inferior to societal norms."

Stigma and bias result from the brain's tendency to create categories as a way to facilitate processing of large amounts of information. Cognitive science has shown we all categorize in this way. Categorization is adaptive, helping us deal with the otherwise overwhelming load of information we continually receive and process. At the same time, this efficiency can lead to judgmental stances and biases if left unchecked.

Stigma around mental illness functions in two ways. For onlookers, stigma creates social distance from stigmatized individuals by positing that mental illnesses, or simply symptoms of emotional distress, reflect moral or character failings, weakness, or laziness. Such social distancing is self-protective; blaming the person with mental illness makes the concept less threatening. The myth persists that "the mentally ill" are more dangerous than "normal" people, even though research in fact suggests they are more likely to be victims of crime. Stigma also elicits shame in people who believe others know about their stigmatized condition, leading them to come across as more tense and less likeable, while also impairing their performance.

The legal profession is particularly prone to being affected by the shunning and shaming effects of stigma. As first years, law students are taught that experiencing strong emotions reflects weakness, and such emotions must be avoided or suppressed so one can "think like a lawyer." In addition, here in the US, state bar examiners began asking questions about mental health, including, for instance, the Connecticut Bar Examining Committee (CBEC) in 1984. By the early 1990s in Connecticut:

> Applicants were required to reveal whether they had ever received treatment for any mental, emotional, or nervous disorder; whether they had ever been hospitalized or committed to an institution (voluntarily or involuntarily) for mental illness; whether they had ever been addicted to alcohol or other drugs; and whether they had ever been treated for substance abuse. An affirmative answer to any of these set the machinery of character and fitness screening in motion.
>
> *Bauer (2001)*

In a promising sign of progress, the US Department of Justice and the CBEC reached a settlement in 2019 regarding Americans with Disabilities Act (ADA) complaints brought against the CBEC, and all questions "regarding an applicant's health diagnosis, treatment or drug or alcohol dependence," were removed from the bar application and are no longer asked of an applicant's employers or personal references. CBEC also agreed to remove its specific regulation titled "Mental Health Inquiry," and further agreed "not to place applicants on a conditional admission status based solely on the applicant's health diagnosis, treatment or drug or alcohol dependence." Similar questions, which have plagued bar applicants in states around the country, were removed from the New York bar exam in 2020, and other states have since followed.

This history of bias and discrimination likely leads many attorneys to shun efforts that target their well-being. For many attorneys, the vulnerability that comes with sharing emotions is too risky in the largely adversarial profession, and this has traditionally been compounded by both the law school learning experience and the bar admission process.

Stigmatization of mental health needs among legal professionals is so deeply ingrained that any professional intervention may be perceived as reflecting a deficit or weakness. The experience of negative emotions (e.g., fear of failing, worry, impending depression, burnout) is often accompanied by a strong sense of shame, which prevents the sufferer from seeking professional assistance. Health-promoting initiatives may further be viewed as contrary to the emotional learning from law school and its reinforcement in practice.

As a result, attorneys have looked to various less adaptive ways to deal with internal distress. Alcohol or drug use may become a habitual "quick fix" for suppressing or avoiding emotional discomfort, with potentially high risk. Shame also inhibits seeking social support from colleagues, leading to further feelings of stigmatization and social isolation, in a vicious downward spiral. Quite tragically, the inability to seek help to address mental health and addiction has led too many attorneys to view suicide as the only way to get relief. The American Bar Association reported in 2022 that approximately 20% of lawyers and staff have considered suicide at some point.

If you find yourself rejecting, dismissing, or tuning out any portion or all of this book, pause and ask yourself, "Why? Why am I tuning out? Why am I dismissing, devaluing, or disregarding this information?" It is possible that unrecognized bias or stigma is influencing your thinking about these topics and your response. For more about addressing mental health stigma in the workplace, see Chapter 5, Understanding and Addressing Workplace Issues Which Impact Well-Being.

BOX 4.1 WORK AS A DISTRACTION FROM LIFE STRESSORS

The pandemic lockdowns exacerbated any propensity to turn to work as a coping strategy because there was often nothing else to do, or options were severely limited. The usual dinners, networking events, and entertainment were all on hold. Gyms were closed. As more than one lawyer put it, "I have nothing better to do, so I might as well work in the evening."

Stoicism and Avoidance

In addition to the deterring effects of stigma, lawyers and other professionals have a propensity to take a stoic approach in the face of crisis and uncertainty. What do many lawyers do when in crisis and feeling a lack of control? They turn to what they do best: Work. They work more. They work harder. They work longer hours. Psychologists call this avoidance. When faced with an unexpected life challenge, we tend to do more of the same, what we are good at, such as working. We do this automatically. You learned early on that through hard work, you can solve problems. When you are dealing with an unexpected crisis, pay attention and ask yourself if this is what you are doing.

> A colleague and mentor once shared a story with me about his work behavior following his wife's cancer diagnosis. The next day, he went into the office and told his colleagues they would not be seeing him around as much and he would not be as accessible. He was going to focus on being a strong support for his wife and would get more involved with work again in about six months. Six months later, he reflected on the months that had passed; not only was he not working less—he realized he had been working more than ever! When faced with the difficult challenge of his wife's cancer diagnosis and uncertain outcome, one over which he had no control and felt powerless, he did what many people do and immersed himself in his work, a place where he was successful and could feel a sense of control and productivity.

Slow down and listen. Lawyers and other take-charge professionals tend to respond to ambiguity with efforts to control everything in their power. During times of stress, uncertainty, and crisis, your family, colleagues, and clients need empathy and to feel heard. While you may be accustomed to having all the answers, or at least feeling like you do, the better approach is one of careful listening, reflection, and transparency, acknowledging the many unknowns, and then focusing on how you plan to move forward.

It is important to note, even though you are ignoring your stress and pretending it is not there, its insidious effects are still taking shape. One risk of not dealing with stressors directly is that some people turn to substances as a way to relax and mute discomfort. For more on the negative physical health, mental health, and cognitive performance effects of stress, see Chapter 3, Attention to Overall Physical and Mental Health.

Time and Delayed Results

Even when you do all the right things, many self-care strategies take time and you do not see immediate benefits. In fact, you may even feel worse initially. You may still feel tired, and still lack energy. You may experience muscle or joint soreness. You may feel hungry, or experience cravings for caffeine, carbs, sweets, nicotine, or alcohol. With increasing age, it may take increasing time and effort to obtain the same results from diet and exercise. Each of these experiences individually can feel deflating, and in combination can overpower even the best intentions toward improving self-care unless you remain vigilant in your efforts.

Beware of Professional Liability Risks

One of the reasons the legal community is increasingly interested in promoting lawyer well-being has to do with the financial and reputational costs related to professional liability issues. Attorneys who are burned out are more at risk of mishandling or failing to manage their caseload. While avoidance may help in the short term with keeping emotions in check, and can lead to a boost in productivity, working more is not an effective long-term well-being strategy. Some problems are not solved by working hard, or solely with logic. We need to step back and take care of ourselves. Over-work without adequate breaks and self-care interventions sets you up for problems down the line, such as burnout, depression, anxiety, substance use, even suicide. If you push yourself to the point of burnout, your work suffers. Colleagues and clients will notice, and you put yourself at risk for filed grievances, legal action, and professional liability.

Self-Care Helps Promote Resilience

What Is Resilience? The word "resilience" is tossed around a lot. It originates in the work of positive psychology pioneer Martin Seligman. It is another one of those words which may not be completely understood by everyone who uses it. *Resilience* reflects personal traits and your overall outlook on life. Importantly, resilience *does not mean* you are immune to highly stressful events; in fact, resilient individuals facing difficult life events may experience temporary symptoms of stress, depression, or anxiety. Along the same perfectionist lines that lead lawyers to strive to prevail at all costs, research has shown how you approach mistakes, and your performance, also has an impact on your well-being. Instead of focusing on the negative, it is important to be able to frame mistakes more positively as a learning opportunity and strategize for the future.

How we approach the uncertainty in our lives makes all the difference in whether we thrive or just get by. The science of resiliency looks at how some people can manage adversity (although still distressed by it) and bounce back relatively unscathed or even stronger than before. The trait which most distinguishes resilient people is their view of the world (i.e., the glass is half full) and their approach to challenging life events and circumstances. Responses to life's challenges tend to be more proactive, positive, and hopeful, with resilient individuals viewing the situation as manageable, circumscribed, and temporary, and viewing themselves as capable of effectuating change. As a result, those who are resilient tend to have a more positive outlook and a problem-solving approach, which allow them to quickly bounce back from difficult life events and return to original levels of functioning. We are not necessarily born resilient. Adaptation, involving acquiring new skills and resources, is a process that often arises in response to stressful life events. This can manifest on the individual level as adopting new coping strategies and becoming more focused on priorities.

Notably, stress-related growth takes this positive response to adversity one step further, with research suggesting that some people over time end up in a psychologically better place than they were prior to a stressful life event. This growth arises out of learning from adversity and engaging adaptive responses, such as adopting healthy coping strategies, working on enhancing or improving relationships, and for some, a new focus on spirituality. This process can result in greater resilience going forward in the people who experience stress-related growth.

On the organizational level, resilience may be reflected in agility and the ability to change course to meet the changing needs of employees and clients, potentially reflected in the adoption of flexible work arrangements and expanded service offerings. The most resilient individuals and organizations will grow when faced with unprecedented challenges, learning new, adaptive ways of managing stress and uncertainty, supporting well-being, and promoting healthy work environments.

Positive Affect Promotes Mental and Physical Health and Performance

Recent research suggests positive affect is related to better cognitive functioning, including memory, decision-making, and strategizing. Positive affect also provides a buffer against chronic stress and negative emotions. Affect refers to our internal experience of emotions and moods. The valence of our thoughts influences our affect, which in turn influences flexibility of thinking and problem-solving ability. Positive emotions broaden our thinking, promoting flexible and creative thought processes. In one study, the buffering effects of positive affect were supported by a finding of improved cardiovascular reactivity in study participants who experienced a positive affect intervention as compared to study participants who were exposed to an intervention which elicited a sad or neutral emotional response. Positive affect is also thought to have a protective effect against other negative health consequences of chronic stress, including immune, endocrine, and neural responses, which in turn can lead to disease. As mentioned earlier, chronic stress or distress can also lead to depression; however, experiencing moments of positive mood during ongoing stressful circumstances can help prevent a lapse into depression by interrupting and inhibiting the negative ruminatory thought cycle. In contrast, the absence of co-occurring positive affect during prolonged, high levels of stress and distress increases the likelihood of becoming clinically depressed.

Beware of Toxic Positivity

Interest in positive psychology has grown exponentially since the early 2000s, along with recognition of the value of positive thinking in terms of promoting our well-being, resilience, and longevity. In recent years, references to "toxic positivity" in the popular press have also increased. We can think of toxic positivity as fostering misdirected efforts to suppress, ignore, or deny negative emotions, in service of staying positive.

Denying negative emotions by pretending to be in a positive mood or saying things like "It's fine" or "I'm fine" or "It's nothing," can be detrimental to your mental health, or that of the person you are speaking with. It can lead to negative self-judgment, guilt, or shame about feeling down, depressed, or worried. It can lead to rumination, or constantly cycling through negative thoughts, which can feed into a negative thought and emotion spiral. And it can lead to emotional suppression, which has its own negative consequences. Research has found that emotional suppression promotes unhealthy cardiovascular activation and appears to increase risk of premature death. In addition, chronic emotional inhibition may lead to poorer thinking ability by virtue of the increased efforts to suppress, which are distracting and reduce mental capacity.

Emotional suppression may also negatively impact your behaviors and interactions with others, either as a result of your own suppression behaviors, if you are not attuned to how the actions of others are negatively impacting you, or if someone else suppresses their anger in response to your behavior. In both scenarios the person whose behavior leads to anger or discomfort is either not challenged to change, or is unaware of the impact of their behavior, risking continued offensive behavior and resulting distress. For more on the importance of recognizing and responding appropriately to emotions in ourselves and others in the workplace, emotional intelligence is addressed in Chapter 5, Understanding and Addressing Workplace Issues Which Impact Well-Being.

Paradoxically, acknowledging and accepting negative emotions can help decrease them (rather than make them worse). It is important to acknowledge a challenge and mourn a loss, experience our sadness, grief, or anger. Sometimes, our worries are based on real-world threats and while we do our best to manage them, they do not completely disappear in the presence of the threat.

The appeal of positive thinking for lawyers comes with risks. There is a risk that unrestrained embracing of positive thinking in the legal community can undermine lawyer and staff mental health by reinforcing deeply embedded beliefs that emotions, and in particular negative emotions (other than anger), reflect weakness and a lack of competence. While it is important to recognize the value in positive affect, a positive outlook, and happiness, we also need to take care to not go to extremes. These "stay positive" efforts, without any acknowledgement of distress, might in effect devalue or stigmatize negative emotions as unacceptable which can paradoxically further increase them and be detrimental to well-being.

Instead of striving for constant positivity, "realistic optimism" is a better way to go, hoping for the best, preparing for the worst, and acknowledging your fear (to yourself, a loved one, a trusted colleague, friend, or neutral professional such as a coach or therapist). In fact, research suggests if we acknowledge and accept negative emotions, they are less likely to harm our overall well-being. Instead of focusing on being happy, we are better served by engaging in behaviors and activities which promote our happiness. For more on the impact of toxic positivity on relationships and psychological safety, see Chapter 8, The Essential Role of Personal Relationships and Social Supports in Well-Being.

Reconsidering the Value of Emotions

All of this information presents challenges to the legal community. Earlier psychological research reinforced lawyer concerns about emotion corrupting thinking, but more recent research suggests positive affect is related to better cognitive functioning, including memory, decision-making, and strategizing, and that acknowledging and accepting negative emotions is also related to better functioning. It is time to reconsider the role of emotion and how emotions are valued and treated. The research supports an integrated approach of utilizing emotions to enhance our experience and understand our thinking.

Finding a Balance Somewhere Between Cynic and Pollyanna. How do we promote well-being while at the same time keeping lawyers grounded, attuned to the finer details of their work, and appropriately skeptical? The answer, as with most things, requires deliberate effort and balance—likely falling somewhere in the middle between crotchety cynic and naïve Pollyanna—remaining both realistic and optimistic, hoping for the best while preparing for the worst. With the knowledge of what well-being looks like and what you as an individual and/or as a leader need to do to promote your well-being and that of your colleagues and organization at large, you can foster self-care, healthy relationships and work environments, assertive and respectful communications, appropriate work–life boundaries, and a healthy dose of skepticism, without falling down the rabbit hole of negativity, cynicism, and possibly despair.

Framing Self-Care as a Targeted Response to Thoughts, Emotions, and Behaviors

Research suggests our subjective experience of well-being is influenced by several internal and external factors. Both internal thoughts and feelings as well as social interactions and experiences are essential to well-being. The cognitive-behavioral framework is helpful when thinking about well-being and targeted self-care interventions. Our thoughts, emotions, and behaviors are all interconnected, each feeding into and influencing each other. The cognitive behavioral model, originating in the work of psychology pioneers Albert Ellis and Aaron Beck, is well-established in the psychological science literature and provides an important foundation for understanding the inter-relationships between our underlying thoughts and beliefs (conscious or not), our experience of emotions, and our behaviors (including inaction).

If you are depressed, you likely experience less energy, are less active, engage in negative thought cycles, and have difficulty thinking clearly or concentrating. If you are anxious, you may similarly have difficulty thinking clearly and concentrating, but you may experience excess energy and restlessness or may avoid stressful situations. If you are sick with a virus, your body is signaling to you it needs rest, and ideally you will respond by acknowledging (thoughts) you are not feeling well and getting the rest you need (behavior), even though you may feel frustrated (emotion) about missing work or other life events. If you don't get any rest after you catch the common cold, you may end up with a more severe illness, such as pneumonia. Similarly, if you are experiencing burnout and do not acknowledge it in your thoughts and modify your behavior to allow yourself to recharge, you put yourself at risk of developing a more debilitating mental or physical illness.

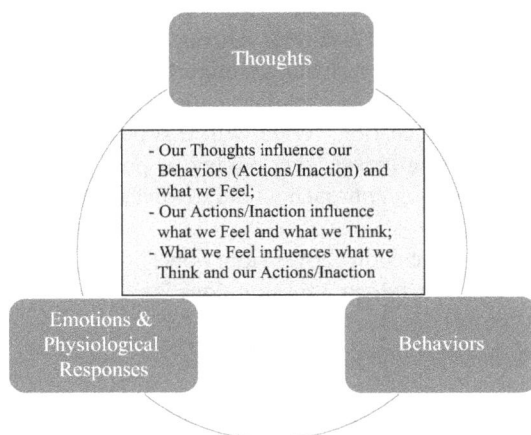

Figure 4.2 The Cognitive Behavioral Framework

The Role of Thoughts and Beliefs in Managing Challenges and Stress

Lawyers with a strong sense of self-efficacy and perceived control believe they have the ability, skills, and resources to address problems and change a negative situation. People who are high in self-efficacy, and who believe circumstances are within their control, tend to be more proactive and problem-focused when dealing with stressful circumstances, which translates into greater resilience. Conversely, if you believe a situation is not under your control and that you are at the mercy of external forces, you are more likely to feel helpless and therefore more susceptible to negative stress consequences.

For instance, if you are a junior associate and your team leader or boss does not provide you with the feedback and autonomy you need to learn and grow, only harshly criticizing as opposed to providing both constructive and positive feedback, your sense of self-efficacy and perceived control may be low. Similarly, if you feel a high degree of responsibility and yet limited authority to make decisions, this conflict will create stress that over time can have a negative impact on your well-being.

Considering how thoughts influence emotional and physiological responses, which in turn influence behaviors, it makes sense that beliefs about perceived control and self-efficacy are so important. Self-care strategies will be most effective if they are tailored to specific individual needs and contexts, targeting the most pressing challenges.

The Importance of Mindset—Shift Your Thinking

"Mindset" is another term used to describe how thoughts influence emotions, physiological responses, and behavior. During times of intense stress and uncertainty, mindset becomes especially important. For instance, when dealing with a difficult workload or workplace situation, it is not helpful to keep rhetorically asking the question "When will this be over?," which reflects a more passive, fatalistic mindset, one lacking in perceived control. A more proactive, self-effectuating approach would involve asking a few questions:

- "What do I have control over right now?"
- "What can I learn from this situation?"
- "What have I discovered about myself?"
- "What do I need to do going forward?"

When it comes to ongoing stressors over which you have no control, you can better manage the situation if you adopt a more positive, proactive mindset. At the same time, when doing so, it is important to set realistic expectations.

A Cautious Approach to Stress Mindset/Stress Optimization

The concept of "stress mindset" has generated interest in the well-being realm, particularly as it relates to organizational psychology. Researchers have suggested that stress is a state of mind and thinking about the benefits of stress can reduce negative effects. This line of research originated in the patient experience context, involving patients who are worried that their stress will make their health condition worse, and later, students concerned that their stress will decrease their performance on an important exam—in other words, these people were stressed about their stress. Importantly, the study participants reflected a very narrow subset of people. Sure, if you are stressed about your stress, we should address this first. Nonetheless, addressing stress about our stress is only a small part of the problem; the stress itself, and the underlying cause of it, must ultimately be addressed.

Most importantly, the biggest risk with this approach to stress is that it puts all the responsibility onto the person who is experiencing stress. This is problematic for two reasons: 1) It leaves out the role of one's work environment. As your employer, I can say:

> "Traci, I realize we expect a lot out of you. You need to bill 5,000 hours a year, the partner leading your group is controlling, explosive, and antagonistic, and we expect you to respond to all electronic communications within 30 minutes. But stress is good for you! You just need to learn how to optimize your stress!"

and, 2) It blames the person experiencing stress, which often keeps people from seeking help early, if at all.

The ability to focus on the positive in life is an important skill. But a hyper-focus on staying positive can alienate anyone who is struggling in the moment and not feeling very positive at all, increasing feelings of isolation, and decreasing the likelihood of reaching out to others for support or help. See Chapter 8, The Essential Role of Personal Relationships and Social Supports in Well-Being, for more on "toxic positivity."

Options for Dealing with Difficult People or Situations

If you find yourself in an unhealthy work environment, you have many options under your control, including:

- Your ability to engage in your own self-care.
- Your ability to speak with trusted colleagues, mentors, HR, supervisors, or firm leaders about your needs.
- Your ability to vote with your feet and seek employment elsewhere.

Instead of feeling victimized or encroached upon by toxic colleagues or workplace culture, it is helpful to think about your existing skills and resources, how you are growing and learning (or are able to do so) during this difficult period, and how you can make the most of the situation. Instead of focusing on how much you are tired of a difficult situation, your energy would be better spent strategizing ways to proactively address it. You have three main options for dealing with a difficult person or situation. You can:

1. *Change the Situation.* You might talk with your team leader or supervisor to request support, flexibility, or more interesting work. You might set boundaries with a colleague, or tell them how their behavior is impacting your ability to do your work.

2. *Change How You Respond to the Situation.* This might involve a change in how you deal with the situation, or through acceptance. If you have tried to be proactive and have come to realize things are not going to change, you can change your expectations for the situation and yourself, change your behaviors accordingly, and engage in self-care strategies to reduce any potential negative impacts. The term "Quiet Quitting" has been in the popular press a lot lately. That response would fall in this category, though I do not endorse it. It reflects a passive response that does nothing to advance your growth, learning, or career.

3. *Leave the Situation.* Finally, if you are unable to change the situation and find it untenable, you can always leave (with a well-thought-out Plan B in mind, of course). The Great Resignation is an example of many lawyers voting with their feet and leaving challenging work environments or unreasonable expectations in search of greener pastures.

Engage in Self-Care to Support Emotional Intelligence

Emotional intelligence reflects an ability to recognize your own internal thought processes, emotional triggers, and flaws, as well as the impact of your words and behaviors on others. It involves empathy, being able to recognize how others are feeling and respond in a way that reflects care and concern. When you are sleep-deprived, stressed, dealing with mental health concerns, or simply over-worked and under-rested, your ability to respond to challenges in an emotionally intelligent way becomes compromised. An emotionally intelligent leader is able to recognize simmering relational conflicts and adeptly identify and address them in a way that maintains psychological safety and respect, leaves people feeling heard and valued, and gains the support of those involved. On the other hand, if leadership and colleague behavior foster competitiveness and distrust, the overall culture will still be unhealthy and harmful to the well-being of all involved. For more on workplace culture, including psychological safety and emotional intelligence, see

46

Chapter 5, Understanding and Addressing Workplace Issues Which Impact Well-Being.

Part II: Self-Care Strategies and Seeking Assistance

The best way to promote well-being is through prevention, engaging in self-care to nourish your mind and body before you experience serious illness or are incapable of performing your work responsibilities. You might be thinking you will grind through until (fill in the blank____, e.g., the house is paid off, the kids are out of college, you secured your vacation home or boat, or achieved a certain level of professional status, etc.), and then you will retire or work less and focus on self-care. The risk here is that your physical health, relationships, or other life circumstances may not cooperate with that plan, and the harder you grind, the more likely they will not cooperate in the long term.

When embarking on a new self-care routine, start small. Set a goal that is realistic, one you know you can accomplish. The success of meeting your goal will energize, motivate, and propel you toward continued self-care and an enhanced routine. Gradually build new goals onto your original goal (which is now a routine) with other challenging but realistic goals. If you expect too much, too soon, you will be setting yourself up for failure. No one needs to tell you failure does not feel good and is discouraging, demoralizing, and saps the energy out of you. Try writing down some goals and ranking them in order from easiest to most difficult to achieve. Start from the easiest and work your way through the list.

Daily Self-Checks Are Essential

Self-checks are an important part of our self-care routine, helping us to recognize early signs of distress or burnout through awareness of our thoughts, feelings, and behaviors. No one is immune from the stress of the legal profession. Chronic stress can be insidious in that often people are unaware of its physical and psychological effects on their own performance or well-being, or the unhealthy behavior patterns that they begin to develop over time. Without self-care, the stressful nature of legal culture takes its toll on all attorneys in one form or another: physical, cognitive, physiological, or emotional. Everyone responds to stress in their own ways.

- *Daily Self-Check.* Begin your daily self-check by asking yourself, "What do I need right now?" and "What can I do about it?" You can then get more specific with your questions… "How are my attention, memory, and concentration?", "How do I feel physically?", and perhaps one of the most difficult for attorneys, "How do I feel emotionally?"

A daily self-check simply involves checking in with yourself, asking yourself how you are feeling mentally, physically, and emotionally. If any one of the three is off, make a plan to address it. Do you need a day off? A long weekend? A vacation? Do you need to check in with your primary care physician or another healthcare provider? Do you need to get more exercise? More sleep? Cut back on your alcohol use? Do you need to set aside time with friends or loved ones? Might it be time to make that call to a therapist or coach?

Better yet, check in with yourself throughout the day. Recognizing when you need a break—and taking one—helps to maximize your efficiency and productivity.

Perhaps all you need is a quick fix (such as reading a favorite comedic line, engaging in a box breathing exercise, taking a walk around the block, or spending a few minutes talking with a loved one, friend, or colleague). Or it may be that you need to plan to work on developing a new routine (such as a new sleep schedule or exercise regimen, or find ways to spend more quality time with the people most important to you). Finally, it may be that you need to reach out to a healthcare provider or another professional to attend to underlying symptoms or concerns.

When addressing mental, physical, or emotional strain, and managing stress, it helps to identify your strengths, weaknesses, needs and preferences. The best interventions will be tailored to the person to ensure a good fit and actual utilization.

Anticipatory Pleasure—Rarely Discussed but Vitally Important for Well-Being

When you are working 60–80 hours a week and barely have time to sleep, foster relationships, or manage household responsibilities, you also likely don't have much time or energy for planning events or experiences. You may go with the flow and go along with whatever someone else in your orbit plans. If this person has compatible interests, great. If not, you may not find yourself especially looking forward to your plans but view them as better than nothing. If you don't plan, and no one else does either, then there may be little to look forward to day to day. This is where anticipatory pleasure comes into play.

Anticipatory pleasure is the experience of positive emotions that arise when thinking about a future event, whether it be a vacation, gathering, an entertainment event, milestone event, or celebration. It may involve planning a vacation, researching destination options and activities, as well as taking moments from time to time to think about and visualize your vacation, and what you hope to experience. In fact, research suggests you may even derive more pleasure from the anticipation of a vacation during the lead up than from the vacation itself. Engaging in mental imagery, such visualizing in detail your vacation destination, or an important event or encounter, enhances the pleasure benefit. It may involve thinking about plans to meet a close friend or loved one for lunch or dinner at a favorite restaurant away from the office, or going to a concert, or another event. If you find yourself feeling burned out at work, ask yourself when was the last time you planned for and took a vacation? When was the last time you looked forward to something?

To further illustrate, one of the unique aspects of the COVID-19 pandemic was how it wreaked havoc on anticipatory pleasure. The early days of the pandemic left us with a *Groundhog Day* effect, with each day—like the days portrayed in the 1993 movie—possibly feeling like an exact replica of the day before, as our options for entertainment, socializing, or doing much of anything, were limited. Most people did not have anything to look forward to, with travel plans, events, entertainment venues, and dining options all canceled or closed.

Even without a global pandemic, you may be experiencing a *Groundhog Day* effect at work, with weekdays and weekends blurring, with days, turning into weeks, turning into months… If this is the case for you, it may be time to plan something fun.

Self-Care Basics

The basics of self-care (some of which can be combined!), take time and planning. You have control over your own behavior—such as creating a structured work schedule, recognizing your need for breaks and taking them, getting regular exercise, engaging in healthy eating, healthy sleep habits, adaptive communication, socializing and connecting with others, deep breathing, mindfulness, yoga and meditation, and… having fun. Develop a routine that works best for you, based on your needs, preferences, and schedule. See Appendix I for a Self-Care Basics Tip Sheet.

Strategies for Managing Stress, Mood, and Anxiety

We cannot be simultaneously stressed and relaxed, just like we cannot be inhaling and exhaling at the same time (try it now!). You can disengage the cycle of worry with a variety of mindful and behavioral exercises. Many of these interventions activate our parasympathetic nervous system and stop the acute stress response. The key is to find the intervention that works best for you. While incredibly effective, meditation is not for everyone. If you find meditation is not helpful, perhaps another more structured intervention would work better for you.

Breathing Exercises—A Simple, Quick, and Effective Way to Relax Anytime, Anywhere

Simple breathing exercises are a great way to stimulate our relaxation response. Breathing exercises activate the parasympathetic nervous system and generate a sense of relaxation by decreasing heart rate and blood pressure, releasing muscle tension, and inducing slower, deeper breathing. Breathing exercises are brief, easy to self-administer, and time efficient. Engaging in deep breathing for just a few minutes is highly effective and continued practice will provide the most benefit. Deep breathing is a great strategy when you are feeling pressed for time, dealing with logistical challenges or difficult people, or sitting in the car, stuck in traffic. With regular practice, you will begin to relax after just one deep breath. You can engage in deep breathing anytime and anywhere... at your desk, while in a meeting, while driving... Taking a deep breath can be subtle so no one will even know you are doing it. Once you master the breathing technique, you will quickly realize that breathing exercises are a simple, quick, and effective way to induce a relaxation response.

Deep Breathing Technique. Before beginning any breathing exercise, it is important to ensure you are breathing correctly. Many people do not know how to deep breathe properly. We learn at an early age to contract (suck in) our abdomen, typically as we inhale, so we look slim and svelte in that bathing suit or form-fitting outfit. This is exactly the *opposite* of effective deep breathing. Proper deep breathing technique involves expanding your abdomen as you slowly inhale, allowing your lungs to fill with air as you continue to inhale. It can be helpful to place your hands on your abdomen as you do this, and feel it expand as you inhale and contract as you exhale.

As you practice breathing exercises, you have different options to choose from, involving variations on whether counting is involved, and timing. A mental health professional or coach can work with you to ensure proper technique and "fit," helping you find an exercise, or exercises, that are tailored to you, your preferences, and your needs. To be effective, it is important to find strategies you are comfortable engaging with and will be likely to utilize.

Many breathing exercises involve counting. One popular exercise in the military is *box breathing*. Box breathing involves beginning by releasing all the air from your lungs. Once your lungs have been emptied, you begin the exercise, inhaling for a count of four, holding for a count of four, exhaling for a count of four, holding for a count of four... repeat three times, or until you feel relaxed.

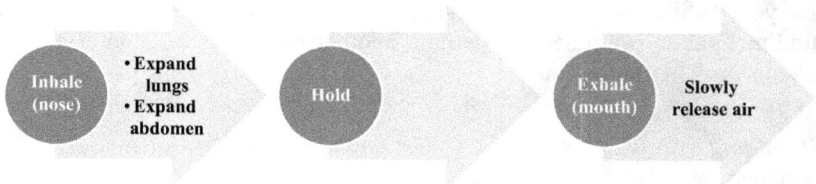

Figure 4.3 How to Engage in Deep Breathing

Box Breathing Exercise

Box breathing exercises provide further structure to breathing practice, which can create a sense of control. Box breathing is used by US Navy Seals and the Marine Corps.

Start by exhaling through your mouth, *releasing all air from your lungs*, then complete the box by following these four steps:

1) Inhale slowly through your nose for a count of 4: "1... 2... 3... 4..."
2) Hold for a count of 4.
3) Exhale through your mouth for a count of 4.
4) Hold for a count of 4.

Repeat in order three times, or until you feel relaxed. Importantly, be sure to *expand* your abdomen and lungs when inhaling, allowing them to fill with air.

Mindfulness/Grounding Exercises—Focusing Attention Using All Five Senses

Mindfulness exercises are a quick and effective way to relieve stress by bringing you out of your worries and into the present moment, giving your brain and your body a rest from the otherwise endless cycle of stress. This effect is achieved by directing your attention to what you are perceiving through each of your senses, one at a time. For a brief, quick and easy, do-anywhere grounding exercise, see Appendix I.

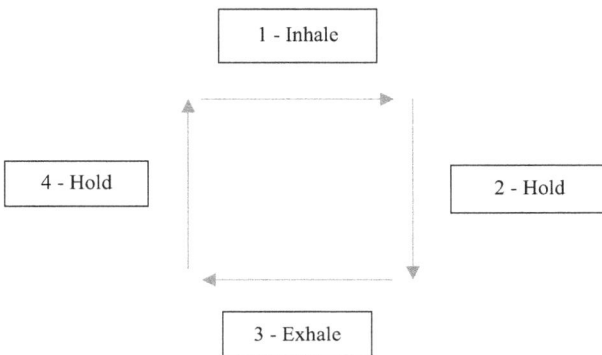

Figure 4.4 Box Breathing

Progressive Muscle Relaxation and Mini-Relaxation Exercises

Progressive muscle relaxation is another effective strategy for activating the relaxation response. These exercises involve systematically relaxing muscles throughout your body. One technique involves the tensing and then relaxing of each muscle group of the body, one at a time, often in combination with deep breathing. While the technique is simple, it may take several practice efforts before you feel comfortable with it and begin to see quick results. Traditionally, these exercises take about 25 minutes, though 15-minute sessions have been found to be just as effective. For an example of a progressive muscle relaxation exercise, see Appendix I.

Mini relaxation exercises were developed in response to a need of the corporate community for exercises that are effective yet brief. Recognizing that busy professionals do not have the time to engage in daily 25-minute relaxation exercises, the mini relaxation was designed to involve four 1.5–2-minute mini relaxation sessions throughout the day. Mini relaxation exercises are based on the longer progressive muscle relaxation exercises mentioned above, but instead involve chunking major muscle groups when tightening and releasing while simultaneously visualizing a favorite peaceful location or scenario, and/or focusing on a relaxing word cue. Mini relaxation exercises are just as effective as a longer 15-minute progressive muscle relaxation initially. In the longer term, however, the 15-minute daily practice is related to greater stress reduction. It all comes down to what is realistic. Mini relaxations will help reduce stress, and are a good alternative to longer exercises, especially if practice will not be maintained with the longer exercises.

Guided Imagery

Guided imagery is another evidence-based relaxation method. It involves using your imagination to engage your senses based on a favorite experience, such as a beach vacation or hiking in the woods. For a self-guided imagery exercise, see Appendix I.

Meditation and Yoga

Meditation is a popular relaxation method, and with good reason. There are several different types of meditation practice, with mindfulness meditation being the most popular, at least in western cultures. It involves practicing non-judgmental awareness. If one type does not work for you, perhaps consider trying another. Mindfulness-Based Stress Reduction (MBSR) is a form of meditation developed by Jon Kabat-Zinn specifically to target stress reduction. It has since been used to treat anxiety, depression, chronic pain, and other chronic illnesses. MBSR incorporates mindfulness meditation and yoga practice, and the training is offered by many medical schools, for staff, professionals (within or outside the school), and patients. Recent research has found that MBSR was as effective as medication for patients with anxiety disorders.

Yoga is another excellent way to manage stress, anxiety, and depression. Yoga involves both physical exercise and mental relaxation and has been found to be associated with stress reduction, improved concentration, memory, focus, and attention, as well as reduced anxiety and depression, and improved immune function.

Physical Exercise

Exercise is a great way to release pent up energy and calm worries—running, jogging, spinning/cycling, rowing, swimming, cardio classes, or weight training are all activities you have ready access to through a local gym or fitness center, or in the case of running or jogging, heading out your door. If you have some equipment at home and need a boost, there are virtual workout options, including YouTube videos and working with personal trainers via video platforms, not to mention companies specializing in providing virtual training workouts with their exercise bikes, rowing machines, and mirrors. Depending on geographic location, plenty of other climate-suited or seasonal outdoor activities are available.

Engage the Great Outdoors

Get outside and take a walk. Walking in nature has been shown to release endorphins and boost your mood. Take in your surroundings using your senses:

- What do you see (e.g., colors, objects, landscape, animals)?
- What do you hear?
- What is the air temperature?
- Do you feel the warmth of the sun or a breeze on your face?
- What is the weather like (e.g., sunny, cloudy, misty, snowy)?
- What do you smell?
- Describe the surface you are walking on.

Distraction with Activities of Interest

Distracting through activities of interest is another great way to get out of your head and into the moment. Think about activities which make time fly for you and leave you wondering where the time went.

Figuring Out What Interests You. Lawyers sometimes struggle with figuring out what their interests are; when you spend most of your waking hours working, or exhausted from work, it can be easy to lose sight of your interests.

If all else fails, think back to when you were a child, or at least a time when you had moments of free time to do whatever you wanted: What drew your attention? What did you most enjoy doing? How do you feel when doing certain things? How competent? How connected? What would you most like to do if no one was watching, evaluating, or appraising?

Practicing Gratitude

Practicing gratitude is another great way to shift negative thinking toward the positive. Daily gratitude journaling can shift your thinking in the moment, but there are long-term benefits as well. Gratitude forces us to focus our attention on things we normally take for granted. It is strongly linked to well-being and satisfaction with life, better physical health, as well as greater levels of positive emotions and more adaptive coping and resilience in the face of stress.

In fact, people who practice gratitude are rated by those around them as more pleasant to interact with and happier. Along with this positive mindset comes an ability to think more broadly and creatively when dealing with challenges. The act of writing itself requires you to put your thoughts into words, which helps with organizing, processing, and accepting your experiences. Gratitude takes time to cultivate, with practice, but can lead to a greater sense of meaning in life over the long term. Meditation and mindfulness exercises facilitate gratitude by focusing attention in the moment and in so doing increase appreciation for the simpler things in life.

Gratitude journaling has been found to promote many physical and psychological health benefits. Mental health benefits include shorter, less frequent depressive episodes; increased positive emotions and optimism; and feeling better about one's life overall. Physical health benefits include decreased physical symptoms; improved immune function; decreased stress-induced cortisol release; and decreased stroke risk. Sleep benefits include longer sleep duration and improved quality of sleep. Exercise benefits include spending more time exercising and exercising more regularly.

- Consider a daily or weekly gratitude journal, listing 1–3 things for which you are grateful. These items can be almost anything; they can be small everyday experiences, moments in nature, others' acts of kindness, people in your life, good physical health, or other benefits you have received. For instance, you might be grateful for:
  o A sunny day after a period of rainy or cloudy days.
  o The warm cup of coffee your loved one brought after you came in from the rain that morning.
  o Your health.
  o A supportive partner.

One thing I am grateful for, surprisingly, is related to the COVID-19 pandemic. Despite all the terrible aspects of the pandemic, I am grateful for having learned (by necessity) to become more comfortable with and adept at using video conferencing. Prior to the pandemic, I fell squarely in the camp that believed any emotionally sensitive meetings, or meetings involving substantive and controversial topics, needed to be held in-person. However, after conducting such meetings remotely during the pandemic by necessity, I quickly realized in-person meetings were not strictly necessary. In fact, in addition to the practical benefits, I also learned that under certain circumstances parties preferred the ability to meet together on screen while at the same time being physically situated in different rooms or locations altogether, when the topic of discussion involved highly charged emotions or power differentials. Zoom can be a great equalizer. It also eliminates travel time and made it easier to manage my work schedule, as well as manage home life.

- Consider different times of day or a specific day for writing in your gratitude journal and pick a time that would be most beneficial for you. For instance, would you benefit most with a morning mental shift, starting your day with a positive frame of reference? Or perhaps you would benefit most from a positive-oriented thinking adjustment when your energy drops mid-afternoon.

Journaling About Life Stressors

Journaling about life stressors for 15–30 minutes a day has been found to decrease stress, rumination (repetitive negative thought cycles), and negative emotions, and to lead to improved mood over time.

Practicing Altruism

Doing for others is one of those win-win scenarios. By engaging in an activity solely for the practical or financial benefit of a person or organization in need, not only is a community need addressed and met, but you may also personally gain an accompanying mood boost and potentially a greater sense of meaning and purpose.

Let Go of the Rest

This last part, letting go, can be quite difficult for lawyers. Although a person or situation may be incredibly frustrating, if you have no control over the situation the best thing you can do is recognize this fact and let it go. As soon as you give yourself permission to do so, you will likely feel an immediate sense of relief.

Self-Care During Times of Stress, Uncertainty, Fear, and When Feeling a Lack of Control

Many people deal with major uncertainty in their lives at one time or another, with the most distressing involving relationships, employment, health, or finances. The events of the year 2020, however, brought uncertainty to the forefront for all, and at an entirely new level. You may have initially tried your usual tactics to ignore and avoid, sticking your head in the sand and hoping COVID-19 and its ramifications would all pass quickly (What were we told initially? Two weeks?). At some point during those first months, you likely realized the challenges brought about by the pandemic were here for the long haul, and your strategies and expectations for daily living, the workplace, and coping needed to be revamped. In fact, for many individuals and workplaces alike, the pandemic induced a laser-focus on self-care.

Facing uncertainty, fear, or a perceived lack of control can be overwhelming. In addition to the usual ongoing legal workplace stressors, personal, familial, political, economic, climate, or global events can heighten fear, and create both prolonged uncertainty and feelings of being powerless. As mentioned above, when it comes to ongoing stressors which we have no control over, we can better manage the situation if we adopt a more positive, proactive mindset and set realistic expectations.

Interrupting the Cycle of Worry and Rumination—And Letting Go

The need for certainty influences how we manage stressors. In the face of any threat, including a toxic workplace situation or the tiresome aspects of the pandemic, you may experience a sense of urgency, just wanting the stressor to be behind you. Thoughts of "When will it end?" may pervade, and a thought cycle of worry and rumination can take you down a negative-spiraling rabbit hole of worst-case scenarios. If not addressed, these negative thoughts can lead to overwhelming feelings of hopelessness and helplessness. When experiencing a negative thought spiral, the cycle of worry needs to be interrupted.

Sometimes, simply trying to shift your thinking is not enough and you need to engage in an activity to intercept the stress response (for more on the stress response, see Chapter 3, Attention to Overall Physical and Mental Health). It is important to pause, breathe, and take a moment to recognize there is hope. The best way to interrupt the worry cycle is to adopt a present-focus—getting out of your head, so to speak, with its negative thought focus on past mistakes or potential future disasters, and into the present moment. The goal is to let go of those unproductive worries so you can focus on the areas over which you do have control. Specific strategies are addressed below.

Over the course of dealing with a major life or workplace stressor, your beliefs about yourself, your world, and others are challenged and perhaps altered. The people and organizations best able to manage, survive, and thrive

56

approach adversity with the beliefs that they can learn, adapt, and change, that their circumstances are temporary, and this difficult period is just some rough terrain in the greater landscape of work or life.

Using Mindfulness and Interoceptive Awareness to Improve Mental Health and Increase Productivity

Interoceptive awareness, or the ability to recognize internal physiological processes, has been found to be related to emotion regulation ability. Research suggests low interoceptive awareness accompanies depression for many, and misinterpretation of interoceptive signals can promote anxiety. In addition, both states are related to increased substance use and potential substance use disorder.

People who are attuned to their subjective feelings of stress have been found to experience better overall psychological and physical health. Similarly, those who are attuned to physiological responses, such as changes in heart rate and breathing, are better at recognizing changes in these responses and accompanying emotions, as well as regulating their emotions. Mindfulness training that focuses on physiological responses has been shown to improve emotion regulation and decrease anxiety, symptoms of depression, and substance use.

These findings help explain why meditation and mindfulness training are so effective for managing stress over time. Lawyers as a group tend toward an external focus, on how one is presenting and coming across to others, on appearing competent, knowledgeable and in control. This external focus leaves little room for self-reflection and scanning for signs of stress or distress. Meditation, however, involves tuning in to, acknowledging, and accepting one's inner experiences, both physical and psychological. Over time, with practice, it becomes easier to recognize disruptions, accept them for what they are, and quickly and effectively manage external stressors and internal stress responses.

Through meditation and mindfulness, we can learn how to enhance and utilize the mind–body connection to improve performance by listen to our bodies, including gut reactions, and being present in the moment. For instance, utilizing our bodies to enhance communication

---

BOX 4.2 CULTURAL PERSPECTIVES ON THE MIND–BODY CONNECTION

In Eastern cultural traditions and philosophies, thought to be the origins of meditation, the mind and body are unified and never considered to be separate. Western culture and medicine traditionally reflect a much more rigid separation of the mind and body.

through gestures, engaging in exercise to enhance mental focus, engaging in synchronous activities with others to create feelings of connectedness and cooperation, and taking in non-verbal information to not only relate to others but also to think better.

Some of the best litigators engage in these processes—such as paying attention to gut reactions about juror receptivity, energetically moving about the courtroom, mirroring juror gestures, and using hand gestures while speaking—to read the room, stay focused, connect with jurors, and enhance juror retention of messaging. When thinking about fostering collaboration, social interoception enhances empathy, which in addition to building social connection and fostering a sense of community, from a productivity standpoint also cultivates collective intelligence.

Additional Resiliency Boosts

Relationships. Relationships are essential for our well-being and resilience, providing us with a sense of community and connection, and a buffer during times of stress, not to mention decreased loneliness. Relationships also require effort. Like a plant, our relationships need to be nurtured to grow and thrive; if they are not cared for, they will wither and potentially die off. When we are busy or feeling stressed, our relationships are often neglected. It can feel like hard work staying connected after working long hours or having a stressful day, but prioritizing relationships will have immediate and long-term benefits. Start small and find ways that work for you. The amount of time is less important than the quality of the time spent. For more on relationships and the importance of social support, see Chapter 8, The Essential Role of Personal Relationships and Social Supports in Well-Being.

Meaning and Purpose. Having a sense of meaning and purpose in work or life can also help you endure the challenges and difficulties that we all inevitably face at one time or another, in our work or personal lives. If the work you do is meaningful to you, consider yourself among the fortunate. At the same time, you should also know that you may be more at risk for burnout. On the other hand, if you do not derive a sense of meaning and purpose from your work, it is important to find other ways to meet these needs. Some possibilities include getting involved with pro bono work, at your firm or through a non-profit in the community, or volunteering for other non-work activities. In addition, valuing work for its intrinsic rewards, via alignment with internal goals such as growth, relationships, health, and community giving, as opposed to external rewards, such as fame and wealth, is linked to greater well-being. For more information, see Chapter 9, Cultivating Meaning and Purpose for Well-Being.

Self-Care Hacks

Sometimes you just don't have time for anything more than the quickest self-care hacks. Check out the list of 21 in-the-moment brief "resets" to decrease stress and improve focus in Appendix I. Find the brief healthy activities (on this list or on your own) which most easily help you "get out of your head," live in the moment for a few minutes, and recharge. Do some experimenting with an assortment of these items. Everyone has their own preferences and finding yours will lead to the best results. Think of some others not listed here! A few brief hacks to get you started include:

- Stretch and engage in deep "belly" breathing for 1–2 minutes.
- Take a 5-minute walk around the office, or up and down some stairs.
- Massage your forehead and scalp.
- Smile or laugh (muscles send signals to the brain which release tension).
- Drink a glass of water or milk.
- Listen to music.
- Engage in a 1–2 minute mindfulness exercise or color in a mindfulness coloring book.
- Meditate for 5 minutes.
- If you are especially tired and also can manage a bit more time: Take a 20-minute power nap (set an alarm).

Promoting Well-Being Goes Beyond Self-Care Strategies

Finances and Other Resources. The state of your finances also influences your well-being. Financial insecurity can create a great deal of stress, anxiety, and related sleep difficulties. It can impact your mood and frustration tolerance, which further impact your relationships. Financial insecurity can lead you to feel trapped in a difficult situation. Conversely, if you are financially secure, or have other supports, you may worry less about money, may have more resources to dedicate toward self-care, and may not find yourself feeling trapped in a difficult workplace or unhealthy personal relationships. For more information, see Chapter 7, The Impact of Financial Resources on Well-Being.

Autonomy, Personal Traits, Workplace Culture and Policies. Finally, how we do our work, including time management and boundary-setting, and how we evaluate our own performance are also essential in protecting our mental and emotional resources. Workplace culture and psychological safety also come into play. As do workplace policies, including those related to flexible work schedules and hybrid or remote work options. For more on these and other workplace-related issues, see Chapter 5, Understanding and Addressing Workplace Issues Which Impact Well-Being.

The Risks of Using Alcohol and Other Substances to Self-Medicate

Alcohol use is prevalent in the legal profession, as a reward or way to unwind after a long day, a way to celebrate when a case is won, or commiserate when something does not go as planned. It is often an essential element at social events. Alcohol slows our mind and body down, and brings on feelings of relaxation and sleepiness. While alcohol can appear to be a quick fix, helping you to relax, unwind, or sleep, its effects are temporary. In addition, long-term regular and heavy use of alcohol is associated with a host of physical and mental health issues.

BOX. 4.3 LONG-TERM REGULAR AND HEAVY USE OF ALCOHOL

Associated health risks:

- Anxiety
- Cancer
- Cardiovascular disease
- Depression
- Dementia
- Gastrointestinal issues
- Immune function impairment
- Liver disease
- Nerve damage
- Sleep disorders
- Suicide

Sleep Disorders. The effects of any given quantity of alcohol on sleep vary from person to person, but even small quantities can have some impact. Alcohol interferes with sleep rhythms and sleep quality, making it harder to fall asleep, or to stay asleep for an extended period without disruption. Long-term alcohol misuse as a sleep remedy can lead to insomnia and a cycle of relying on stimulants such as caffeine to wake up in the morning and focus at work, and alcohol to wind down in the evening. Alcohol has also been found to be related to obstructive sleep apnea, which involves throat muscles relaxing and obstructing the air passageway, making it difficult to breathe, or causing temporary pauses in breathing, which leads to impaired sleep with moments of waking, and snoring.

Physical Health. Alcohol is a known carcinogen. The American Cancer Society recommends not drinking any alcohol because of its relationship with several cancers, including breast, colon, liver, and some esophageal cancers. Excess alcohol consumption is also a risk factor for liver disease (cirrhosis), brain damage and dementia (Korsakoff syndrome), cardiovascular disease (high blood pressure, heart attack, stroke), nerve damage, a variety of gastrointestinal issues, and decreased immune function.

Dichotomous View of Mental Health

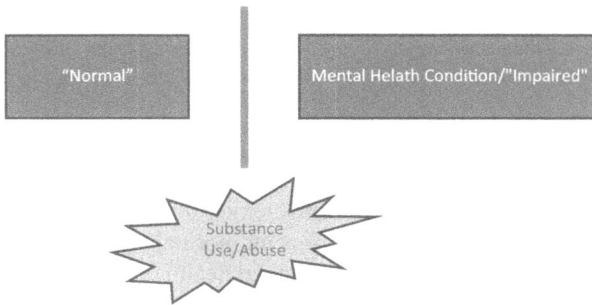

Figure 4.5 Dichotomous View of Mental Health

Mental Health. Excess alcohol consumption is a risk factor for onset of depression and anxiety, and is known to exacerbate existing symptoms, both because of alcohol-related brain changes as well as impulsivity and judgment lapses leading to post-drinking regret.

Seeking Assistance for Mental Health and Substance Use Issues

Understanding Mental Health

Many lawyers take a black-and-white approach to mental health, one that is reinforced by popular literature and social media—either you are healthy, or you are not. Either you have it together or you don't. Interestingly, substance abuse is viewed by some as separate and distinguished from mental health.

Mental Health and Well-Being Continuum

We all have experienced fluctuations in our physical health over the years, whether it be viral or bacterial infections or more serious conditions. Consider a common cold (which can lead to symptoms ranging anywhere from mild nasal congestion to more severe sinus and chest congestion, coughing, difficulty breathing, and in the most severe cases hospitalization). In addition, the level of symptoms you are experiencing reflects or signals your healthcare needs. Consider blood pressure, cholesterol, or blood sugar levels. Your numbers may be unremarkable, at a pre-clinical stage, low, moderate, or at a "you must do something about this right now!" level. If you recognize and address your symptoms early, a health crisis can often be averted.

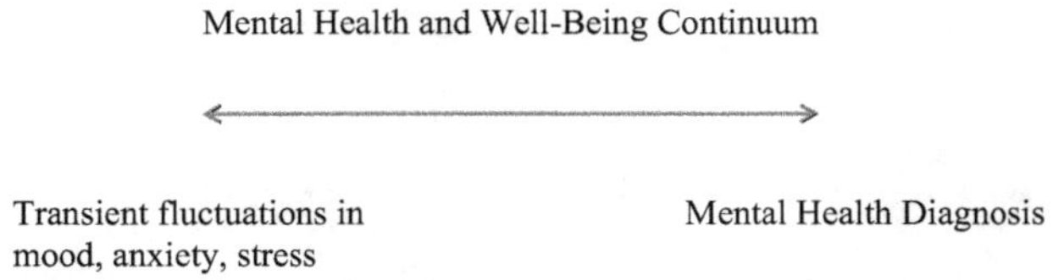

Mental Health and Well-Being Continuum

←————————————————————→

Transient fluctuations in   Mental Health Diagnosis
mood, anxiety, stress

Figure 4.6 The Mental Health and Well-Being Continuum

The same holds true for mental health. We can think of mental health as a continuum, just like physical health, which varies by person over time. Mental health can range from experiencing normal transient fluctuations in mood, anxiety, and stress to a formal mental health diagnosis. Even if you do not have a mental health diagnosis, life events and circumstances can impact your overall mental health and well-being. Fluctuations in stress levels, mood, and anxiety occur throughout our lives. Paradoxically, even positive life events can trigger negative emotions and anxiety. And as with physical health, the degree of mental health symptoms at any given time reflect your mental health intervention needs.

Regardless of where you fall on the continuum, it is important to be attuned to how you feel when faced with stressors in your life, so you can manage your mood and anxiety and prevent longer-term consequences. Most diagnosed mental health issues, if caught early, can be effectively managed with cognitive behavioral therapy and/or medications. But when external stressors are high, symptoms can be more difficult to manage. If addressed early, more serious mental health and substance use conditions can be averted.

- *Changes in Yourself.* You may be feeling emotionally drained, sad, or worried because of circumstances in your workplace or personal life. You may notice you are slower to get out of bed in the morning or getting to bed later in the evening. You may be having difficulty sleeping. Perhaps you are experiencing more headaches, neck, and back pain. Difficulty concentrating may be a daily experience. You may find yourself re-reading the same paragraph multiple times or distracted by worries that have begun to inject themselves into your thinking throughout the day. You may be having difficulty motivating yourself.
- *Changes in a Colleague.* Similarly, you may notice a colleague is not as responsive as usual, and when they do respond it may be more curt or less thorough. Your colleague may appear more short-tempered and irritable, or perhaps they appear to have less energy or are no longer participating in office social activities. They may appear somewhat disheveled in the morning instead of their usual

put-together appearance, with messy or wet hair, unshaven, more casual attire, bloodshot eyes, or dark-circled puffy eyelids.

Recent research highlights the importance of being in tune with your internal experience, finding that people who reported stress levels consistent with their internal physiological stress markers (i.e., heart rate) also experienced better overall levels of well-being, including psychological health, and decreased inflammatory markers. You might begin by simply striving to become more attuned to your psychological experience, while keeping it separate from your professional activities.

Providing and Seeking Assistance

One of the most difficult things for most people to recognize is when they are not at their best or need professional help. Sometimes it takes the kind words of a colleague, friend, or loved one, asking how you are doing, asking if you need anything, perhaps gently mentioning they've noticed differences in your behavior, appearance, responsiveness, or work quality. The same applies when reaching out to a colleague when you are concerned about their mental health.

It can be difficult to hear these things, but recognizing it comes from a place of support and caring can help prevent defensiveness and allow for digesting what has been heard. Even if you (or your colleague) do become defensive, after a cooling off period you may come to realize what the person was saying makes sense.

You may even recognize the need for help yourself but put off getting it because you are too busy or do not know where to look. When you do finally acknowledge you need help, decide to pick up the phone and make that call, or send that email inquiry, it can be nerve-wracking, or deflating. Seeking help reflects internal strength and is to be commended. Perhaps start by reaching out to someone you trust, a loved one, friend, lawyers' assistance program, or trusted colleague, to get support and discuss next steps, such as how and where to find treatment.

Consider seeking professional assistance if you are:

- Experiencing chronic internal distress, such as recurrent negative thoughts or distressing emotions, or are feeling stuck or immobilized.
- Engaging in external maladaptive behaviors such as irritability, interactional difficulties, substance abuse, unproductivity at work, or other work-related problems.

Therapy does not have to be long term. Many people benefit from just a few sessions, and I often suggest thinking of it as a "tune-up." When looking for a therapist, you have many options.

Where to Look for Treatment

- Ask you primary care provider or another trusted medical provider for a referral.
- Insurance provider networks.
- Your employee assistance plan (EAP).
- A lawyer's assistance program (such as Lawyers-Concerned-for-Lawyers in the US), which can provide some assistance, or refer you to community providers for psychotherapy or substance use treatment.
- Word-of-mouth referrals from family, friends, and trusted colleagues.
- Online resources and directories.
- Local (in the US—state or regional) databases, information lines, and hotlines.
- National suicide prevention helplines (for example, US 988 Suicide and Crisis Lifeline; UK National Suicide Prevention Helpline; The Canada Suicide Prevention Service; Lifeline Australia; Samaritans of Singapore).

Options for Treatment

Types of Providers—doctoral level, master's level, psychotherapists, and prescribers. Mental health providers may conduct psychotherapy, prescribe medications, or both. Just figuring out the type of provider you want to see can be challenging. There is a wide array of providers, at least in the US, and distinguishing them all can be confusing. Doctoral level providers include psychologists, psychiatrists, and more rarely social workers. Psychologists typically earn their degree over the course of five to seven years in a graduate school doctoral program, including a year of internship, and then obtain at least a year of postdoctoral training for licensure. Psychologists provide psychotherapy and assessment, and in recent years some have obtained additional education and training to prescribe medications for mental health conditions. Psychiatrists, who have an MD degree, involving the completion of medical school, residency, and typically fellowship, prescribe medications and some may also provide psychotherapy. A number of primary care physicians will prescribe medication for anxiety or depression. In addition, there are several types of master's level psychotherapists (having obtained a two-year master's degree) in social work, marriage and family therapy, or counseling. The American Psychological Association is in the process of working toward licensure of an additional provider category encompassing those with a master's degree in clinical psychology.

Levels (Types) of Care. Treatment options for mental health and substance use range from weekly individual or group outpatient psychotherapy to more intensive outpatient therapy, to inpatient treatment. Weekly individual outpatient psychotherapy sessions typically last 45–60 minutes, once a week, with some more specialized treatment or group therapy sessions lasting 90 minutes or meeting more frequently. Intensive outpatient treat-

> ## BOX 4.4 LEVELS OF TREATMENT FOR MENTAL HEALTH AND SUBSTANCE USE IN THE US
>
> Weekly outpatient: 45, 60, or 90 minutes
>
> Group therapy: 60, 90, or 120 minutes
>
> Intensive outpatient treatment programs: A few hours a few days a week (i.e., three hours, three days)
>
> Partial hospitalization programs: Five days a week for several hours
>
> Inpatient programs

ment programs and partial hospitalization programs are both outpatient with the former meeting a few days a week for a few hours, and the latter meeting every weekday for several hours. In addition to public hospitals, there are private hospitals which can be easier to access in terms of finding an in-patient bed, but are also quite costly. In the US, options vary by whether the provider or treatment center accepts insurance, and the type of insurance accepted. People who can pay out of pocket have a large selection of options and can often secure an appointment or in-patient bed more quickly.

Forms of Psychotherapy. There are many different forms of psychotherapy, reflecting differing theoretical orientations. Evidence-based therapies tend to be grounded in some form of cognitive, behavioral, or cognitive-behavioral therapy (challenging thoughts and modifying behaviors). Humanistic therapies are also present-focused, with an emphasis on autonomy and growth through work with a therapist who exhibits authentic and unconditional acceptance and care. Insight-oriented therapies focus on uncovering unconscious motivations and interpretations, and learning more about yourself through gaining an understanding of your interactions with your therapist. Many psychotherapists engage in an integrative approach, utilizing a combination of theoretical approaches tailored to the individual and their needs.

In addition to these more traditional forms of psychotherapy, which typically involve addressing thoughts, behaviors, and emotions, biofeedback therapy involves raising awareness of physiological responses (interoceptive awareness), such as those that arise during the stress response, so that you can more easily detect symptoms and respond with a relaxation exercise or other self-care strategy.

What to Expect from Psychotherapy: Private, Confidential, Non-Judgmental

Lawyers struggle with seeking help. To begin with, mental health stigma within the profession is a substantial deterrent. The negative effects of stigma are compounded by lawyer perfectionism and intense fear of failure, which make it difficult to reveal vulnerability by asking for help. Even if you do find your way to a therapist's office, it may be difficult to open up and share closely held thoughts and feelings, depending upon your expectations of the therapist and therapy process.

Therapy is very different from meetings with other lawyers. Sometimes when a group of lawyers gets together, a more negative mindset prevails, with everyone jockeying for position, judging, looking for one or more flaws in those around them (tapping into those skills used to discredit a witness) so they feel they have a leg up. If you enter therapy with the same mindset and expectations for your therapist, your self-protective stance and potential intense need to feel in control of the situation and to not appear weak can interfere with therapy, even if you have the best of intentions.

A therapist is your ally. Your therapy session is a time when it is truly all about you. The therapist is there to listen, help you think about things differently, help you change behaviors, help you build coping strategies, and help you process troubling experiences. Your therapist is there to help you navigate life issues in a supportive yet objective manner.

How to Choose an Effective Therapist

Finding a professional with whom you are compatible is important. The best predictor of successful therapy is the quality of the relationship with your therapist, known as the *therapeutic alliance*. The therapeutic alliance reflects three relationship factors which are considered to be key to therapy success. When meeting with a new therapist and evaluating the therapy experience, ask yourself whether your therapist:

1) respects you.
2) understands you.
3) has the skills to help you.

All three are essential. Even if your therapist respects and understands you, if you need help with a specialized area (such as an eating disorder, substance use disorder, gambling disorder, etc.) and the therapist does not have experience in this area, their ability to help you will be more limited. Two or three meetings is sufficient to develop a good sense of this alliance. If after two or three sessions you are not feeling it, do not hesitate to look elsewhere.

Be Proactive

An important takeaway throughout this chapter, and book, is the value of being *proactive*. Think about the things you can do to manage or change a difficult situation. If you need to dedicate more time and energy to self-care, start today. If you need help with a mental health issue or substance use problem, contact a mental health professional. If your needs are more in the workplace realm (for more on workplace challenges, see Chapter 5, Understanding and Addressing Workplace Issues Which Impact Well-Being) consider seeking support from a trusted colleague. Working with a coach is another option. A coach can help identify personal priorities, strengths, and weaknesses, understand the organizational context in which you are operating, and develop goals, strategies, and skills to promote positive and healthy change in yourself, your work, and the workplace, including improved productivity, improved work relationships, and a better work environment. Just get going.

Bibliography

Ahmedani, B. K. (2010). *Determinants of stigma: A comparison of health, mental health, and drug use conditions* (Order No. 3417692). Available from ProQuest Dissertations & Theses Global. (746094514). www.proquest.com/dissertations-theses/determinants-stigma-comparison-health-mental-drug/docview/746094514/se-2

American Psychological Association. (2009). *Different approaches to psychotherapy.* www.apa.org/topics/psychotherapy/approaches. Adapted from the *Encyclopedia of psychology*, Kazdin, A. E. (2000). American Psychological Association.

Arnold, A. J., Winkielman, P., & Dobkins, K. (2019, November 26). Interoception and social connection. *Frontiers in Psychology, Mini Review.* https://doi.org/10.3389/fpsyg.2019.02589

Aspinwall, L. G. (1998). Rethinking the role of positive affect in self-regulation. *Motivation and Emotion, 22*(1), 1–32. https://doi.org/10.1023/A:1023080224401

Bauer, J. (2001). Character of the questions and the fitness of the process: Mental health, bar admissions and the Americans with disabilities act, 49. *UCLA Law Review, 93,* 104.

Cassens Weiss, D. (2009, April 30). Reportedly laid-off lawyer is an apparent suicide at Kilpatrick Stockton. *ABA Journal.* www.abajournal.com/news/article/kilpatrick_stockton_lawyer_reported_dead_from_a_gunshot_wound

Cassens Weiss, D. (2022, May 10). About one-fifth of lawyers and staffers considered suicide at some point in their careers, new survey says. *ABAJournal.com.* Retrieved online at https://www.abajournal.com/news/article/19-of-surveyed-lawyers-and-staffers-said-they-considered-suicide-at-some-point-in-careers

Dalpati, N., Jena, S., Jain, S., & Sarangi, P. P. (2022). Yoga and meditation, an essential tool to alleviate stress and enhance immunity to emerging infections: A perspective on the effect of COVID-19 pandemic on students. *Brain, Behavior, & Immunity Health, 20,* 100420. https://doi.org/10.1016/j.bbih.2022.100420

Dunkley, D. M., Blankstein, K. R., Masheb, R. M., & Grilo, C. M. (2006). Personal standards and evaluative concerns dimensions of "clinical" perfectionism: A reply to Shafran et al. (2002, 2003) and Hewitt et al. (2003). *Behaviour Research and Therapy, 44*(1), 63–84. https://doi.org/10.1016/j.brat.2004.12.004

Emmons, R. A., & McCullough, M. E. (2003). Counting blessings versus burdens. *Journal of Personality and Social Psychology, 84*(2), 377–389.

Emmons, R. A., & Stern, R. (2013). Gratitude as a psychotherapeutic intervention. *Journal of Clinical Psychology, 69*(8), 846–855. https://doi.org/10.1002/jclp.22020

Farina, A., Gliha, D., Bourdreau, L. A., Ale, J. G., & Sherman, M. (1971). Mental illness and the impact of believing others know about it. *Journal of Abnormal Psychology, 77*(1), 1–5. https://doi.org/10.1037/h0030496

Flett, G. L., Madorsky, D., Hewitt, P. L., & Heisel, M. J. (2002). Perfectionism cognitions, rumination, and psychological distress. *Journal of Rational-Emotive and Cognitive-Behavior Therapy, 20*(1), 33–47 (2002). https://doi-org.yale.idm.oclc.org/10.1023/A:1015128904007

Folkman, S., & Moskowitz, J. T. (2000). Positive affect and the other side of coping. *American Psychologist, 55*(6), 647–654. http://doi.org/10.1037/0003-066X.55.6.647

Fredrickson, B. L. (2004). The broaden-and-build theory of positive emotions. *Philosophical Transactions of the Royal Society of London Series B, Biological Sciences, 359*(1449), 1367–1378. https://doi.org/10.1098/rstb.2004.1512

Fuller, K. (2022). *Physical effects of alcohol and risk of disease.* American Addiction Centers. https://americanaddictioncenters.org/alcoholism-treatment/physical-health

Glasbergen, R. (2004). Stress management is for wimps! [Cartoon]. Permission granted from Glasbergen Cartoon Service. https://www.glasbergen.com/image-search/cartoons/search/toon-1838

Goffman, E. (1963). *Stigma: Notes on the management of spoiled identity.* Prentice-Hall.

Goldfried, M. R., & Davison, G. C. (1994). *Clinical behavior therapy,* Chapter 5, Relaxation training (pp. 81–111). Wiley Inter-Science.

Hewitt, P. L., & Flett, G. L. (1991). Perfectionism in the self and social contexts: Conceptualization, assessment, and association with psychopathology. *Journal of Personality and Social Psychology, 60*(3), 456–470. https://doi.org/10.1037/0022-3514.60.3.456

Hoge, E. A., Bui, E., Mete, M., Dutton, M. A., Baker, A. W., & Simon, N. M. (2022, November 9). Mindfulness-based stress reduction vs escitalopram for the treatment of adults with anxiety disorders: A randomized clinical trial. *JAMA Psychiatry.* https://doi.org/10.1001/jamapsychiatry.2022.3679

Humphrey, A., Szoka, R., & Bastian, B. (2021, March 8). When the pursuit of happiness backfires: The role of negative emotion valuation. *Journal of Positive Psychology.* https://doi.org/10.1080/17439760.2021.1897869

Mannarini, S., & Rossi, A. (2019, January 11). Assessing mental illness stigma: A complex issue, opinion article. *Frontiers in Psychology,* Sec. Psychology for Clinical Settings. https://doi.org/10.3389/fpsyg.2018.02722

Mosel, S. (2022). *Anxiety and alcohol: Does drinking cause anxiety and panic attacks?* American Addiction Centers. https://americanaddictioncenters.org/alcoholism-treatment/anxiety

Najavits, L. M. (2002). *Seeking safety: A treatment manual for PTSD and substance abuse.* The Guilford Press.

Niazi, A. K., & Niazi, S. K. (2011). Mindfulness-based stress reduction: A non-pharmacological approach for chronic illnesses. *North American Journal of Medical Sciences, 3*(1), 20–23. https://doi.org/10.4297/najms.2011.320

Paul, A. M. (2021). *The extended mind: The power of thinking outside the brain.* Mariner Books.

Pennebaker, J. W., & Seagal, J. D. (1999). Forming a story: The health benefits of narrative. *Journal of Clinical Psychology, 55*(10), 1243–1254.

Ponce, A. N., Lorber, W., Paul, J. J., Esterlis, I., Barzvi, A., Allen, G. J., & Pescatello, L. S. (2008). Comparisons of varying dosages of relaxation in a corporate setting: Effects on stress reduction. *International Journal of Stress Management, 15*(4), 396–407. https://doi.org/10.1037/a0013992.

Price, C. J., Thompson, E. A., Crowell, S., & Pike, K. (2019). Longitudinal effects of interoceptive awareness training through mindful awareness in body-oriented therapy (MABT) as an adjunct to women's substance use disorder treatment: A randomized controlled trial. *Drug and Alcohol Dependence, 198,* 140–149. https://doi.org/10.1016/j.drugalcdep.2019.02.012

Rosch, E. (1978). Principles of categorization. In E. Rosch & B. B. Lloyd (Eds.), *Cognition and categorization* (pp. 27–48). L. Erlbaum Associates. https://search.library.yale.edu/catalog/51858

Seligman, M. E. P. (2011, April). Building resilience. *Harvard Business Review.* https://hbr.org/2011/04/building-resilience

Selye, H. (1973). The evolution of the stress concept: The originator of the concept traces its development from the discovery in 1936 of the alarm reaction to modern therapeutic applications of syntoxic and catatoxic hormones. *American Scientist, 61*(6), 692–699. www.jstor.org/stable/27844072

Sleep Foundation. (2022). *Alcohol and sleep.* www.sleepfoundation.org/nutrition/alcohol-and-sleep

Sommerfeldt, S. L., Schaefer, S. M., Brauer, M., Ryff, C. D., & Davidson, R. J. (2019). Individual differences in the association between subjective stress and heart rate are related to psychological and physical well-being. *Psychological Science, 30*(7), 1016–1029. https://doi-org.yale.idm.oclc.org/10.1177/0956797619849555

Strupp, H. H., & Binder, J. L. (1984). *Psychotherapy in a new key: A guide to time-limited dynamic psychotherapy.* Basic Books, A Division of HarperCollins Publishers.

Summer, J. (2022, September 29). *Napping: Benefits and tips.* Sleep Foundation. www.sleepfoundation.org/sleep-hygiene/napping#:~:text=In%20general%2C%20the%20best%20nap,grogginess%20and%20actually%20worsen%20sleepiness

Varshney, M., Mahapatra, A., Krishnan, V., Gupta, R., & Deb, K. S. (2016). Violence and mental illness: What is the true story? *Journal of Epidemiology and Community Health, 70*(3), 223–225. https://doi.org/10.1136/jech-2015-205546

Waterschoot, J., Morbée, S., Vermote, B., Brenning, K., Flamant, N., Vansteenkiste, M., & Soenens, B. (2022, January 13). Emotion regulation in times of COVID-19: A person-centered approach based on self-determination theory. *Current Psychology.* https://doi.org/10.1007/s12144-021-02623-5

Understanding and Addressing Workplace Issues Which Impact Well-Being

The Great Paradox of Legal Culture

Recently, I asked an attorney what they would most like to change about their workplace culture. The person paused for a moment, tilted their head up and to the right, and said, "Hmmm, I never thought about it that way. It just is." The legal profession has been slow in recognizing the importance of workplace culture, and to this day early career and younger attorneys tend to lead the charge in this realm. While segments of the profession, labeled well-being champions and catalysts, have recently begun to think about the importance of a healthy work environment, many others have not. *It just is.* A lot of lawyers simply go to work, do their work, try to bill enough hours, and eventually go home, with little energy left to consider well-being.

Organizational Culture Defines Values, Behaviors, and Wellness Priorities

Our environment and the people we surround ourselves with play an important role in our overall mental health and well-being. Our work environment provides context for our lived experience. It becomes the lens through which we see the world. Our environment also impacts our mood, as we absorb the various stimuli around us, whether it be workplace politics and interpersonal interactions, perceptions of the expectations and values of leaders, client interactions, opposing counsel interactions, or reviewing and contemplating the details of what may be considered to be the horrendous experiences of clients.

For lawyers, who as a group tend to spend most of their waking hours at work, the workplace takes on an outsized role in life. Interestingly, and significantly, the legal profession tends to draw people who are highly competitive, risk-averse skeptics, and then reinforces these traits in law school and beyond. Competitiveness, risk-aversion, and skepticism take on an immense role in shaping legal culture—how firms operate, how colleagues interact, leadership styles and mentoring (or lack thereof) of associates, and attitudes toward self-care and well-being. External appearances, and in particular an air of competence, are essential.

 DOI: 10.4324/9781003285519-5

The valuing of these traits, what might be called negativity-focused traits, is quite understandable. The stakes in law are usually high, without room for error. One wrong move and someone's rights might be violated, and their freedom taken away, or another client could be out of a great deal of money. These high stakes, combined with common lawyer traits, can be a recipe for overbearing, negative, competitive, and micromanaged office culture. Just the opposite of one that enhances motivation.

The Paradox and Liability Risk

A culture defined by negativity—in the forms of skepticism, cynicism, competition, and constant striving for personal recognition—does not foster collaboration, innovation, or help-seeking. In fact, research has found these attitudes lead to more cheating behavior and unethical behavior.

This represents the great paradox of the legal profession: the very traits which are considered important for good lawyering not only foster a negative work environment, but they also can create professional liability risk. And they certainly do not do anything to facilitate innovative ideas and problem-solving. When these inherent traits are compounded by stress, the outcome can be toxic and shattering, both personally and professionally.

One of the reasons the legal community is increasingly interested in promoting lawyer well-being has to do with the financial and reputational costs related to professional liability issues. Attorneys who are burned out are more at risk of mishandling or failing to manage their caseload. In addition, office culture and working relationships influence willingness to speak up at work, ask for help, challenge the status quo, and offer ideas. Office culture also impacts the likelihood a lawyer or staff member will recognize and approach a colleague in distress to see if they need help and offer resources. If mental health and help-seeking are stigmatized, colleagues will be more inclined to "stay in their own lane" and hope the person figures it out on their own, not wanting to shame their colleague/friend or appear intrusive. For more on mental health stigma, self-care, seeking assistance, and how to recognize a colleague in distress and offer help, see Chapter 4, Self-Care Strategies and Overcoming Barriers to Healthy Routines.

Unique or Challenging Pressures in the Legal Profession

Legal practice and law firm culture come with their own unique pressures. In addition, workplace pressures further vary by size of the organization, geographic location, setting and area of specialization, as well as the types and rigidity of policies in place, and the people who work at the organization.

Billable Hours. The billable hour requirement is an obvious and well-known pressure in the private practice sector. The billable hour requirement inherently creates pressure and stress, setting forth minimum requirements for bonuses and positive performance evaluations. In addition, many junior associates worry their work product doesn't warrant the billable hour price tag, that they are not working efficiently enough, or, in contrast, that they are not billing enough time. Some mid-size and smaller law firms have begun experimenting with alternative fee arrangements, yet there may be limited motivation for firms to change the status quo when law firm structure is so dependent on it.

> When I was a summer associate who had free access to Lexis/Westlaw as a law student, a young associate would ask to use my Lexis/Westlaw login. The associate was worried about taking too much time on assignments and did not want the firm to notice based on their legal research login times and costs.

Adversarial Nature. The profession by nature is adversarial. Litigation tends to be more blatantly adversarial, but transactional work involves its own fair share of subtle power plays. While some people thrive on adversity, it can be stressful and exhausting for others. High-price-tag or high-profile civil litigation, high-profile criminal litigation, and divorce litigation all tend to involve some of the greatest levels of brazen adversity.

Long Hours. Your time is often not your own. Whether you are prepping for a complex litigation case or closing a deal, there may never seem to be enough hours and you may find yourself working nearly around the clock. Depending on firm size and practice area, you may experience an ebb and flow of work demands, which allow you to rest and recuperate between projects, or you may experience the greatest demands at certain times of the year. Alternatively, you may experience a never-ending flood of transactional work or new cases, which all need to be balanced and prioritized. Long work hours are *de rigueur.*

Rainmaking Requirements. Rainmaking expectations can be a challenge. If you are in a private practice setting, eventually you will be expected to bring in new business to earn your keep or advance to partnership. Sales is a skill not taught in law school, and some people are much better at it than others. While these skills can be learned, networking and sales do not come easily to all lawyers (especially those who tend toward introversion), and in fact many lawyers are taught there is a fine ethical line that can be crossed related to marketing and sales. For lawyers who struggle in these areas, efforts to generate business do not feel good, and for some (rightly so or not) these efforts are indicative of poor taste, low quality work, or inauthenticity, which presents a hurdle to overcome if one is to be successful.

Ethical Challenges. Ethical challenges can be untenable. At times, especially when working on high stakes or high-net-worth projects, or cases involving questions of maltreatment or abuse, ethical challenges can arise. Because no case is ever black-and-white, it can be difficult to stand your ground, particularly if you believe your job or career is on the line. Sleepless nights may be spent wrestling with competing values, goals, and interests.

Vicarious Trauma. Vicarious trauma is a risk for lawyers repeatedly exposed to client stories, images and videos depicting abuse and torture. These repeated exposures can lead to traumatic stress symptoms in lawyers representing clients who have been severely victimized. Vicarious trauma will be addressed later in this chapter.

Work Setting Trade-Offs. There are trade-offs when seeking the perfect fit in a different work setting or practice area. Lawyers working in criminal, immigration, and other civil law practice areas involving trauma and abuse may find their work meaningful, but must manage the psychological pressures and consequences, such as vicarious trauma, of repeated exposure. On the other hand, unending transactional work can seem dry to some, leading to boredom and a sense of lack of fulfillment.

Outside of private practice, hours may be more regular, and without billable hour requirements or rainmaking responsibilities, but this often comes at the price of flexible work schedules and autonomy, particularly in government jobs. Corporate settings may offer a middle ground in terms of hours worked, flexible schedules, and personal autonomy, but there may be more ethical pressures, or the most complex and perhaps interesting litigation cases may be farmed out to law firms, leaving lawyers in more of an administrative role which may be less personally fulfilling.

A Client-as-King Approach Impairs Time Management. Law is a professional service industry which is often governed by the belief that "the client is always right." Young lawyers, particularly at larger firms, learn early on that their time is dictated by the client, as opposed to the associate setting expectations for the client. As a former Big Law associate once said,

> "When your client decides their needs are paramount, they become paramount."

This client-as-king approach has time management implications. One of the issues that I am frequently asked to address is associate time management. There are several strategies for managing time, but similar to other issues related to well-being, associates need to be supported by leadership in these efforts, including in their autonomy and boundary-setting efforts. More on setting boundaries and managing time can be found later in this chapter in the section on time management.

Organizational policies and leadership role modeling can set healthier expectations for associates and provide guidance about how to manage client expectations.

> A former Big Law mid-level associate in a London office shared their experience working on a large project with a senior associate and a few junior associates. When a client request came in at 5:00 pm on a Friday, the junior associates balked and one of them went to the partner overseeing the project. When the

partner learned they were responding to a client demand that was important but not otherwise urgent, the partner phoned the client and said "my people cannot work on this for you before Monday."

This response exemplifies appropriate boundary-setting. An associate does not have the authority or clout to do so, but partners do. The organization and its leaders need to set appropriate client expectations at the outset. This is not to say that lawyers should never work on weekends; at times matters are truly urgent and do require immediate attention, regardless of the day of the week.

A Perpetual Job Interview. Only a small percentage of incoming associates will make partner, if for no other reason than it is financially inefficient to have a top-heavy firm structure. As a result, many associates feel like they are on a continuous job interview, always striving, trying to advance to the golden carrot—partnership. This sense of continuous evaluation creates a great deal of stress. It is also a deterrent for many associates in terms of setting boundaries or speaking up, reinforcing the culture of long hours and constant accessibility.

The Self-Perpetuating "Pay Your Dues" Culture. Change can be difficult when the culture is self-perpetuating, with senior attorneys believing young associates need to pay their dues just like the older attorneys did early on in their careers. It takes a degree of selflessness to acknowledge the system as you experienced it could be improved, and make a change for the positive for those that follow.

Work environment plays a crucial role in overall health and well-being. The office is a place of positive and negative interactions and experiences which give rise to thoughts, feelings, and behaviors, which then further influence degree of satisfaction with the workplace and overall well-being. An

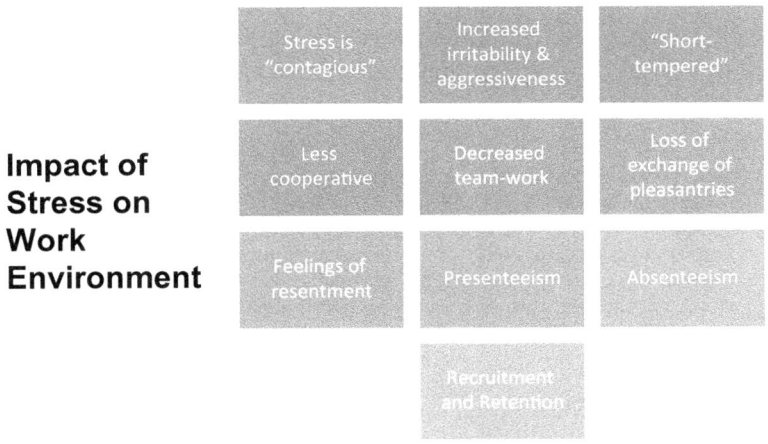

Figure 5.1 Impact of Stress on Work Environment

adversarial workplace, devoid of pleasantries and filled with abrupt interactions, aggressive outbursts, or toxic leaders can take a toll. So too can unrelenting workloads and nearly non-stop work hours.

A lot of attention has been given to "Quiet Quitting" in the popular press in 2022. It is an emotionally salient term that grabs our attention. The term seems to mean different things to different people. For some, it refers to checking out mentally at work, and doing the bare minimum. Although the term is new, the issue of sitting at your desk and not being super productive is not. Lawyers have been sitting at their desks for years while in desperate need of a break and not being especially productive, yet putting in the requisite "face time" (an old-school term for time spent at the office purely for the purpose of appearing hard-working and committed to the organization). The term "presenteeism," another reference to unproductive time spent at one's desk and a play on "absenteeism," later came into fashion. Presenteeism reflects time spent at the office when you are physically or mentally ill-equipped to work that day, time which would have been better spent recovering at home. It might reflect coming to work with a severe cold, fever, or stomach virus, or a hangover. It might reflect coming to work while experiencing burnout or fatigue, or debilitating depression or anxiety.

Often, unproductive time spent at work is a consequence of unmitigated stress and burnout. Stress is contagious. When you interact with someone who is strung out, their high-strung energy permeates your physiological and psychological space. You may notice your heart rate increasing, your worries starting to spiral. And if there is a group of you, everyone in the room may experience the same responses. It takes internal awareness to recognize your response and manage it. There are times when you cannot just leave the room, so you may need to practice those breathing or grounding exercises mentioned in Chapter 4, Self-Care Strategies and Overcoming Barriers to Healthy Routines. Significantly, depression is estimated to cost billions each year due to work absenteeism, diminished productivity, increased healthcare costs, and early death.

Consider this hypothetical scenario:

> When you are immersed in a stressful work environment with no escape or end in sight, you may find colleagues or yourself becoming more irritable and aggressive, creating a self-perpetuating cycle. This irritability and aggressiveness can lead to an overall lowered frustration tolerance and angry or aggressive outbursts. As this happens, the workplace culture begins to deteriorate, and people become less cooperative. As cooperation decreases, teamwork begins to suffer. Pleasantries are exchanged much less frequently; interactions tend to be direct and at times curt. Over time, resentment builds on the part of staff and attorneys, while motivation and loyalty begin to wane. You may find the percentage of unproductive time spent sitting at your desk is increasing, and perhaps signs of burnout, anxiety, or depression setting in. Absences may begin to

increase. Eventually, fantasies about leaving the job become reality, increasing turnover. As word gets out about a particularly bad workplace culture, recruitment and retention become more difficult, especially for firms that do not have the salaries, benefits, and cachet of some national or international law firms.

Although positive practices (related to work environment, managerial effectiveness, job satisfaction, work–life balance, recognition, and reward) are not traditionally valued by the legal profession, research suggests these practices are in fact related to performance, work climate, turnover, as well as senior leader evaluations of effectiveness—even in the financial services industry which has a similarly limited view of well-being and healthy work environments.

Burnout

What Is Burnout?

The World Health Organization (WHO) recognized and classified burnout as an "occupational phenomenon" in 2019. Ever since, the term "burnout" has been used more frequently, in the media and in legal circles. Burnout refers to the impact on functioning of ongoing, unrelenting workplace stressors. It reflects tension experienced by a person arising out of their workload, work pressures, or work environment. Importantly, this classification is not a medical diagnosis, nor is burnout recognized in the American Psychiatric Association's *Diagnostic and Statistical Manual*. Although the popular press has referred to various types of burnout, the WHO has reiterated that the ICD classification of burnout solely and narrowly reflects "phenomena in the occupational context."

Interest in burnout exploded in 2020. The timeliness of the 2019 classification was prescient, occurring in the same year that the COVID-19 pandemic was beginning to take flight. While there was great interest even before "coronavirus" became a common household term, the global pandemic shone a bright light on workplace issues contributing to burnout, and the impact burnout was having on productivity. Long hours, limited autonomy and control over work, as well as decreased sense of community, are some of the issues experienced by lawyers and staff. The additional seemingly endless uncertainty and threats brought about by the pandemic, and constant risk-benefit calculations, further drained emotional and cognitive resources, and decreased tolerance for stress.

The fact that "burnout" is neither a medical nor a mental health diagnosis is probably one of the reasons why the concept has been embraced by the legal community; without a diagnostic implication, experiencing burnout carries less stigma and feels safer to acknowledge.

According to the WHO website, burnout further reflects a "syndrome" which arises as a result of "chronic workplace stress," stress which "has not been successfully managed." There are three primary elements to burnout:

1. *Exhaustion.* You may be feeling as though your energy stores have been depleted, and you do not have the reserves to keep pushing forward.
2. *Depersonalization or Emotional Detachment, Negativity, or Cynicism.* You may feel disconnected, or emotionally detached from your work, perhaps as though you were an observer of yourself doing your work, or you may view everything through an especially negative or distrusting lens (even for lawyers).
3. *Diminished Sense of Personal Accomplishment.* You may feel as though you cannot get anything accomplished and may feel ineffective or experience feelings of inadequacy.

Burnout Symptoms

In addition to the three elements mentioned above (depleted energy; mentally detached/negativity; and feeling ineffective), you may notice other symptoms in yourself or a colleague, such as hostile behavior, increasing cynicism, irritability, and a low frustration tolerance. You may notice you are having difficulty concentrating on your work, are becoming progressively more unproductive, and, therefore, are simultaneously ever more preoccupied with what you are not getting accomplished.

Over time, sleep may become impaired, and depression might set in. Physical symptoms of burnout often mirror those of chronic stress, including fatigue, insomnia, gastrointestinal issues, and headaches. If the circumstances leading to burnout are not addressed, over time chronic illnesses can develop as well. Fortunately, the same interventions that are utilized to manage chronic stress are also helpful for addressing burnout.

What Causes Burnout?

Burnout reflects tension experienced by a person arising out of their work environment, workload, or work pressures. It arises as a result of what psychologist and burnout research pioneer Christina Maslach has called a "mismatch" between a person and their work environment. Burnout has been conceptualized to reflect six areas of "incongruity" in the workplace: 1) Workload; 2) Control; 3) Reward; 4) Community; 5) Fairness; and 6) Values.

The six workplace aspects which may lead to burnout can each stand alone. Yet, in many legal environments each of these aspects is compounded by many of the others.

78

**BOX 5.1 JOB DEMANDS WHICH
INCREASE BURNOUT RISK**

Lawyers frequently struggle with many of the following overlapping job-related demands which increase burnout risk:

- High work demands/spending a great deal of time on work or pre-occupied with work/ongoing, unmitigated work stressors.
- Perceived or actual lack of control over work stressors/low autonomy.
- Lack of recognition or feeling valued.
- Toxic work environment.
- Unsupportive or unfair work environment/different "rules" apply to different people.
- Ethical conflicts/competing values/work not meaningful.

High Workload Demands. Many lawyers experience both workload overload and low control. An endless, intense workload, and spending a great deal of time on work with never enough hours in the day, week, month to complete it, over time can lead to feelings of exhaustion, a negative attitude, and a sense of ineffectiveness in lawyers. Even when not working, any "free" time may be spent preoccupied with work. Work content may be especially mentally taxing, emotionally draining, or it may be monotonous. Never-ending deadlines and long working hours may leave little or no time to rest and recharge. Legal culture has been a burnout machine for decades, all-consuming and stifling of individual needs and identities. With the advent of mobile technology, demands for instant responsiveness soared, compounding many of the already existing issues.

Lack of Control/Low Autonomy. In addition, if lawyers do not believe they have any control over their workload or the work itself, this is a separate risk factor for burnout; responsibility for a project, without the authority to make substantive decisions, creates conflict and stress. Similarly, feeling powerless to address workplace challenges, such as hours, workload, timing of assignments, flexibility in schedules, or work environment can lead to feeling hopeless and helpless.

Lack of Recognition/Not Feeling Valued. Add to this the fact that many legal environments do not provide adequate recognition, and the risk of burnout continues to increase. Simply not feeling valued by supervisors, leaders or the organization, and a lack of recognition for hard work, efficiency, and productivity, can lead to burnout over time. Some firms do reward and recognize hard work and long hours with salary increases, bonuses, entertainment perks, car services, and meals. These monetary rewards and workplace perks—recognizing that the comfortable ride and a meal may be appreciated when leaving the office at 10:00 pm without having to plan dinner or transportation home—do not address the important psychological need for interpersonal recognition, and the sense of feeling valued for hard work, long hours, and a job well done.

Toxic Work Environment. Similarly, a toxic work environment, where supervisor–lawyer/staff interactions are difficult at best, can lead to exhaustion, detachment, and inefficacy, especially if lawyers or staff believe they cannot do anything to change the situation or stop abusive behavior. More about toxic leaders and work environments will be addressed later in this chapter.

Unfair/Different "Rules." When different rules apply to different people, whether it has to do with privileges, responsibilities, or opportunities, resentment increases, along with the risk of other burnout symptoms. Lawyers and staff may personally experience a lack of fairness in the workplace or witness it in terms of how others are treated. Socioeconomic background and lineage, race, ethnicity, gender/gender identity, or sexual orientation may underlie subtle differential treatment—just enough to create tension and disconnection, but perhaps difficult to identify, pinpoint, and address.

Ethical Conflicts/Competing Values. Workplace roles, responsibilities, or expectations may create ethical challenges or give rise to value conflicts. Dealing with disconcerting ethical challenges, struggling to balance competing values, and/or not deriving any meaning from one's work are all additional recipes for burnout.

If you have been working around the clock for an extended period, if your workplace is highly stressful or toxic, if you feel unsupported or under-valued, if you lack autonomy or control over your work, if you are faced with ethical challenges or do not find your work meaningful, or if your practice area takes an emotional toll on you, any one or a combination of these factors can contribute to burnout.

Burnout Is a Workplace Issue

Burnout reflects conflict at the intersection of workplace demands and individual needs. The WHO classification of burnout as an occupational phenomenon in 2019 was an important step toward helping employers recognize that the responsibility for promoting health and well-being does not rest solely on the individual. Burnout is not a clinical diagnosis or an individual "phenomenon."

Thankfully, the legal profession is finally embracing the need to address burnout and promote lawyer well-being, mobilized by the skyrocketing mental health needs brought on by the COVID-19 pandemic. Although recognition of the well-being crisis in the legal profession had been (slowly) increasing prior to the pandemic, most interventions have been on an individual level, as opposed to creating meaningful organizational change. Simply providing access to nutrition counseling, yoga, meditation, or other self-care strategies is not enough to sustain the profession. If workplace culture is toxic, even if yoga and meditation are offered and utilized, people will eventually experience burnout.

We Have Burnout—Now What? When a large percentage of lawyers and staff are experiencing burnout, this signals a need to evaluate and address workplace culture. If we recognize burnout is a workplace phenomenon, brought on by difficult working conditions or circumstances, then we must also recognize the need for it to be addressed on an organizational level. The burden cannot be solely on the individual attorney or staff member. And while human resources staff will inevitably be involved, real change will be more likely to occur if the need for change is acknowledged, prioritized, and addressed at the leadership level.

Legal Employers Can in Fact Be Nimble. The pandemic not only increased awareness of the central importance of supporting well-being to promote productivity; firms also became nimbler and began to recognize that once-previously-unthinkable efficiency- and productivity-related workplace changes can be implemented quickly and effectively. The most obvious of these changes was the rapid transition to remote work. Remote work saves time and money in travel and commuter costs. Many young lawyers prefer remote work. Nonetheless, remote work and video conferencing were not on most lawyers' radar prior to 2020 in a profession that values in-person "face time" as "evidence" of hard work and productivity. There was (and perhaps still is) an overarching belief that important work needs to be accomplished in person, and meetings involving complex matters, conflict, and strong opinions require everyone to be sitting around the table in a room together. There was, and still is, a fear that if people work from home, they will slack off and not be as productive or work fewer hours.

Generational Divides Can Be Barriers to Positive Change. Lawyers from different generations tend to have differing views on the adequacy of virtual technology, but as time passes and people become more comfortable with video applications and platforms, the generational divide appears to be narrowing in this regard. Attorneys of all ages have come to realize virtual meetings save a great deal of travel time when long distances are involved, eliminating geographical barriers to attendance. Experts from around the country and the world can attend meetings and make contributions. Moreover, in some instances, parties to a disagreement appreciate the ability to be in their own physical space, while addressing the conflict in a virtual meeting.

Many Lawyers Are Taking Stock of Their Work Situation. The pandemic led to a near-universal "taking stock," and many lawyers have begun to question why they are spending long, stressful hours working. Generational differences in how work is valued, and what role it plays in one's overall identity have been highlighted as a part of this taking stock period. Younger generations tend to see work as just one part of their larger identity ("I am a male, father, spouse, son, friend, lawyer, chef, marathon runner, volunteer"), while older generations tend to see work as their identity ("I am a lawyer"). Both sides need to find a way to bridge the gap. Marginalized identities are also more at the forefront in the minds of younger generations, who do not want to hide or suppress their gender identity or mute their cultural background, traditions, and mannerisms. Although larger firms have responded to associate dissatisfaction and turnover threats by increasing associate salary, for many young lawyers, money is not the answer.

The Great Resignation is not about laziness, it is about hope for a better future, hope that work can be productive and satisfying without being all-consuming. When evaluating potential legal employers, young lawyers want more than yoga classes and a meditation app. While self-care strategies are essential, they simply are not enough.

A 2021 survey from *Bloomberg Law* asking lawyers why they are planning on leaving their employer revealed some surprising and telling findings. Significantly, the top three reasons did not reflect remuneration. These were:

1) Better work–life balance.
2) Reduce work stress.
3) Increase focus on personal life.

Notably, "Better salary/compensation" came in at number 4. "Better work–life balance" topped the list, with 45% of respondents endorsing this item, and "Reduce work stress" came in at a close second with endorsement from 43% of survey respondents. Thirty-nine percent of those responding endorsed "Increased focus on personal life," which came in third. Reasons 5, 6, and 7, respectively, were "fewer hours," "better work environment," and "more opportunity for advancement."

The benefits of healthy work environments are two-fold; a healthy workplace both 1) enhances productivity and 2) prevents burnout by promoting a positive culture and addressing problematic workplace issues. Real change in the legal profession needs to be much bigger than the current self-care approach, and will happen one employer at a time. Real change needs to start at the top, with firm leaders embracing promotion of a healthy workplace while taking steps to address systemic problems and barriers to well-being. Perhaps younger generations will not find the employer oasis of their dreams, but might there be a compromise arrangement that is feasible for lawyer and employer alike?

Addressing Burnout: No One-Size-Fits-All Solutions

Prioritizing Self-Care. Despite the fact that it is a workplace phenomenon, burnout is also a sign that self-care needs to be addressed. When feeling unproductive, it can be very difficult to give yourself permission to take a break, even though you may desperately need one. It may seem counter-intuitive, but you will accomplish more if you allow yourself to take a break and recharge. The same project that may have been taking you three hours to complete, once refreshed, may only take 30 minutes to an hour. Depending on the extent of your symptoms, a break may be anything from 15 minutes to a vacation. How you address burnout will depend on your individual needs and circumstances. See Chapter 4, Self-Care Strategies and Overcoming Barriers to Healthy Routines for more information.

What Are the Written and Unwritten Rules, the Expectations, and Unspoken Values in Your Workplace? As an employer, you can begin by taking a close look at the unspoken values and biases in your workplace. Strengths, pain points, and needs vary across settings. What are your organizational values, including the unspoken values? If identifying and addressing these issues is easier said than done, often a neutral third party can access this information and help to gently address problem areas and people.

What are your expectations for associates and staff, including the unspoken expectations? What are your expectations related to:

- Billable hour requirements?
- Efficiency?
- Time spent working in the office at one's desk?
- Workload and accessibility after hours?
- Fostering client relations?
- Rainmaking?
- Prioritizing work above family?
- Self-sacrifice in the name of work, or a particular client, or type of case?

What are the organizational values regarding healthy work environments?

- How are people expected to treat each other and behave around one another?
- How are people treated on a day-to-day basis?
- What do working relationships look like?
- What are typical daily and weekly hours worked?
- Do lawyers have autonomy over their work?
- Do lawyers have the ability to say "no" to assignments, within reason, without negative repercussions?
- Do lawyers take their vacation time?
- Do the same "rules" apply to everyone?
- Is it okay for men to take paternity leave?
- Is it okay for women to ask for flexibility to manage childcare responsibilities?

The best change strategy will include the voice of rank-and-file lawyers and staff. The simple act of asking for input, and responding to it, leaves people feeling heard and valued. Involving organizational leaders in healthy workplace messaging and dialogue is key. Ask lawyers and staff about their workplace experience, including the areas above. As them what they like about the workplace, and what might be changed or improved. Starting with an anonymous survey is a good place to begin, ideally tailored to your specific organization. You can follow-up afterward with small group discussions about the results, in groups comprised of some configuration of leadership, lawyers, and staff. By simply allowing, enabling, and participating in this conversation, you are opening the door to better communication, improving your workplace culture, and taking an important step toward lawyer well-being. More on promoting healthy work environments, preventing burnout, and addressing toxic culture to follow later in this chapter.

Toxic Leaders, Toxic Culture

Sometimes the work environment itself, rather than the subject matter, is the major stressor. Toxic leaders take a toll on the workplace environment and associate and staff well-being. A 2022 thematic analysis by Sull and colleagues involving 1.3 million Glassdoor.com employer reviews of 40 large US corporations identified *The Five Toxic Culture Attributes* that "poison" corporate culture. Not unsurprisingly, there are overlaps with risk factors for burnout discussed earlier:

1) *Disrespectful* (defined as a "lack of consideration, courtesy, and dignity for others").
2) *Non-Inclusive* (including inequity related to LGBTQ+ status, disability, race, age, gender, "cronyism and nepotism," and "general non-inclusive culture").
3) *Unethical* (defined as "unethical behavior, dishonesty, or lack of regulatory compliance").
4) *Cutthroat* (defined as "backstabbing behavior and ruthless competition").
5) *Abusive* (defined as "bullying, harassment, and hostility").

Respect and Inclusivity

The five categories of toxic leaders simply reflect emerging themes across employer reviews, but the categories also represent familiar themes when lawyers talk about problematic colleagues. The identified behaviors may be engaged in by a leader, or by associates, or other entry- and mid-level lawyers who are vying for assignment of a case, partnership, or another distinguished role. When thinking about your workplace culture, are people treated with courtesy, consideration, and dignity, or do communications tend to be abrupt, direct, and without any reflection of care or concern about the person being addressed? Inclusivity certainly encompasses the many important issues under the broad diversity, equity, and inclusion umbrella, but it can also include things like cronyism, nepotism, playing favorites, and cliques. A person may be excluded because someone does not like them, because they have different opinions on an issue, or because they are viewed as a competitive threat. Do people feel they are treated with fairness? Do they feel valued? Is appropriate recognition given for a job well done? Are they included in key decision-making processes? Do they experience stonewalling when making suggestions, asking questions, or requesting meetings?

Ethics, Ruthless Competition, and Toxicity

Unethical behavior, such as regulatory non-compliance, creates strain and puts a great deal of pressure on lawyers who want to succeed but do not feel comfortable with flouting regulations, guidelines, and social mores. Unethical behavior may include misleading or deceptive behaviors on an interpersonal level, such as undermining, sabotaging, not giving credit where credit is due, or representing someone else's work as one's own. When we think about cut-throat competition, lawyers are at significant risk. On the whole, lawyers are a highly competitive group, with a distinct competitive streak. Competition is not a bad thing; it motivates us and helps us produce some of our best work. But put a group of highly competitive people together and there is a risk they can feed off each other, with ever-increasing competitive behaviors which can potentially escalate to toxic levels. Associates vying for a plumb case or for partnership may be engaging in this subtle sabotage without others even knowing it.

The Exploding Hostile Lawyer, Overt Abuse, and the
Perpetuation of Negative Workplace Culture

We are all familiar with the partner (either through friends and colleagues, lore, or our own experience) who explodes on a dime, yells, screams, berates, and belittles, and perhaps throws things. This behavior is toxic for obvious reasons. It creates a tense workplace with people on edge, or who hide in their offices and use a lot of energy navigating the partner in an effort to not set them off. Such an atmosphere does not foster open communication, creative thinking, positive energy, or relationships. The office climate becomes strained and negative, and there is also a risk of downstream effects where the target of the abuse then takes out their frustration on a lower-level attorney or staff member, thus perpetuating the abuse and a negative office culture. Often

85

these partners remain, likely because they are important rainmakers for the firm, but also because no one wants to confront the bully.

The abusive "exploding lawyer" is all too familiar to many young associates. A sharp first-year associate at a large, big-city law firm once shared about typical interactions with a hostile, bullying partner they worked with:

> I would be given an assignment and would deeply research the issue, come up with some creative arguments, and would draft a brief. The partner and I would meet to discuss the work, and he would then explode, yelling about how terrible the brief was and demanding changes. I would go back and make all the changes he requested, and we would meet again to review the latest draft. This time, the same thing would happen, he would explode and tell me how terrible the work was, only this time he would ask me to revise the document back to the way it was when I originally submitted it to him. This was the way he operated. Everyone knew it, but no one did anything about it.

In other words, the partner ultimately wanted the brief to reflect the original submission, but in the process not only did this leader and supervisor not acknowledge the contribution of his associate, but repeatedly verbally assaulted and demeaned the associate in the process as well. Over time, the associate knew what to expect with this partner, and did not take it personally, a key factor in the associate's resiliency.

For others, facing and bracing oneself for these types of interactions day-in and day-out can be draining and may lead to burnout. Bullying, harassment, and hostility leave an indelible negative mark on workplace culture. To survive, those who are targets of the behavior may perpetuate it by taking out their frustrations on lower-level attorneys and staff, they may withdraw and not engage in leadership development behaviors or creative problem-solving, or they may leave the organization. If an attorney feels trapped in their job, they may turn to substances to self-medicate and manage their distress, which can then lead to addictions, poor work performance, or professional liability.

The Quietly Manipulative Lawyer and the Insidious Toxicity of Passive-Aggressive Behavior

On the other hand, a more subtle, manipulative abuse can also occur, involving condescending and demeaning behavior, undermining, and sabotage. Passive aggressive behavior is a tactic which makes it very difficult for the target to address because it leaves room for interpretation. Such tactics include stonewalling or silent treatment (not responding to calls or emails, or refusing to discuss certain topics), using indirect aggression by raising topics with the intention of creating discomfort or a sense of exclusion, making sarcastic comments, or negative comments about a topic more broadly which is highly relevant to the person being targeted. Passive aggressive behavior can also include pretending to not know something or not have any information as a way to subvert the efforts of someone else. This behavior can be more difficult to identify because it is not overt and obvious, yet it takes a negative toll on the workplace, creating distrust, impeding communication, potentially inciting a similar, or more aggressive, response from their targets, and creating stress.

Toxic leadership and culture in more subtle and nuanced forms can be quietly manipulative, disrespectful, or involve stonewalling, as in the following scenario:

> During meetings, the team leader would not acknowledge my presence or respond directly to my questions or recommendations. Once I was done speaking, this leader would simply go on to give their opinion and make directive declarations, disregarding anything I said, and often in contradiction to it, without any acknowledgement of me, my effort, and work.

Cutthroat, ruthless competition is another toxin which further erodes workplace culture. It is another example of symptoms of a psychologically unsafe environment which discourages cooperation and collaboration and encourages self-promotion and self-protective behaviors to the exclusion of all others. It can lead to a lack of consideration or courtesy, and a failure to treat others with dignity and respect. In addition to stonewalling, responses to questions may be misleading and deceptive. People may not be treated fairly, may not be made to feel welcome, and may be left out of key decision-making processes. Ideas may be criticized, dismissed, or disregarded in one meeting only to be embraced later by someone else as their own. Abusive behavior does not have to be overt; it can come in the form of undermining and sabotage.

These toxic behaviors are caustic to workplace culture, and can lead to cycles of escalation, burnout, and high attrition rates. People respond in different ways; some respond in kind, leading to escalation, some may eventually lose their cool and respond more overtly in frustration (leaving them open to being labeled as the problem, especially when colleagues and supervisors miss the subtle toxicity to which they are responding).

Stonewalling behavior may be an intentional, manipulative, power-play strategy, or it may be the result of someone not knowing how to respond in a challenging situation. In any case, addressing it directly can help you get to the root of the behavior and determine the best way to respond and manage the situation going forward. Even when not intended to manipulate, stonewalling behavior or a refusal to talk with someone who asks because you don't want to be in an uncomfortable situation prevents you from gathering data that could be helpful for you in managing the people and situation involved. It also leaves the person who asked for a meeting feeling unheard and unvalued, and perhaps not respected depending on the circumstances.

If you want to build a healthy work environment which draws top talent and promotes creativity, autonomy, and independence, you will also want to challenge toxic behaviors and work to promote healthy communication.

Responding to Toxic Culture

The Importance of Intervening

Any behaviors leading to a negative or toxic environment need to be immediately addressed. The behaviors may reflect benign processes, such as not recognizing or appreciating the negative impact of one's behavior on others, or more generally not knowing how to effectively communicate. These behaviors may also be a product of discomfort with conflict and avoidance thereof. Someone who lacks self-confidence may also engage in these behaviors when feeling threatened. Or the behaviors may be more targeted and malicious. When looking at the five categories, we can see how a ruthless competitor might engage in disrespectful, non-inclusive, unethical, or abusive behavior in attempts to stifle the perceived competition. Or how an egotistical person might engage in all of these behaviors because they view themselves as higher up on the food chain and entitled to do whatever they so choose.

In any case, any underlying cause(s) of the behavior needs to be determined so that it can be successfully addressed. The identification of the most problematic behaviors is important, but it is equally important to find the underlying factor which led to the behavior in the workplace. The cause may reflect an intersection of organizational policies, values, and pressures with individual traits, mental and physical states, and life circumstances.

If not adequately addressed, at some point, your top talent may decide to return those recruiter phone calls to see what else is out there in the job market, after having exhausted all possible means to address the situation internally. Those lawyers who are the most proactive, motivated, creative, and independent-minded problem-solvers, once they recognize they have done all they can to try to improve the situation, will eventually seek out other opportunities. They will leave behind a group of people who toe the line in order to keep the toxic leader happy, and are less likely to engage in creative or proactive thinking and problem-solving.

Which leads me to a related point—when looking for a new position or simply staying abreast of the postings, you may notice a certain position at a certain organization appears to be perpetually posted. This may reflect an internal leadership problem that is not being addressed, resulting in a negative or toxic work environment.

How to Intervene

If you know there is tension on a certain team, it is worth exploring by the team leader or more senior level leader, an internal human resources professional, or an outside, neutral professional.

1) *Leaders, Speak Up.* Leaders need to speak up and call people out when they witness toxic behavior, and support the person who is the target of the behavior. Depending on the severity of the behavior, using humor or a playful tone can diffuse tensions while still getting the message across, though sometimes a more serious tone and approach is warranted. Often the toxicity itself, power dynamics, or disparate status prevent people from managing toxic colleagues or leaders on their own without intervention from the top. Be clear and direct. Explain how the behavior is impacting colleagues and the work environment. Let the person know this behavior is not acceptable. Offer to help find resources for learning more about effective communication, leadership, or addressing mental health needs.

2) *Address Issues as They Arise.* You may know there is a problem on a team, but not know why. Perhaps one person has been "difficult." Take the time to explore what is going on. Talk with people. It might be the result of the subtle, manipulative, undermining behavior that tends to go unnoticed by anyone who is not the target. Instead of avoiding the situation, it is best to tackle it head-on. Lawyers are very comfortable with conflict that is well-defined by the rules of the game and not interpersonal. On the other hand, most prefer to ignore interpersonal conflicts and hope they go away. This approach can lead to erosion of the workplace culture.

3) *Be Approachable, Open, and Transparent.* Signal that you are an ally to associates and colleagues, and create psychological safety by being approachable, a good listener, open, and transparent. Reflect back what you are being told to convey your attention (and also to make sure you are hearing it correctly). Provide a safe, receptive, and responsive place for associates and staff to discuss difficulties and help problem-solve solutions.

4) *Associates, Find an Ally.* While it is important to speak up and be assertive, when dealing with a toxic colleague or leader you may need to reach out to an ally in a leadership position, someone whom you trust, to explain what is going on and ask for guidance, or help in managing or changing the situation. You are not going to be able to change a toxic leader on your own; they feed on your subordinate status and relative lack of power, and you may fear putting your position or career in jeopardy. If the toxic person is of equal status, they

may do everything they can to demean, minimize, and jeopardize your role, in an effort to claim superiority or a coveted assignment.

5) *Consider Taking the "Pulse" of Office (or Practice Group/Team) Culture.* Gather data on how associates and staff experience your firm culture. Often perceptions of senior leaders, as compared to those of rank-and-file attorneys and staff, are disparate when it comes to views of office culture, psychological safety, and in general how great it is to work in your office. You might consider utilizing a neutral party to administer an anonymous survey or interview stakeholders. It may be that overall, the office culture is positive, but a particular practice area or team may continually experience problems or attrition.

Not Toxic, but Not Positive Either

Perhaps you are fortunate in that your workplace is not hampered by a toxic partner or colleague. At the same time, some of the normative ways of relating in legal culture can still be draining. The legal profession is known for its pervading sense of competitiveness. When the adversarial approach taken to deal with opposing counsel spills over into interactions with colleagues, in combination with lawyers' existing competitive and perfectionistic traits, this can lead to an intense workplace culture. Competitiveness in and of itself is not bad; in fact, it is a motivator. But when competition becomes a primary way of relating, even if not at toxic levels, it can interfere with relationships and limit connectedness.

Consider this likely familiar scenario: Sometimes, when you get a group of lawyers in a room, everyone begins to puff up and survey the room, evaluating the "competition" and where everyone else fits within a hierarchy. Conversation reflects this competitive stance, with inevitable efforts to one-up. This approach can lead to feelings of power and control, but it does nothing to foster relationships or promote connectedness or intimacy (keep this in mind when you leave the office and want to maintain or build outside relationships). This approach does not foster collaboration. Although relationships may arise out of these gatherings and interactions, a chess game of sorts, these relationships tend to be more instrumental and based on what each player can do for the other rather than on personal connection. As such, these relationships may be less likely to provide social support during challenging times and may in fact dissipate if one of the parties is experiencing difficulties in their work or personal life. Finally, this approach creates a negative work atmosphere. (And if condoned by leadership, colleagues begin to believe they need to respond in kind if they are going to survive, which then perpetuates the problem.)

90

Emotional Intelligence Is Not an Oxymoron

> To be a good lawyer, you need to think objectively and not be swayed by emotion.

Law professors had it right in that we do not want to act purely on our emotions, feelings, and psychological needs. Nonetheless, the best decisions incorporate emotional knowledge into logical reasoning, without necessarily acting on emotions or giving them paramount importance. Ideally, depending on the situation (e.g., work versus personal life), emotions may be given more or less weight. Emotional intelligence reflects an ability to recognize your own internal processes, triggers, and flaws, as well as the impact of your words and behaviors on others. It involves empathy, being able to recognize how others are feeling and respond in a way that reflects care and concern.

An emotionally intelligent leader is able to recognize simmering conflicts and adeptly identify and address them in a way that maintains psychological safety and respect, leaves people feeling heard and valued, and is more likely to gain the support of all involved.

In recent years, lawyers who have begun to adopt self-care strategies and create boundaries in their lives are now embracing well-being in the legal profession, eager to share what they have learned. Although the idea of well-being resonates, thinking around well-being has often been much more fragmented, as in "well-being means doing x, y, or z," without the frame of the big picture, involving the context of workplace culture. This insider recognition of the importance of well-being is encouraging, nonetheless. At the same time, caution needs to be taken to ensure this movement does not reflect a microcosm of the more concerning problems of the legal profession, under the guise of wellness. A well-being arena that is highly competitive or at times even adversarial, with jousting among professionals, can be jarring to observe and experience. Professional behavior which role models collaboration, instead of coming from a place of competition, would be ideal. Old habits are difficult to change, however, and many lawyers struggle to shift from an adversarial stance to a more collaborative one, even with the strong desire to do so.

Litigators who transition their practice to non-adversarial or alternative dispute resolution (ADR) often find the transition difficult. This process takes time, and often requires a great deal of training, to learn not only the skills involved in ADR, but also how to think differently about cases. It also requires self-reflection and an ability to evaluate and recognize one's own internal thoughts and emotional responses, as well as how these in turn impact the other people in the room, and to modify behaviors accordingly. It is these behaviors (adversarial or collaborative) which most impact the climate in the room. The same holds true for promoting well-being.

If leadership and colleague behavior foster competitiveness and distrust, the overall culture will still be unhealthy and harmful to well-being. No amount of self-care will be able to mitigate the negative effects of an unhealthy workplace culture. Notably, when psychologists advance through their doctoral training, psychotherapy historically has been required, more recently recommended, by many doctoral degree programs. This is because we can best facilitate change and help others when we know ourselves, warts and all.

The most effective leaders have insight into their internal responses, the impact of their behavior on others, and the internal experiences of those around them. If they don't, many consider working with a coach to understand and manage workplace thoughts, emotions, and behaviors.

Addressing Time Management Challenges

Time management is not just a productivity issue, it is also a well-being issue. An inability to make efficient use of time, set boundaries, and know when your work is "good enough," can create unnecessary stress, and lead to overwork and exhaustion.

Recently, a lawyer who decided to return to law firm life after a stint with a non-profit made this observation:

> In starting back into a law firm environment, there are a few things that strike me as odd. I used to believe that the "busy lawyers" who did work all the time—no matter where they were—were so adaptable, important, and very smart to be able to markup documents while sitting at a professional development program [or other meeting]. But looking at lawyers doing this now made me think—they are inefficient at their work, they are not giving the proper attention to their client matters by multi-tasking, and that they are unintentionally putting their clients' information at risk by having others potentially see certain documents.

Multi-tasking is inefficient. Our brains can only focus on one thing at a time. If you try to work on client matters and attend a professional development seminar at the same time, neither task will be performed well. You won't give the client the undivided attention they need, expect, and are paying for, and you likely will not learn very much from the workshop. While it is easy to say, "don't multi-task," the problem is much bigger, reflecting caseload, time management skills, as well as expectations and support of supervisors.

Prioritization and Knowing When Enough Is Enough. Early career associates struggle with knowing when their work product is "good enough." When faced with a never-ending flood of work, whether it be as a young prosecutor, or a transactional or litigation associate, decisions need to be made about what projects will take priority in terms of when they will be worked on in relation to other projects, as well as the amount of time spent on each project. The ability to recognize when a project is completed is an important skill. This requires a combination of taming one's inner perfectionist, as well as a degree of self-confidence and self-direction, leading to an ability to quickly address the salient issues of a "small potatoes" project to be able to move on and spend more time and energy on the "big fish" that awaits. Being nimble in this manner is essential to keep things moving. Your inner perfectionist does not necessarily recognize that after a certain point the costs of your time and energy begin to outweigh any benefit of continued work on a project. The ability to recognize this helps you with not getting bogged down in details that may not be relevant, or will only have minor consequences relative to the big picture and other work that needs to be addressed.

- So, when is your work "good enough"? The point at which your efforts will not bring enough value to warrant continued work on a document. How do you know when you have reached this point? Unfortunately, there are no quick-fix easy answers. This wisdom usually develops over time. You will begin to recognize when you have reached "good enough" more quickly and confidently with experience.
- The calculation involves weighing a few different variables, including the stakes involved in the case, the likely level of scrutiny, and whether even minor errors can lead to major consequences. Cases and deals that are high profile and/or involve large sums of money, or are controversial in some way, are the types of cases that may involve increased scrutiny and leave little room for the smallest of errors. (We are not talking about malfeasance or unethical behavior, which are always inappropriate regardless of level of scrutiny.) It can feel like every project falls within these categories, which makes it difficult to let go and move on.
- When prioritizing your time, you want to ensure your work is legally sound. At the same time, consider spending less energy looking for obscure legal rules or gathering other information which will not add much to your position, especially when weighed against time involved. Consider spending less time re-drafting a document to the extent that it can be submitted for a literary award.

Setting Boundaries. Determine the time of day when you are most productive and strive to set aside time for uninterrupted work. When faced with constant work demands, ideally you will experience some degree of autonomy in your work, an ability establish boundaries around your availability, and an ability to say "no" to new assignments. Admittedly, some workplaces are more receptive to associate autonomy than others, but it also requires a degree of assertiveness on the part of the associate. This card needs to be played judiciously (especially when it involves saying "no" to an assignment), and cannot be over-used, but it is also an important skill to be able to recognize when you will be at a tipping point if you take on more work. See Appendix II, Setting Boundaries, for specific strategies.

Leadership Support Is Essential. Time management is an ongoing concern for associates and leadership. Time management strategies may sound helpful in theory, but associates don't have much leverage without leadership support.

- Written and unwritten policies which promote autonomy and empower associates to block off time for productive work, and sleep—read: not expecting them to be immediately responsive all the time—can reduce stress, allow for moments to recharge, and improve focus and productivity.
- Mentoring can also go a long way in helping associates learn where to focus their time and energy, and when their work is "good enough." There is only so much time in the day and efficiency will allow for more work to be accomplished across associate caseload. Ideally, efficiency will also give associates some room to take short breaks to recharge, which in turn will further improve efficiency.

Multi-Tasking Can Increase Professional Liability Risks. As the lawyer quoted at the beginning of this section importantly observed, in addition to the inherent inefficiency, working on client matters while in a public space with many other people around can create breach of confidentiality risks, whether it be in a seminar, at a school play, or on an airplane.

Other Strategies for Fostering Productivity and a Healthy Work Environment

Set Realistic Expectations. Importantly, do not expect perfection from yourself or others.

Stay Attuned to Toxic Urges. At times you will inevitably slip back into what I will call *Adversarial Type-A Competitive Mode* (ATACM, or "attack 'em"), but with insight, time, and effort, these instances should become less frequent and less intense. A healthy work environment encourages transparency, fosters collaboration, and promotes psychological safety. If you are chanting "Rah-Rah-Rah Well-Being," but you are unable to foster collaboration with others and engender psychological safety, your words will fall on deaf ears. Consider working to identify where any need to control and/or perfectionist tendencies most interfere, and when your competitive feathers become ruffled. These traits are common in the legal profession, but there are others to consider as well. Once you have identified any other problem-areas, you can be attuned to, and learn more about, how you respond when these are triggered, and perhaps develop more collaborative approaches. For more on the impact of stress and personal traits on health and productivity, and the importance of self-care strategies for maintaining emotional intelligence, see Chapter 3, Attention to Overall Physical and Mental Health and Chapter 4, Self-Care Strategies and Overcoming Barriers to Healthy Routines.

Strong Advocacy Can Be Civil. It is important to keep in mind that civility and strong legal advocacy are not mutually exclusive. There is a distinction between assertiveness and aggressiveness, though sometimes the two become enmeshed. An assertive lawyer is confident, clear, calm, firm, and respectful when making demands. Listening and hearing what the other side has to say is not a sign of weakness; in fact, it can even lead to a better resolution for your client overall. An aggressive lawyer leans more on threatening tone and behaviors, personal attacks, and not listening to—or even ignoring—the other person. Respect for the other person is lacking in this approach and it usually leads to an escalating cycle of attacks from both sides. People respond by digging in their heels, becoming more positional and farther away from a meeting of the minds than when they began.

Avoid Conferring Responsibility Without Authority. An associate with a great deal of responsibility also needs some degree of autonomy and authority to make decisions and judgment calls. This authority needs to be earned, but as soon as it is clear an associate has what it takes, the reins should be gradually loosened and lifted. With more autonomy, work can be done more quickly and efficiently, while simultaneously building confidence and a sense of self-efficacy in the associate, further enabling professional growth. This also comes into play when accepting or refusing assignments.

Empowerment. Empowerment is an important component of a productive and healthy workplace. When work is supported, meaningful, and self-directed, one's organizational commitment, job satisfaction, and psychological well-being all increase, and burnout decreases.

People tend to have a more positive experience of the workplace, better overall physical and psychological well-being, and decreased likelihood of burnout when they also:

- Have a strong sense of competency or belief that they can perform their tasks skillfully.
- Find their work meaningful.
- Have the authority and autonomy to carry out their responsibilities.
- Have some degree of influence on workplace decisions and outcomes.
- Are supported and empowered in their roles by their organization.

Empowerment through organizational pathways is important, such as through:

- Information sharing.
- Access to professional development and advancement opportunities.
- Access to resources.
- Supervisory coaching support, including positive feedback.

Supportive workplaces make it easier to manage demanding and aggressive clients and other stressful work-related challenges. Empowerment through support includes positive feedback from supervisors and colleagues, something that is often over-looked in busy, high-intensity, high-pressure work environments such as those found in the legal profession.

Providing positive feedback may seem gratuitous and inefficient, but it is an important motivator, one that enhances feelings of affiliation, identification, and belonging, which in turn are related to increased levels of commitment to the organization. A sense of empowerment in terms of how one views their role, abilities, and influence, as well as degree of support from supervisors and the organization, can make the difference between high performance and burnout.

Showing Appreciation Goes a Long Way. Even if workplace culture is not toxic, it may still be lacking in terms of recognition. This is not necessarily, or solely, financial recognition in terms of raises, bonus, and benefits. For many lawyers, it may simply be an interpersonal acknowledgment. Lawyers are great at letting people know when things are not going well, but positive reinforcement for a job well-done is much less common. You just do your job, and if there is a problem you will hear about it. Reaching out to an associate to say "Hey, great job handling that case last week!" or "You raised some interesting ideas in our meeting this morning, we need to explore those further" can go a long way in helping someone feel valued, appreciated, not to mention motivated. If you are unable to acknowledge in person, a phone call, email, text, or other internal network message are all fine options.

Finally, when striving to change workplace culture, recognition of collaborative and inclusive behaviors among colleagues signals leadership support for healthy workplace changes.

Is Your Firm a Psychologically Safe Workplace?

If you are reading this and did not skip this section after seeing the words "psychological safety," that is a good sign. The old-school buck-up-or-get-out attitude of the legal profession balks at such "soft" concepts. But long-standing cracks in the system have been under greater scrutiny since 2020.

Increasing numbers of early career attorneys are choosing quality of life over compensation when it comes to unrelenting long hours in unsupportive, at times "unsafe" work environments. After two to three years of grueling work, with new experience and diminished or eliminated law school debt, many associates begin to look elsewhere for a better work environment, better hours, and improved work–life balance, even if this comes with a lower pay scale. Unhealthy work environments negatively impact productivity, as well as attorney and staff retention.

An essential aspect of a healthy work environment is psychological safety. Despite decades of research on the value of a healthy work environment, law firms have been slow to arrive at the psychological safety table. In addition to the rampant lawyer fear and loathing of vulnerability, an important pragmatic reason is likely the inherent nature of the profession... mistakes can have high stakes consequences, in terms of personal freedom or economic outcomes.

An overarching theme in a psychologically safe workplace is a "social climate of trust." Amy Edmondson introduced the concept of "psychological safety" in 1999 as "[a] shared belief held by members of a team that the team is safe for interpersonal risk-taking." She has since expanded her conceptualization of psychological safety to include three levels, the individual level, the team level, and the organizational level, recognizing the necessity of trust at all three levels in a healthy, productive workplace.

A Safe Place to Learn, Grow, and Problem-Solve

Psychological safety is particularly important for early career associates because it promotes what is known as "learning behavior": seeking feedback, sharing information, asking for help, talking about errors, and experimenting. If simply reading the word labels for these behaviors makes your head ache and your chest constrict, your workplace, team, or specific work relationships may not feel safe to you. The competitive nature of the profession, as well as the perfectionist need to convey a competent and a flawless image, inhibit help-seeking behavior. There may be a fear that seeking feedback, asking for help, and discussing mistakes suggests insecurity or incompetence. On the other hand, the desire to get ahead may deter information sharing, so as not to inadvertently give someone a competitive advantage.

In many legal office climates, these fears are very real and well-founded. At the same time, when we feel threatened our thinking constricts and we become more inflexible, in both our thinking and our behavior. This narrowed thinking and inflexibility further limit engagement in any behaviors perceived to be risky, and thus reinforce a rigid office climate that in effect prioritizes appearances and "saving face" over learning and growth. Learning and growth require risk-taking, self-assessment, curiosity, and inquiry, which enable the detection of errors, promote problem-solving (which may involve gathering feedback and information), and ultimately allow for any necessary correction. These are important skills, and not only for new associates.

Proactive people gather information, and exchange information and resources with their colleagues, which then promotes trust, relationship-building, and a safe environment for creative problem-solving. Colleagues, however, will not share information or speak up when they observe errors, disagree, or have alternative views if they believe they will be punished, rejected, or shamed for doing so, or simply be seen as incompetent. Moreover, for people to take the personal risk and reveal errors or make suggestions for improvement, they also need to believe their team can make use of the information. Associates may experience a degree of psychological safety with fellow associates working on the same case, but if their team leader will not be receptive, or worse will react negatively, associates will not be willing to take the risk and reveal errors or share creative problem-solving ideas.

A Safe Place for All

Psychological safety also reflects office climate and the ability to be yourself while feeling comfortable and valued. It relates to issues of diversity and how welcoming your firm is, not only to differing perspectives, but differences in how people look, behave, relate to others, and identify with their biological sex and sexuality. Similarly, a climate of trust characterized by interpersonal trust, respect, and cooperation, information exchange, as well as shared language and social codes, is strongly related to firm performance. The ability to communicate openly throughout the various phases of a project, allowing for discussion, brainstorming, and differing perspectives related to decisions, leads to better performance as a team.

Psychological Safety in a Remote World. In this new age of increasing remote work, psychological safety is especially important when working remotely across countries and cultures. It is more difficult to read people via electronic communications, including video technology. Leaders who promote mutual respect, inclusivity, and open communication can help build the trust needed for successful virtual collaborations.

Guiding "Beliefs" Which Reflect Psychological Safety

The question becomes, how do we create a safe environment, one that promotes learning behaviors throughout the career span, while at the same time fostering high-quality work? Expectations around learning and competence influence our ability to engage in learning behaviors. Did you expect perfection from yourself the moment you passed the bar? After a few months, or years, of work? Do you expect the same of those who work for you? Do you believe once you or colleagues reach a certain point of "competence" you then focus your time and energy elsewhere? The reality is, when we stop learning and growing, we stagnate, as professionals and as people.

Edmondson identified "a set of related beliefs" which can help evaluate for psychological safety at the team level. These include beliefs that team members:

- Will not be rejected by their colleagues for being themselves.
- Care about each other and are interested in their colleagues as people.
- Have positive intentions.
- Respect the competence of each member of the team.

Of note, team psychological safety influences the learning behaviors (i.e., willingness to ask for help, provide help, challenge the status quo, point out errors) mentioned earlier, which in turn impact performance. The most effective leaders will role model these behaviors while creating an environment in which interpersonal risks which come from a place of positive intention will not be punished, thus facilitating proactive behaviors which in turn lead to successful performance.

Making the Most of Negative Feedback

Psychological safety and related interpretations made by individual attorneys or the entire team regarding the intentions of colleagues influences receptivity (or lack thereof) to feedback, and whether negative feedback is interpreted as amicable or hostile. For example, if your nemesis gives you negative feedback, you will likely view their intentions as hostile rather than to be helpful, and you will be much less likely to reflect on the feedback or respond positively. Yet, it may in fact be very useful data. Regardless of the other person's intentions, you can learn a lot from feedback.

Some of the most valuable feedback we receive comes from our interactions with the people who most irritate us. Instead of dwelling on everything that is wrong with the other person, you will gain the most benefit from stepping back, taking a deep breath, and reflecting on the information you received. Think about how it meshes with your beliefs, values, personal style, or reactions. Is there a kernel of truth to what you are being told about your behavior or work product? Even if the messenger may be misinterpreting your intent or missing the point, is it possible their interpretation is also valid? How can you utilize this information to improve going forward, becoming a more formidable legal expert and a better communicator and colleague?

Toxic Positivity in Leadership Undermines Psychological Safety

On the leadership level, team, or organizational level, one clear sign of a lack of psychological safety is a leader who only wants to hear about how well everything is going and does not want to know about anything problematic. This attitude creates an environment of threat, with reluctance to ask for help, offer to help, or make suggestions for improvement. Over time, this stifling environment can begin to feel untenable, and strategies for dealing with it may include looking for work elsewhere or protecting oneself by remaining closed off and narrow minded. For more on the negative effects of toxic positivity on social support efforts and psychological safety, see Chapter 8, The Essential Role of Personal Relationships and Social Supports in Well-Being. See Chapter 4, Self-Care Strategies and Overcoming Barriers to Healthy Routines, for more on the psychological and physical heath impacts of toxic positivity.

Additional Psychological Safety Challenges
Unique to the Legal Profession

Admitting you have concerns, or do not have the answers, have a different perspective, or believe you will not fit in if you reveal your true self, are all quite threatening personally and professionally. This is true for everyone, across professions, but appears to be particularly salient for the legal profession with its unspoken but well-known rules, policies, and expectations related to behavior and competence. These unspoken guidelines play a large part in how safe lawyers and staff feel, and the nuanced aspect makes problematic unspoken rules, policies, and expectations more difficult to address. While research on psychological safety has been conducted across professions, research in the legal profession is lacking. In recognition of the unique aspects of legal practice, further research in this area would be enlightening.

In the end, creating an environment in which people feel safe to raise concerns, differences, errors, or the need for help, is not easy. Not only is the culture shift itself difficult, but doing so in a way that does not swing the pendulum too far in the other direction also requires a strategic approach.

Finding a Balance between Control and Creativity. While divergent thinking, creativity, and risk-taking are highly valued in some professions, these characteristics are not necessarily valued in the legal profession. In fact, they may sound rather threatening. The challenge for the legal profession is to find the sweet spot between structure, order, and control, and free-wheeling

100

creativity and risk-taking. Setting aside time for creative problem-solving with colleagues can lead to novel approaches and is much different than on-the-fly risk-taking. Relational leaders build a culture of trust, which enables learning from failures and improves decision quality.

A Note on Workplace Gratitude Exercises

In addition to its many physical and mental health benefits, gratitude journaling has be shown to lead to better interactions with others and to have positive relationship benefits. Friends, loved ones, and others who regularly interact with people who initiated gratitude journaling report experiencing the journaler to be more pleasant to be around, more helpful, more trustworthy, more outgoing, and more optimistic. The very nature of gratitude, which is prosocial and relational, is said to lead to stronger social bonds and relationships. Perhaps the act of directing our attention to the altruism and generosity of others takes us out of our single-minded, self-focused pursuits by broadening our thinking and experience, which creates room to recognize our small role in something much bigger, and to experience an improved sense of connection with others.

Notably, as a result of mainstream recognition of the value of expressing gratitude, beginning meetings with a gratitude exercise has become quite popular. The type of exercise varies and can involve asking everyone to state three things they are grateful for (perhaps since the last meeting), or in the interest of time, one thing for which they are grateful. As mentioned earlier in Chapter 4, Self-Care Strategies and Overcoming Barriers to Healthy Routines, gratitude exercises are highly effective at helping us appreciate the little things in the present moment, and shifting our mindset to a positive focus, which in turn influences mood in a positive direction.

Workplace Gratitude Exercises Are Not an Intervention for Creating Psychological Safety. It is one thing to write in your gratitude journal each day or week, and another to share with a group, particularly if someone has been dealing with professional or personal challenges. Exercises such as this can be valuable in a psychologically safe environment, but they cannot in themselves create a psychologically safe environment, especially when a team leader/meeting leader does not foster a safe environment otherwise. Such exercises can instead heighten awareness of the lack of psychological safety in the room. A less threatening approach would be to open the floor to anyone who wants to share positive news. Unless the environment is truly psychologically safe, inviting people to report positive news, if they want to, should be as far as this exercise goes.

The best interventions are targeted to specific needs and circumstances. For more on self-care and creating change, including developing a workplace pledge or challenge, see Chapter 4, Self-Care Strategies and Overcoming Barriers to Healthy Routines, and Chapter 10, Creating Change.

Diversity, Equity, and Inclusion

Well-being is interwoven with issues of diversity, equity, and inclusion, and a discussion of well-being would be incomplete without acknowledging the impact of the complex individual, interactional, and cultural factors related to diversity, on workers and healthy work environments. Learning and growth in this area is lifelong. When considering how to address these complex and important issues here, a more practical and useful approach for purposes of this book might be to focus on interactional skills and behaviors.

As Anton Hart wrote in 2020, addressing teaching issues of diversity, "If there is a single, main principle to be underscored, it is that—in teaching and in learning—listening with openness is of at least coequal importance with speaking with thoughtfulness and wisdom." Hart's main premise is that curiosity, although psychologically threatening to both the curious person and the subject of curiosity, can guide our thinking and interactions, and help us to appreciate the underlying biases and processes which influence our interactions and the reasons why we choose certain words and to make certain statements.

This approach is compelling. It is unrealistic to expect everyone to become an expert in issues of diversity, equity, and inclusion. At the same time, it is very reasonable to expect everyone to be respectful, thoughtful, and reflective human beings. If we approach all our interactions with a lens of respect, self-reflection, and empathy, being conscious of our motivations and the impact of our words and actions on others, we can navigate complex relationships with respect and humility, two essential components of fostering equity and inclusion.

This premise is particularly relevant to the legal community. Issues of diversity, equity, and inclusion involve an inherent subjective, emotional component. With the strong focus on competence in legal culture, it is all the easier to hide behind knowledge and the "facts" to manage anxiety related to these difficult issues, instead of moving into the threatening emotional domain. Yet, in doing so, we limit our ability to relate to our colleagues, and may inadvertently cause them psychological pain, stress, and feeling psychologically unsafe. By staying in the cognitive realm, you may avoid messy emotions and feel more in control, yet this sense of security comes at a cost. It is through curiosity and emotional vulnerability that we begin to build intimacy and safety, and to truly connect with others.

BOX 5.2 THE CONNECTIONS AMONG MICROAGGRESSIONS, STRESS, HEALTH, AND PSYCHOLOGICAL SAFETY AT WORK

As mentioned in Chapter 3, Attention to Overall Physical and Mental Health, ethnic disparities in hypertension have been attributed to chronic stress in non-White Americans. Moreover, daily stress related to discrimination has been linked to poorer psychological and physical health in the long term. A constant state of vigilance due to threats of discrimination and microaggressions is thought to be a source of chronic stress, which might explain the higher rates of hypertension in Black as compared to White Americans.

A work environment filled with colleagues who are not educated and attuned to issues of diversity, equity, and inclusion can lead to a psychologically *un*safe workplace by perpetuating racist (or other stereotype- and bias-based) beliefs and microaggressions. In addition to promoting job dissatisfaction and stifling creativity and collaboration, microaggressions can lead to feelings of vulnerability, psychological and emotional distress, traumatic stress, and a multitude of psychological and chronic health difficulties. Microaggressions create an additional and entirely unwarranted layer of stress and trauma on already strained lawyers and staff.

Vicarious Trauma

Lawyers are at risk for experiencing trauma through their work with clients via ongoing exposure to disturbing stories and various forms of evidence, including graphic photos and videos, particularly when those lawyers are high in empathy. As with a client who has been victimized, lawyers who represent them might experience several symptoms, including overwhelming anxiety and feelings of vulnerability, nightmares, intrusive thoughts and images, thoughts based in fear, and suspicion about the motives of others. The psychological impact from working with trauma victims can have a negative impact on sleep, thoughts, and emotions for months or even years. Psychologists Lisa McCann and Laurie Pearlman identified these psychological effects in professionals who work with trauma victims, coining the term "vicarious trauma."

Several areas of law have been identified as being at risk, including family, criminal, child protection, and immigration, as well as other areas of civil law addressing deliberate harm, abuse, and neglect. For instance, lawyers who prosecute child pornography may need to review large quantities of images depicting disturbing graphic material. Immigration attorneys working with asylum seekers may need to listen to repeated graphic stories of inhumane treatment. Family lawyers may be exposed to difficult stories about child abuse and domestic violence. The stories clients share often challenge beliefs, values, and assumptions about human nature and the fairness, justness, and safety of our world, as well as one's sense of identity, spirituality, and self-efficacy.

When your work involves listening to clients talk in detail about their traumatic experiences, including situations involving threatening behavior, emotional, physical, or sexual abuse, assault, or murder, your mental health can be put at risk. Some of your clients may be experiencing post-traumatic stress disorder (PTSD), involving intrusive thoughts or images, painful emotional reactions, or nightmares, and over time you may find yourself experiencing the same. You may feel angry, sad, lonely, or anxious.

A personal trauma history can lead to greater distress when working with traumatized clients. Feeling overwhelmed or experiencing hopelessness increase the risk of turning to unhealthy coping strategies, including relying heavily on alcohol, drugs, gambling, or other addictive behaviors. This risk further increases if you have a history of substance misuse, problem gambling, or other problematic coping behaviors.

Left unaddressed, as with mental health and well-being in general, the effects of vicarious traumatization on your work can set you up for professional liability claims. If you begin to recognize the effects of vicarious trauma in a colleague, try to gently offer to help your colleague find assistance. If you are struggling, reach out to a trusted colleague for support, and/or a mental health professional who can help you identify, acknowledge, and process the difficult thoughts and emotions you are experiencing, and learn effective coping strategies. For more on seeking assistance, see Chapter 4, Self-Care Strategies and Overcoming Barriers to Healthy Routines.

Leadership Defines Legal Culture

Leaders wield a great deal of power, not only related to business practices but also related to organizational culture. Rank-and-file lawyers and staff look to leader behaviors as a model for how to work and relate to others. Leader behaviors shape organizational culture, ranging from communication practices to whether people take vacation. Research suggests practices that promote psychological safety, autonomy, trust, respect, communication, as well as having a voice and feeling valued are all related to a positive work environment, job satisfaction, and productivity, all factors important to individual and organizational well-being.

Outsized Significance of Competency

A fair amount of research and writing has been dedicated to the role of self-determination theory in lawyer well-being. Self-determination theory is a theory of motivation based on our needs for competency, autonomy, and relatedness. Further research has looked at the role of leadership autonomy support, which helps to frame how to meet these three needs. Leadership autonomy support refers to leadership behaviors which reflect an interest in the perspectives of the people who work for you, allowing them the opportunity to express a preference or make a choice, and encouraging self-directed behavior. While these approaches have been found to be related to well-being, work engagement, job satisfaction, and positive work behavior, there appears to be more to the role of competency when it comes to lawyer well-being.

Competency is central to the lawyer identity, and its superlative importance is reflected in all aspects of law school and law firm culture. The reason budding lawyers quickly learn to guard their emotions, limit emotional expression, maintain their poker face, not ask for help or show any level of need or vulnerability, is because these behaviors are believed to reflect competency, or a lack thereof. When we consider the competency aspect in self-determination theory, there is the instrumental component—lawyers need to be trained to do their jobs, need courtroom experience, need client contact, need exposure to the big picture of the projects they are working on—but we cannot ignore the important psychological safety aspect.

A junior associate's ability to participate freely in a discussion, raise ideas, raise counter-points or a difference in opinion, while experiencing a sense of being respected, supported, and valued, are elements of psychological safety which promote competency and need to be acknowledged. This is where research from different areas of the literature converge and help us to better understand how to create a supportive, healthy, and productive work environment in an otherwise highly competitive profession. Amy Edmondson's research on psychological safety, Dweck's research on mindset, Salovey and Mayer's emotional intelligence theory, Deci and Ryan's work related to self-determination theory, as well as Seligman's research in the areas of positive psychology, are all informative and together help frame the essential elements of a healthy and productive work environment.

Feedback, Positive and Negative, Is Important for Associate Development

It goes without saying attorneys are known for their skepticism, and this constant negative focus often leaves little room for positive feedback. If something goes wrong, or is not what a supervisor had in mind, you will certainly hear about it. But if something is quite good, that is to be expected and often such success goes without mention.

In 2008, the *Harvard Business Review* reported that a Baker McKenzie survey of associates found:

> First, associates wanted better-quality feedback on their performance, in terms of having greater depth and breadth of feedback. "Breadth" meaning more comprehensive feedback that covered all the key areas of performance. "Depth" meaning feedback that goes beyond generalizations, to examples that are specific and useful. Second, associates wanted more clarity on what was expected of them at the current job level, and what was expected at the next job level, and what knowledge and skills were required to get there. And thirdly, they wanted to know what development opportunities the firm had to offer to help them get there.

Feedback should be broad, deep, clear, and concise. If constructive, it should include a specific explanation of any negative impact on work product, you, colleagues, the organization, or clients, and what can be improved going forward. Positive feedback can be as simple as a one-sentence statement. For a job especially well-done, consider public recognition (which may be as simple as offering praise or congratulating at a team meeting or sending out an email to everyone on the team).

Minding Mindset: Growth, Fixed, Organizational, Strategic

Growth vs. Fixed Mindset

You are probably familiar with the term "mindset." Carol Dweck's research investigates the influence of our thoughts on our problem-solving, learning, and productivity. Dweck is known for her research exploring the importance of our beliefs about our skills, talents, and intelligence, as well as our ability to change. If you believe people are born with a certain level of ability and intelligence, you might be said to approach your work, your abilities, and other people with a "fixed mindset." A challenge of this mindset is the all-or-nothing frame. Either you have what it takes, or you don't. You win, or you fail. The focus tends to be more on external "failure" than on what went wrong and what could have been done differently. Energy is more likely to be spent trying to look "good" (i.e., "successful," "competent," "in control," "powerful," etc.), instead of trying to learn and grow as a professional and a person. A growth mindset, on the other hand, is based on our belief that our abilities can be developed through learning from mistakes, strategic approaches, consultation with and asking for help from others, and hard work.

In reality, our thinking reflects a combination of growth and fixed mindsets. Shaming someone for having what is perceived to be a fixed mindset is

106

not helpful. Nor is it helpful to espouse a growth mindset in theory but not in practice. Mindset is a continuous work in progress. It helps to be attuned to when your thinking is veering more towards the fixed, such as when triggered by an unexpected event or circumstance filled with uncertainty, so you can adjust as needed.

Organizational Mindset

Organizational culture reflects the underlying norms and values that define behavior within a team or organization. Research suggests organizational culture can be defined and categorized based on "mindset." Just as individuals may tend toward a growth or fixed mindset, organizations similarly operate within this framework.

On the organizational level, a growth mindset encourages risk-taking, and will utilize failures as opportunities to learn and grow. Is failure an overwhelming loss or a new opportunity? This way of thinking about failure is a foreign concept for lawyers. There are times when things do not work out as planned. How are these situations handled? Is any consideration given to whether help was sought? To whether resources were available? To whether leadership could have handled things differently? In most cases, probably not, because everyone is involved in a self-protective dance. But if the overall culture supports learning from mistakes, less energy may be expended on the blame game and more on figuring out how to learn, grow, and come back stronger next time.

- *Growth Mindset and Prevention of Catastrophic Failures.* It goes without saying that some mistakes are much more consequential than others. When moving toward a learning stance for dealing with mistakes, the goal would be to foster communication, help-seeking, learning, and growth around smaller-scale issues, concerns, questions, and mistakes, as a way of preventing larger-scale failures. A growth mindset recognizes the reality that we all are lifelong learners.
- *Growth Mindset Promotes Communication, Psychological Safety, and Job Commitment.* Organizations with a growth mindset also recognize the importance of collaboration among colleagues, instead of competition. Companies which embrace a growth mindset are perceived as more collegial and foster a sense of commitment in employees. A psychologically safe work environment can help foster collaboration instead of competition.
- *Risk Taking and Innovation.* Two additional "virtues" of a growth mindset are also not particularly appealing to the legal profession. These are "supporting risk taking" and "fostering innovation."

107

Risk-taking is an important component of innovation, whereas fear of failure and perception of lack of competence hinder risk-taking. These findings help explain why the legal profession is not known for innovation. The risk averse, slow, and steady legal profession is not known for its taste for embracing mistakes, risk-taking, and innovation.

Strategic Mindset

More recently, Dweck and colleagues' mindset research has expanded to explore the value of a "strategic mindset." This involves having an awareness of your own thoughts and being inclined to recognize, understand, and act upon them to help yourself through a challenging situation, or when you have not met your goals. Questions you might ask yourself include: "What can I do to help myself?", "How else can I do this?", or "Is there a way to do this even better?" Asking yourself these questions is associated with strategic action leading to increased commitment to, progress toward, and achievement of goals that are long term, important, and unfamiliar, as well as increased performance speed. Strategic thinking is something lawyers already bring to the table when it comes to their work, but perhaps not so much when it comes to self-care, monitoring stress, distress, and illness levels, and organizational culture.

Learned Helplessness and Mindset

Martin Seligman introduced the term learned helplessness. He found that when exposing dogs to inescapable shocks, the same dogs did not try to escape from shocks in a later situation in which they could have learned and figured out how to escape. Similarly, early career associates can quickly learn that they cannot change their work situation or conditions. This may sound appealing to leaders, but when this mindset permeates all aspects of work it limits proactive and creative problem-solving.

Is it possible learned helplessness and fixed mindsets are at play when it comes to promoting change in the legal profession? Are hiring and promotion decisions based solely on "talent" versus potential or ability? What message does the familiar human resources title which includes "talent" convey to lawyers, staff, and new hires? Does the risk-averse nature of the profession promote a sense of learned helplessness in aspects of one's work? The same question applies to workplace culture and expectations.

Final Thoughts for the Skeptics

Growth mindset might be a tough sell for many lawyers and law firm leaders. But learning from mistakes, development through consultation with others, asking for help, and strategic approaches, as well as calculated risks and well-thought-out innovative approaches, may be just what you or your firm need to improve workplace culture and jumpstart job commitment, motivation, productivity, and enhanced problem-solving.

Eliminating Mental Health Stigma in the Workplace

A psychologist colleague once told me a story about a lawyer they knew in the early 1980s:

> An associate attorney disclosed to a managing partner on a Thursday that the associate was in psychotherapy; the following Monday, the associate's office door was locked, and the office emptied.

While employment discrimination laws may now prevent this behavior, this mentality has unfortunately been slow to change in the legal profession. It reflects underlying biases which foster mental health stigma and leads many attorneys to shun efforts that target their well-being. For more on the role of stigma as a deterrent to self-care and seeking assistance for mental health issues, see Chapter 4, Self-Care Strategies and Overcoming Barriers to Healthy Routines.

When mental health is misunderstood, experiences of intense emotion, frustration, worry, or symptoms of more serious mental health disorders may be perceived as signs of weakness, incompetence, or a lack of intelligence—in a colleague or oneself. The experience of many negative emotions (e.g., fear of failing, anxiety, impending depression, burnout) is often accompanied by a strong sense of shame, which prevents the sufferer from seeking professional assistance. In addition, for many attorneys, the vulnerability that comes with sharing emotions is too risky in the largely adversarial profession. Intense emotions can also be perceived as personally threatening, especially when you do not know how to manage them, in yourself or a colleague.

As a result, instead of tuning in to the signals received from mind and body, lawyers quickly learn to ignore, suppress, or avoid emotions, which can lead to hostility, irritability, social withdrawal, burnout, and substance abuse, not to mention physical health issues. For more on understanding mental health and seeking assistance, see Chapter 4, Self-Care Strategies and Overcoming Barriers to Healthy Routines.

Reducing Stigma Through Education About Mental Health and Well-Being

Stigmatization of mental health needs among legal professionals is so deeply ingrained that any professional intervention may be perceived as reflecting a deficit or weakness. Health-promoting initiatives may initially further be viewed as contrary to the emotional learning from law school and its reinforcement in practice.

The best way to combat stigma is through education and role modeling, in terms of how to recognize mental distress in oneself or a colleague, and what to do about it. Importantly, support for mental health and well-being programs and policies needs to start from the top, with backing from managing partners, executive directors, CEOs, general counsels, and other senior leaders. Mental health awareness can be supported through words and action. This may be done by way of a few different channels, such as:

Role Modeling. Role modeling may take different forms, such as speaking out about the importance of mental health and self-care or demonstrating support for people who are dealing with mental health issues, other well-being challenges, or are dealing with a loved one's mental health crisis. Some senior leaders choose to share their own experiences with mental health challenges or navigating stressful events in their personal lives. This is not necessary, but it certainly epitomizes lead by example. Caution should be taken, however, when inviting rank and file to do the same. You don't want to create unintended pressure for people to self-disclose. Because of the realities of stigma, as well as power dynamics, the career and personal risk is much greater for rank-and-file lawyers and staff when disclosing mental health challenges.

Education and Awareness. Raise awareness by educating lawyers and staff about mental health, self-care, and barriers to help-seeking, through programming and other resources. Education resources may take many forms, including speakers and workshops, on-site mental health fairs, supporting mental health organizations, providing specific mental health resources (both old-school brochures and online access) and dedicated mental health space in a weekly or monthly newsletter. Announcements about mental health and well-being programs coming from senior leaders, and attendance by senior leaders, will be much more effective than if this messaging comes solely from human resources staff. Better yet, mandate attendance at some or all of these programs. Education should include how to recognize when colleagues or loved ones are experiencing mental health issues, how to respond with empathy, and how to assist by connecting with resources or professionals.

Implementing a Dedicated Well-Being Committee or Hiring a Well-Being Leader. Dedicating resources and authority to a committee or internal well-being leadership position for the sole purpose of promoting mental health and well-being serves two purposes: carrying out initiatives, as well as signaling leadership support of the initiatives. This can be achieved through the establishment of a well-being or wellness committee, or the hiring of a Director of Well-Being/Chief Well-Being Officer, with a title that reflects the value the firm places on such a role, its purpose, authority, and function.

Inviting Feedback and Suggestions from Lawyers and Staff. This may be a worrisome proposition for some leaders who like to be in control. But it is an important one. When people experience a chance to be heard, and believe they have a voice in how things are handled, they tend to be more satisfied with outcomes, even if the outcome is not exactly what they had wanted. Inviting feedback and suggestions also signals that leadership values the opinions, needs, and experiences of rank-and-file lawyers and staff. The goal would be for everyone to feel comfortable voicing their thoughts and opinions on issues related to their work environment, work demands, and personal needs. The reality is most people will not feel comfortable doing so openly. Interestingly, senior leaders often have a perspective on employee satisfaction and how things are going that does not reflect the reality of employee experience. Allowing people to provide feedback and suggestions anonymously will make honest participation, or any participation, more likely. If this approach is taken, it is also essential to share findings and how such findings will be addressed. Otherwise, the entire process will be viewed as a futile exercise that was not taken seriously or valued by leaders.

Robust Insurance Coverage. One deterrent to seeking mental health treatment is related to inadequate insurance coverage. This is a separate and enormous policy issue, further reflecting how society has traditionally under- or de-valued mental healthcare, which goes beyond the scope of this book but is relevant when comparing insurance plan offerings for your workplace. Despite parity laws, some insurance plans are still much more generous with mental health coverage than others. In addition, the depth and breadth of provider networks vary by insurer, and often reflect reimbursement rates. In some states (particularly in areas where cost of living is high), it can be very difficult to find mental health providers within one's insurance network because of poor reimbursement rates. Offering a health plan which provides robust mental health coverage is a reflection of support for mental health.

Be Proactive

As mentioned in Chapter 4, Self-Care Strategies and Overcoming Barriers to Healthy Routines, an important takeaway throughout book, as well as this chapter, is the value in being *proactive*. Think about the things you can do to manage or change a difficult situation.

Even the US Surgeon General recently recognized the importance of workplace well-being, sharing a model just before this book went to press. If you are a law firm leader, you are in a position to create change. If you are a new associate, you may feel trapped. Although as an associate you may not be in a position to directly make changes, one thing you can do is find a leadership ally whom you trust and can talk with about workplace culture and policies. When talking with this ally, consider making suggestions which would be beneficial to not just you, but also from the perspective of the firm, or your team (look for the win-win), or simply use the time to brainstorm. If all else fails, working with a coach is another option.

Bibliography

American Psychological Association. (2016, June 1). *Workplace well-being linked to senior leadership support, new survey finds.* www.apa.org/news/press/releases /2016/06/workplace-well-being

Argyris, C., & Schon, D. (1978). *Organizational learning: A theory of action perspective.* Addison-Wesley.

Brobst, J. A. (2014). The impact of secondary traumatic stress among family attorneys working with trauma-exposed clients: Implications for practice and professional responsibility. *Journal of Health and Biomedical Law, 10*(1): 1–54.

Cameron, K., Mora, C., Leutscher, T., & Calarco, M. (2011). Effects of positive practices on organizational effectiveness. *Journal of Applied Behavioral Science, 47*(3), 266–308. https://doi-org.yale.idm.oclc.org/10.1177/0021886310395514

Canning, E. A., Murphy, M. C., Emerson, K. T. U., Chatman, J. A., Dweck, C. S., & Kray, L. J. (2020). Cultures of genius at work: Organizational mindsets predict cultural norms, trust, and commitment. *Personality and Social Psychology Bulletin, 46*(4), 626–642. https://doi.org/10.1177/0146167219872473

Carmeli, A., Tishler, A., & Edmondson, A. C. (2012). CEO relational leadership and strategic decision quality in top management teams: The role of team trust and learning from failure. *Strategic or-Ganization, 10*(1), 31–54. https://doi.org/10. 1177/1476127011434797

Carter, R. T., Mazzula, S., Victoria, R., Vazquez, R., Hall, S., Smith, S., Sant-Barket, S., Forsyth, J., Bazelais, K., & Williams, B. (2013). Initial development of the race-based traumatic stress symptom scale: Assessing the emotional impact of racism. *Psychological Trauma: Theory, Research, Practice, and Policy, 5*(1), 1–9. https://doi.org/10.1037/a0025911

Chen, P., Powers, J. T., Katragadda, K. R., Cohen, G. L., & Dweck, C. S. (2020). A strategic mindset: An orientation toward strategic behavior during goal pursuit. *PNAS Proceedings of the National Academy of Sciences of the United States of America, 117*(25), 14066–14072. https://doi.org/10.1073/pnas.2002529117

Collins, C. J., & Smith, K. G. (2006). Knowledge exchange and combination: The role of human resource practices in the performance of high-technology firms. *Academy of Management Journal, 49*(3), 544–560. https://doi.org/10.5465/AMJ. 2006.21794671

David, S., & Congleton, C. (2013). Emotional agility: How effective leaders manage their negative thoughts and feelings. *Harvard Business Review,* November 2013, 1–5.

Dweck, C. (2015, September 22). Carol Dweck revisits the "growth mindset," commentary. *Education Week, 35*(5). https://www.edweek.org/leadership/opinion-carol-dweck-revisits-the-growth-mindset/2015/09

Dweck, C. (2016). What having a "growth mindset" actually means. *Harvard Business Review, Managing Yourself, January 13, 2016.* https://hbr.org/2016/01 /what-having-a-growth-mindset-actually-means

Dweck, C. S., & Leggett, E. L. (1988). A social-cognitive approach to motivation and personality. *Psychological Review, 95*(2), 256–273. https://doi.org/10.1037/0033-295X.95.2.256

Editors. (2014). How companies can profit from a "growth mindset". *Harvard Business Review*, November 2014. https://hbr.org/2014/11/how-companies-can-profit-from-a-growth-mindset

Edmondson, A. C. (1996). Learning from mistakes is easier said than done: Group and organizational influences on the detection and correction of human error. *Journal of Applied Behavioral Science, 32*(1), 5–32.

Edmondson, A. C. (1999). Psychological safety and learning behavior in work teams. *Administrative Science Quarterly, 44*(2), 350–383.

Edmondson, A. C., & Lei, Z. (2014). Psychological safety: The history, renaissance, and future of an interpersonal construct. *Annual Review of Organizational Psychology and Organizational Behavior, 1*(1), 23–43. https://doi.org/10.1146/annurev-orgpsych-031413-091305

Elliott, E. S., & Dweck, C. S. (1988). Goals. *Journal of Personality and Social Psychology, 54*(1), 5–12.

Emmons, R. A., & McCullough, M. E. (2003). Counting blessings versus burdens: An experimental investigation of gratitude and subjective well-being in daily life. *Journal of Personality and Social Psychology, 84*(2), 377–389. https://doi.org/10.1037//0022-3514.84.2.377

Emmons, R. A., & Stern, R. (2013). Gratitude as a psychotherapeutic intervention. *Journal of Clinical Psychology, 69*(8), 846–855. https://doi.org/10.1002/jclp.22020

Gibson, C. B., & Gibbs, J. L. (2006). Unpacking the concept of virtuality: The effects of geographic dispersion, electronic dependence, dynamic structure, and national diversity on team innovation. *Administrative Science Quarterly, 51*(3), 451–495.

Gong, Y., Cheung, S.-Y., Wang, M., & Huang, J.-C. (2012). Unfolding the proactive process for creativity: Integration of the employee proactivity, information exchange, and psychological safety perspectives. *Journal of Management, 38*(5), 1611–1633. https://doi.org/10.1177/0149206310380250

Greenberg, P. E., Stiglin, L. E., Finkelstein, S. N., & Berndt, E. R. (1993). The economic burden of depression in 1990 [Abstract]. *Journal of Clinical Psychiatry, 54*(11), 405–418.

Groysberg, B., & Abrahams, R. (2015, August). The whys and hows of feedback. Harvard Business School Background Note 416-013. (Revised February 2017). https://www.hbs.edu/faculty/Pages/item.aspx?num=49483

Hicken, M. T., Lee, H., Morenoff, J., House, J. S., & Williams, D. R. (2014). Racial/ethnic disparities in hypertension prevalence: Reconsidering the role of chronic stress. *American Journal of Public Health, 104*(1), 117–123. https://doi.org/10.2105/AJPH.2013.301395

International classification of diseases, eleventh revision (ICD-11) for mortality and morbidity statistics (Version: 05/2021). QD85 Burnout. https://icd.who.int/browse11/l-m/en#/http://id.who.int/icd/entity/129180281

Jenkins, M. (2013). Teaching law students: Lessening the potential effects of vicarious trauma. *Manitoba Law Journal, 37*(1), 383–402.

Keyes, C. L. M. (2002). The mental health continuum: From languishing to flourishing in life. *Journal of Health and Social Behavior, 43*(2), 207–222. https://doi.org/10.2307/3090197

Keyes, C. L. M., & Lopez, S. J. (2005). Toward a science of mental health: Positive directions in diagnosis and interventions. In C. R. Snyder & S. J. Lopez (Eds.), *Handbook of positive psychology* (pp. 45–59). Oxford University Press. ProQuest Ebook Central. https://ebookcentral-proquest-com.yale.idm.oclc.org/lib/yale-ebooks/detail.action?docID=3052021

Larson, J. S. (1996). The World Health Organization's definition of health: Social versus spiritual health. *Social Indicators Research, 38*(2), 181–192. https://doi.org/10.1007/BF00300458

Laschinger, H. S., & Read, E. (2017). Workplace empowerment and employee health and wellbeing. In C. L. Cooper & M. Leiter (Eds.), *The Routledge companion to wellbeing at work* (pp. 182–196). Routledge Companions.

Maier, S. F., & Seligman, M. E. (1976). Learned helplessness: Theory and evidence. *Journal of Experimental Psychology: General, 105*(1), 3–46. https://doi.org/10.1037/0096-3445.105.1.3

Maslach, C., & Leiter, M. P. (2016). Understanding the burnout experience: Recent research and its implications for psychiatry. *World Psychiatry: Official Journal of the World Psychiatric Association (WPA), 15*(2), 103–111. https://doi.org/10.1002/wps.20311

Mayer, J. D., Salovey, P., & Caruso, D. R. (2008). Emotional intelligence: New ability or eclectic traits? *American Psychologist, 63*(6), 503–517. https://doi.org/10.1037/0003-066X.63.6.503

McCann, I. L., & Pearlman, L. A. (1990). Vicarious traumatization: A framework for understanding the psychological effects of working with victims. *Journal of Traumatic Stress, 3*(1), 131–149.

McEwen, C. A., & McEwen, B. S. (2017). Social structure, adversity, toxic stress and intergenerational poverty: An early childhood model. *Annual Review of Sociology, 43*(1), 445–472.

Monje Amor, A., Xanthopoulou, D., Calvo, N., & Abeal Vázquez, J. P. (2021). Structural empowerment, psychological empowerment, and work engagement: A cross-country study. *European Management Journal, 39*(6), 779–789. https://doi.org/10.1016/j.emj.2021.01.005; *citing* Kanter, R. M. (1977). *Men and women of the corporation.* Basic Books.

Nahum-Shani, I., Henderson, M. M., Lim, S., & Vinokur, A. D. (2014). Supervisor support: Does supervisor support buffer or exacerbate the adverse effects of supervisor undermining? *Journal of Applied Psychology, 99*(3), 484–503. https://doi.org/10.1037/a0035313

Pearlman, L. A., & Mac Ian, P. S. (1995). Vicarious traumatization. *Professional Psychology: Research and Practice, 26*(6), 558–565. https://doi.org/10.1007/BF00975140

Ryan, R. M., & Deci, E. L. (2000). Self-determination theory and the facilitation of intrinsic motivation, social development, and well-being. *American Psychologist, 55*(1), 68–78. https://doi.org/10.1037/0003-066X.55.1.68

Ryan, R. M., & Deci, E. L. (2000). Intrinsic and extrinsic motivations: Classic definitions and new directions. *Contemporary Educational Psychology*, *25*(1), 54–67. https://doi.org/10.1006/ceps.1999.1020.

Salovey, P., & Grewal, D. (2005). The science of emotional intelligence. *Current Directions in Psychological Science*, *14*(6), 281–285. https://doi.org/10.1111/j.0963-7214.2005.00381.x

Salovey, P., & Mayer, J. D. (1990). Emotional intelligence. *Imagination, Cognition and Personality*, *9*(3), 185–211. https://doi.org/10.2190/DUGG-P24E-52WK-6CDG

Schein, E., & Schein, P. (2017). Chapter 10: How leaders embed and transmit culture. In *Organizational culture and leadership* (5th ed., pp. 181–206). Wiley/John Wiley & Sons, Inc.

Seligman, M. E. (1972). Learned helplessness. *Annual Review of Medicine*, *23*(1), 407–412.

Shapiro, A., & Keyes, C. L. M. (2008). Marital status and social well-being: Are the married always better off? *Social Indicators Research*, *88*(2), 329–346. www.jstor.org/stable/27734704

Slemp, G. R., Kern, M. L., Patrick, K. J., Kent, P. J., & Ryan, R. M. (2018). Leader autonomy support in the workplace: A meta-analytic review. *Motivation and Emotiom*, *42*(5), 706–724. https://doi.org/10.1007/s11031-018-9698-y

Stone, D., & Heen, S. (2015). *Thanks for the feedback*. Portfolio Penguin.

Sull, D., Sull, C., Cipolli, W., & Brighenti, C. (2022, March 16). Why every leader needs to worry about toxic culture. *MIT Sloan Management Review*, Measuring Culture/Research Highlihgt. Reprint # 63409. https://sloanreview.mit.edu/article/why-every-leader-needs-to-worry-about-toxic-culture/

Thomas, K. W., & Velthouse, B. A. (1990). Cognitive elements of empowerment: An "interpretive" model of intrinsic task motivation. *Academy of Management Review*, *15*(4), 666–681. https://doi.org/10.2307/258687

US Surgeon General. (2022, October). Current priorities for the US surgeon general. *The surgeon general's framework for workplace mental health and well-being.* www.hhs.gov/surgeongeneral/priorities/workplace-well-being/index.html

World Health Organization. (2019, May 28). *Burn-out an "occupational phenomenon": International classification of diseases.* www.who.int/news/item/28-05-2019-burn-out-an-occupational-phenomenon-international-classification-of-diseases

CHAPTER 6

Managing Work–Life Balance for Well-Being

When talking with lawyers about the importance of taking extended time away from work to rest, recharge, and reconnect with friends and loved ones, a familiar response is:

> "I don't have time to take a vacation."

As a lawyer, you work hard. Work takes up most of your time during your pre-retirement adult life. At times, it may feel as though your calendar and mobile devices are running your life, rather than organizing and simplifying it. You may have a family life and responsibilities, which often include care-taking responsibilities (child, elder), household chores, and finding time for self-care, a significant other and friends, and non-work interests and hobbies. You may feel like you are running on a hamster wheel, not knowing how or where to jump off, or at least slow it down. You may find you are always tired, but can never get enough sleep, or quality sleep. You know you should be getting some exercise, but you just can't seem to find the time. You have days when you just can't focus, but you don't have time to take a break. As a profession, lawyers are a high strung, strung out, over-worked, often under-paid group. One lawyer recently asked:

> "Will we ever be able to solve the work–life balance problem?"

Work–family conflict has been found to be related to decreased physical and psychological health (e.g., depression, anxiety, burnout, alcoholism), decreased satisfaction with life, decreased marital and family satisfaction, and, from the organizational perspective, decreased job satisfaction, decreased job commitment, and increased turnover. There are many internal, behavioral, and environmental factors at play. Here we will look at some of the foundational aspects of work–life balance.

But what exactly is work–life balance? Is it realistic? Is it achievable?

> Early in my career, when I was an associate at a law firm, my senior associate supervisor had young children at home. She would leave around dinner time to take care of her family responsibilities, then jump back online 8:30–9:30 pm and start sending me assignments. I was expected to do the work right away,

DOI: 10.4324/9781003285519-6   116

and not wait until the next day. This meant very long days and late nights. Sure, we ordered dinner in from top restaurants and had a car service on call to drive us home, but these amenities came at a cost to personal time, social life, and self-care.

This narrative "from a mid-career lawyer" is rather normative, but that does not mean it is healthy. It reflects a lack of autonomy and voice on the part of the associate. And a lack of interest in the associate experience on the part of the supervisor. The message is: This is the way it has always been done, so we will keep doing it this way. Granted some assignments are time sensitive, but are there times when an assignment received after 9:30 pm can be worked on first thing in the morning? We may not be able to completely eliminate long hours, but by being attuned we can at least try to limit them whenever possible, instead of accepting them as the status quo.

Work–family conflict. Work–family balance. Work–life balance. Work–family integration. Work–family enrichment. Work–family facilitation. You may be familiar with some or all of these terms and know implicitly and perhaps vaguely what they are referring to, yet none by itself fully captures the experience. Broadly speaking, these terms reflect theoretical perspectives in the work–family/work–life literature, which view the intersection of work and personal life through lenses of conflict, enrichment, or balance. The large body of work–family research sheds some light on the many ways our work and home lives can clash, and how our management of the conflicting responsibilities can affect our physical and psychological health.

Notably, there is no perfect phrase to describe these balance challenges; wording has evolved over time from "work–family" to "work–life," in an effort to acknowledge that everyone, not just parents with childcare responsibilities, can struggle with balancing work and personal life responsibilities, relationships, obligations, and interests.

Work–family conflict theory views competing work and family roles through a negative lens, reflecting a conflict between the two mutually incompatible roles, and a recognition that participation in one role by necessity makes it more difficult to participate in the other role. As the level of participation in one role increases, so too does the degree of conflict experienced, with a resultant inability to participate in the other role. Our time and energy resources are limited, and anything utilized as part of our participation in, say, our work role, depletes our reserves available for use in our family role.

Work–family enrichment, on the other hand, views dual work and family roles through a positive lens and reflects the many ways our work and family roles can enhance each other, such as through development of communication, negotiation, and time management skills at work which can also be utilized at home, or benefit family life in other ways. The degree of harmony or conflict among work and family roles has a multitude of personal, work, and family implications and is related to:

- Work and family stress.
- Physical and psychological health.
- Exhaustion and burnout.
- Productivity.
- Presenteeism and absenteeism.
- Organizational commitment.
- Job satisfaction.
- Organizational citizenship behavior (i.e., how we treat others, likelihood of stepping up voluntarily for non-job tasks).
- Intention to leave one's job.
- Marital happiness.
- Family functioning.
- Satisfaction with family.

Work–family interface difficulties have been found to be related to poorer psychological health (e.g., depression, anxiety, burnout, substance use disorders), decreased satisfaction with life, poorer physical health, and, from an organizational perspective, decreased job satisfaction, decreased job commitment, increased turnover, and increased turnover intent.

Time Pressures. Lawyers have always worked long hours. But with the advent of mobile technology, it is becoming increasingly difficult to cultivate protected downtime. While technology and mobile devices have provided flexibility and enhanced our productivity, downsides include expectations of constant availability and responsiveness. Pressures from supervisors, leadership, and clients make it very difficult to separate work and home life and to not always be "on."

Lawyers vary in their approach to time management and boundary setting, with some seeking to craft rigid boundaries between work and home life, even if this means spending very long hours at the office. Others attempt to utilize mobile technology to their advantage, as a way to stay on top of things via email while out of the office, extend the workday, and be available to clients at all hours—while squeezing in some family time at home. Interestingly, it has been suggested that this more integrated approach to work and home life appears to be best suited to men in a traditional heterosexual relationship, where the wife or another caregiver manages all childcare responsibilities, as well as to lawyers who no do not have childcare responsibilities. This is consistent with historical employer expectations of work being a man's number one priority, with his wife at home managing all the child, household, and social responsibilities, supporting her husband in his work role in any way possible. Think 1950s housewife a la *Leave It to Beaver*.

Role Conflicts. Awareness of role conflict arising out of competing work demands, priorities, and family responsibilities began to increase with changes in the workforce demographic, namely the rise in dual-earner couples. In 2021 in the US, both parents were employed in 62% of heterosexual and single-sex married couple families with children under age 18, according to the US Bureau of Labor Statistics.[1] Data from the OECD (Organisation for Economic Co-operation and Development), which reflects employment rates across industrialized countries for people who have obtained at least a college degree, reveals that on average 85% of 25–64-year-olds were employed in 2020. In the US and Australia, this number was 82%, while in the UK 86% of this group were employed. Most countries ranged between 73% (South Africa) and 90% (Slovenia). India was an outlier, with 62% of this group employed in 2020.

Role-conflict awareness has only increased with the introduction and subsequent widespread use of mobile technology, and more recently, changing cultural norms and expectations around the involvement of both parents in child-rearing and other household activities. The task of juggling competing goals, priorities, and responsibilities is particularly challenging for dual-earner couples, single parents, those with elder-care responsibilities, and people navigating some combination of competing role responsibilities. These role-conflict challenges are yet another source of stress, with negative implications for physical and psychological health. Stress in one domain can become excessive and "spill over" into another domain, such that stress at home, due to family conflict or parenting difficulties, can lead to additional work stress.

Is Work Interfering with Family, Family Interfering with Work, or Both?

Work–family research further considers the directionality (work → family; family → work) of the conflict between mutually incompatible work and family roles: Is work interfering with family life, or family interfering with work, or is it bi-directional? The answer varies depending on person and context, but for many lawyers work tends to interfere with family life more often than vice versa. In addition, the type of interference varies. It may be internal, related to your preoccupation with one role, such as work, while "within the role boundaries" of another role, such as family. If you spend a lot of psychological energy (thinking, researching, problem-solving, empathizing) carrying out your responsibilities in one role, you may find yourself preoccupied with the tasks of that role and unable to disengage after transitioning to another role. You may find you are always thinking about work or recycling the same thoughts related to a workplace issue outside of work. You may be physically present with friends or loved ones, but not engaged in the conversation, or not paying attention to the soccer game you left work to attend. Or, by the time you leave the office, you may not have the emotional bandwidth to support loved ones and friends in crisis. On the other hand, with a newborn or a sick family member at home, you may find yourself distracted with thoughts, emotions, or worries about family matters while at work.

Are Work–Family Challenges Rooted in Behavior, Time Constraints, or Internal Experience?

Incompatible Role Behaviors. Behaviors essential to either work or family may not be appropriate or compatible with the other role. As a lawyer, it can be difficult to turn off your skeptical lens and adversarial approach when you leave your workspace, yet neither of these promote positive and open communication when used to cross-examine loved ones or friends. Specifically, using work-related aggressive, competitive, rational/unemotional tactics to deal with family conflicts, remaining in this mode when interacting with your spouse, children, or other loved ones, can disrupt or damage relationships. It goes without saying that while this approach can be effective at work, is it not at all helpful in fostering trust and nurturing relationships at home. Conversely, using an open, nurturing approach to deal with an adversarial competitor is equally ineffective. Although feeling and expressing empathy goes a long way in strengthening personal relationships, left unchecked it can leave you vulnerable during an adversarial workplace negotiation.

Incompatible Schedules. There are only 24 hours in a day, and we are forced to make choices about how we utilize each hour. Long work hours, or work deadlines, may prevent you from participating in day-to-day family life, or attending important family events, celebrations, and other gatherings. Your work schedule may also prevent you from doing things like preparing a healthy meal, getting some exercise, or taking care of household-related responsibilities. On the other hand, family responsibilities, such as dealing with the death of a parent or caring for a sick child, may prevent you from attending an important meeting at work. Necessary, and difficult to schedule, daytime appointments related to your own personal physical or mental health may also interfere with your work schedule.

Limited Mental and Emotional Energy. Your competing responsibilities may further lead to strain, with pressures related to your responsibilities in one role making it difficult to perform the other role. For instance, you may be too mentally exhausted from work at the end of the day to meaningful engage with your family or loved ones, or you may be having difficulty concentrating at work because a new baby has interfered with your sleep schedule, resulting in sleep deprivation. Burnout can come into play here as well. Burnout is a workplace phenomenon addressed in Chapter 5, Understanding and Addressing Workplace Issues Which Impact Well-Being. The draining effects of burnout do not disappear when you leave the workplace and can spill over into your family life. Burnout manifests as a combination of negative thoughts and emotions, deleteriously impacting your energy levels and ability to concentrate.

Work–family research is extensive and involves multiple constructs—conflict, interference, enrichment, integration, and balance. Importantly, despite the role conflict challenges that arise, there are also positive aspects of engaging in work and family roles, which will be addressed later in this chapter.

Personal Traits such as Perfectionism and Optimism Influence Levels of Work–Family Conflict-Related Distress

Unhealthy Perfectionism Is Not a "Strength." Perfectionism is conscientiousness on steroids. Lawyers by necessity are highly conscientious, and the profession tends to attract people whose dispositions are high in this trait or its sibling, perfectionism. Perfectionism can lead to inefficiency, such as procrastination, constant reviewing and revising of work product, and delays in finalizing work product and agreements. Although conscientiousness is essential to competent lawyering, there comes a time when the costs of additional review and delay outweigh any potential benefits of revision. The law school classmate interview advice for answering the dreaded "What is your greatest weakness?" question—"It's perfectionism. I can't stop myself and will work myself to the bone for your firm"—is misguided and highlights flawed thinking about the value of workaholism and a never-good-enough attitude. For more on time management and taming your inner perfectionist, see Chapter 5, Understanding and Addressing Workplace Issues Which Impact Well-Being.

Personal traits such as perfectionism have been found to influence strain and overall distress levels in attorneys and others who are dealing with work–family conflict. While some aspects of perfectionism can be beneficial (e.g., high standards, striving for excellence, doing one's best) and might enhance your job performance as an attorney, unhealthy aspects of perfectionism (e.g., not being satisfied with one's performance, self-critical) can lead to poorer psychological health, which, in turn, can impair your job performance.

My dissertation research data collected from 236 Connecticut lawyers in 2005 revealed that unhealthy perfectionism exerted a pervasive negative influence on the psychological well-being of the attorneys in the sample. Unhealthy perfectionism was significantly and directly related to overall poorer mental health regardless of gender; specifically, anxiety, depression, and somatization. Lawyers who reported experiencing the highest levels of unhealthy perfectionism, and who were also in the highest third in terms of work responsibilities interfering with family, also experienced significantly higher levels of psychological distress. Notably, the distress level of these

Changes in Relationship Between Level of Work-Family
Stress and Psychological Symptoms in Lawyers As Degree
of Perfectionism Increases (Cipriano, 2007)

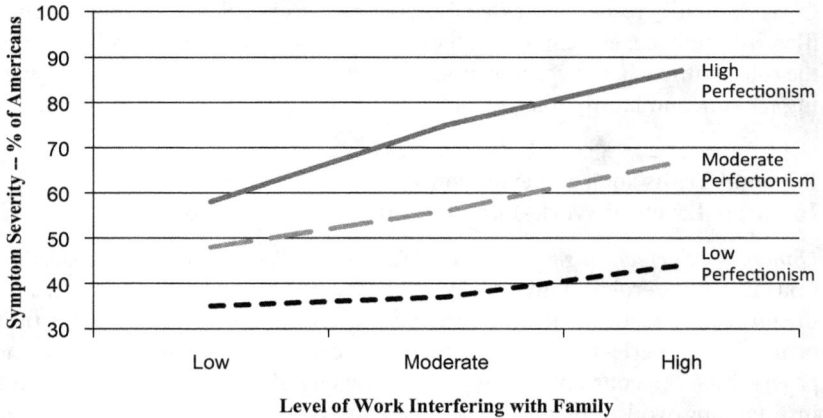

Figure 6.1 Lawyers Who Were in the Top Third on Self-Rated Perfectionism and
Work Interfering with Family Reported the Highest Levels of Overall
Distress (89th Percentile)

lawyers fell within the 89th percentile—meaning they were more distressed
than 89% of the US population. One possible explanation for these findings is
that unhealthy perfectionism (i.e., not being satisfied with one's performance)
leads to increased work hours, which creates role strain, which then leads
to poorer psychological health outcomes. Unhealthy perfectionism may also
simply lead to unrealistic expectations and feelings of inadequacy in both
one's work and family roles, which creates role strain as a result of trying to
do it all in both arenas, yet not being able to meet one's expectations in either,
which again may lead to poorer psychological health.

On the other hand, optimism is an important positive trait related to lower
levels of stress and better health. In the same study, optimism was found to be
a stress buffer for both men and women, but interestingly the effect was much
more dramatic in men who were both lower in optimism and experiencing
higher levels of preoccupation with work interfering with family life.

While both women and men benefit from being highly optimistic when
juggling incompatible work and family roles, it appears that high levels of
optimism are even more important for men's psychological well-being. One
possibility might be that men are less likely to discuss difficulties and emotions with others and therefore are less likely to receive workplace or social

support around these issues. A lack of supports makes having an optimistic outlook even more important.

The Influence of Identity on Management and Experience of Work–Family Issues

Worker vs. Parent

Depending on whether your personal identity is based more in your profession or your family role, the direction of any interference you experience may vary. If "lawyer" is your primary identity, then you would be more likely to experience work interfering with your family life in some way, whereas if "parent" is your primary identity, you may experience the opposite. It may be that your identity encompasses both roles fairly equally. Or, you may prioritize one role or the other at different times, such that work is prioritized right after law school graduation and bar passage, but family is prioritized right after the birth of your first child. You may spend the same amount of time at work in both scenarios, but you may be more preoccupied with work or feeling mentally drained when you are at home in the former, while in the latter you may be more preoccupied with family and physically exhausted while at work. Presenteeism may come into play, if you are physically present at your desk but are too exhausted or distracted to maintain productivity levels.

Gender Norms

Women are more likely to deal with work stress by working longer and harder. They are also more likely to be struggling to balance long work hours with family responsibilities, and difficulties with turning off their workplace behaviors when interacting with family. In addition, women are more likely to experience distress when family responsibilities interfere with their work role as compared with men. When considering gender role stereotypes, all these findings make sense. Women are constantly battling the assumption that they are not truly committed to their job. A frequent refrain exemplifies this thinking: "There appears to be a pattern in which women work at a law firm for three years after graduating, then take an in-house position and immediately become pregnant. Everyone else must then pick up the slack." Putting aside the merits of this statement, getting pregnant does not in itself reflect a woman's lack of commitment to her job, and fortunately employment discrimination laws align with this view. Yet, as a result of the pervading, insidious, stigmatizing beliefs about women in the workplace, female attorneys often try to avoid, or are distressed by, any behaviors which might feed into this negative stereotype. For example, if a man misses a meeting to take care of a sick child, he is more likely to be granted leniency, as in "What a good guy, taking one for the team." On the other hand, if a woman does this, she is more likely to be met with, "Hey, where is she, doesn't she know there is important work to be done here?!"

In terms of difficulties juggling long work hours, we know women remain at work longer than men to deal with work pressures, but we cannot discount how gender role expectations come into play and whether women are receiving extra pressure from a spouse or children to be home more. Similarly,with respect to adversarial interactions at home, the threshold for acceptance of these behaviors in men is much higher than it is for women. It is worth considering whether the finding related to spillover of "workplace behaviors" at home may be an artifact of gender norms and expectations around assertiveness and other leadership behaviors which are simultaneously expected of women at work and nonetheless frowned upon. Do men have the same difficulties turning off these behaviors, yet this is somehow more acceptable and less noted?

It is no wonder many high-achieving middle-aged women are childless—as many as 33–42% according to one 2002 study. For those women who choose to have children, many do so to the detriment of their career and salary. When conflicting roles become unmanageable, women are more likely than men to adjust their careers (i.e., reduce their work hours) to accommodate family life and responsibilities. We saw this phenomenon play out early on during the COVID-19 pandemic, when lockdowns and school closures meant children were home, or home-schooling.

Interestingly, men also struggle with gender norms in the workplace. Research on men's work–family challenges is more limited, and less attention is paid to the research that does exist. While the traditional gender-role expectation of men is that they will devote all their time and energy to work (and prefer to do so), recent generations are expressing a desire for more family time, including the ability to share in household chores, childcare responsibilities, and simply the ability to know and connect with their young children. And yet, even if an employer has a progressive parental leave policy, many men do not feel comfortable taking leave to care for and spend time with a newborn. This discomfort likely reflects a discrepancy between written policy and unwritten behavior codes (with expectations for male colleagues rooted in traditional gender-role stereotypes and masculine identity norms).

LGBTQ+ Families

Work–family research is historically rooted in traditional gender norms, without much recognition for non-traditional family configurations and same-sex couples until recently. Existing research suggests that while same-sex couples divide work and family responsibilities more equally, they also experience the same work–family challenges as heterosexual parents, in addition to unique stressors and stigma. Some of the stigma-related pressures include not being invited to work-related social events, an absence of same-sex partner benefits, and pressure to not reveal same-sex family status at work. Additional stress on LGBTQ+ attorneys and staff results from navigating work–family conflicts and challenges, while at the same time passing as heterosexual and hiding family information.

Race and Ethnicity

Research into racial and ethnic differences in the experience and impact of work–family role challenges is, unfortunately, notably lacking. One recent study found that Black women experienced greater levels of depression as compared to White women when family role responsibilities interfered with their work role responsibilities. This finding is also consistent with what we know about gender and racial stereotypes, and the cognitively efficient but unacceptable tendency to default to negative assumptions when someone fits into a stereotyped category.

Positive Benefits of Dual Work and Family Involvement

Despite all the challenges, the work–family enrichment literature suggests people who participate in both work and family roles, and are satisfied with both roles, might be happier and have better overall physical and psychological well-being than they would if they only participated in one of these roles.

Your work or family life can also serve as a buffer to stress arising out of the other role. When faced with a family crisis, your work can provide a distracting yet productive outlet, as well as support. This diversion can help limit both the escalation of your distress, as well as the negative effects of existing stress, particularly when you are engaging in tasks reflecting your skill and mastery. The same holds true in the other direction. After a long, challenging day, spending time immersed in rewarding family life can similarly stop the escalation of stress, providing much-needed space to unwind and recharge. In addition, research suggests that your positive experiences in one role can *enhance your experience and performance* in the other role, such as through developing patience, or learning behavioral management skills.

Promoting Work–Family Enrichment Through Balance

There are various ways to think about work–family balance. Traditionally, work–family balance has been viewed as an absence of work–family conflict or a satisfaction with how well work and family roles are integrated. Work–family balance has also been conceptualized more broadly in the literature as successful navigation of work and family roles that goes beyond individual experience; it takes into account context, such as one's impact on others (i.e., is someone else picking up the slack in the work or home domain?) and whether you are in fact meeting expectations for carrying out negotiated role-related responsibilities both at work and at home. The research and definitions have evolved over time, though more rigid definitions reflect devotion of equal amounts of time and energy to work and family roles. This last approach may be easier to measure empirically, which potentially helped legitimize work–family research in its infancy, but it does not reflect the reality that most people cannot, or choose not to, always attend to each role with equal amounts of time and energy. Such rigidity is neither practicable nor feasible in the long term.

Being Mentally Present. An important aspect of modern work–family balance theory is the ability to be mentally present in whichever role you are engaged. It is also a more fluid concept which takes your situational context into account, involving a degree of flexibility to meet role-related needs as they arise, and reflecting adjustments in role-related expectations as needed.

> ⇒ *Contemplation Exercise.* Are you able to effectively manage both your work and family roles? Can you do so in a way that does not involve constant, high levels of stress arising out of conflicts between the roles, while at the same time effectively carrying out your responsibilities in both domains? What are the quality and impact of the interactions within your work and family roles? When at work or at home, are you fully immersed in the moment and the tasks or activities at hand?

Workplace Policies and Practices Can Alleviate Work–family Stress

By taking a bigger-picture approach to work–family issues—instead of narrowly viewing issues of work–family conflict as solely the responsibility of the individual and a reflection of poor choices—we bring it into the realm of organizational culture, policies, and practices. Written and unwritten policies within an organization can either facilitate or encumber challenges arising out of incongruous work–life roles. Workplace policies which help lawyers and staff with managing non-work responsibilities can increase productivity, loyalty, and positive workplace involvement.

Such policies may allow for flexible arrangements in terms of hours worked or remote options, they may give supervisors discretion to negotiate individualized flexible arrangements, or they may be in the form of leave, vacation time, childcare provisions, or management and staff trainings related to wellness, work–life balance, leadership, and time management. Importantly, such policies by themselves, no matter how generous, are not sufficient to promote work–life balance or culture-change. Flexible policies (such as those related to hours or location of work), can breed loyalty, increased productivity, and "organizational citizenship behavior," if they are accompanied by a perception that the organization supports work–family balance and well-being.

Attitudes and behaviors of direct managers are particularly important here. For example, if paternity leave exists, but those who take it are scoffed at or are less likely to receive plum assignments, career advancements or increased remuneration when they return, the culture does not support the policy. Similarly, if vacation time is encouraged, but a supervisor is constantly checking in and working remotely while on vacation, this sets the expectation that everyone on the team will do the same, if they dare take time off in the first place.

⇒ *Contemplation Exercise.* Does your workplace culture, and particularly the attitudes and behaviors of direct managers, support and encourage the use of policies designed to enhance work–life balance and well-being?

Notably, flexibility and autonomy can also paradoxically lead to longer work hours. Lawyers, staff, and others who are entrusted with a great deal of independence and ability to take time off, with the expectation that they will get the job done in a competent and timely manner, often work longer hours than they might have if their employer imposed more structure around hours worked and paid leave. The same goes for working remotely. There are a couple of forces at play here. One is the moral commitment involved when one is provided a high degree of autonomy and flexibility in getting the job done. The other has to do with colleagues and especially team members. If the norm around you is to work long hours, or if the team is waiting on you, expecting your contribution, the tendency is to work until the job is done. This is all well and good, except when the cases and projects are never-ending. It becomes difficult to take time off for vacation when the perception is this will hold back the rest of the team. Workplace culture often reinforces long work hours and limited full-disconnected time off, regardless of official policies. Change will not occur unless leaders and supervisors walk the walk and show support for those who are brave enough to take some time to recharge and connect with the important people in their lives.

What Else Can You Do?

Finding work–life balance is a complex process, it is individualized yet also dependent on external workplace pressures, norms, and policies. Work–life balance is achievable, as long as you remain flexible in terms of your expectations and goals. Some lawyers decide to open their own practice in an effort to maximize flexibility and autonomy, but may similarly find themselves working long hours and having difficulty balancing work and family roles. Greater autonomy and authority often come with greater responsibility, necessitating a keen ability to use time wisely and set appropriate boundaries while remaining reasonably accessible to clients. For many, the autonomy and authority of being one's own boss is worth any work–life balance downsides. For others, being a part of a larger organization is energizing and empowering, and worth the long hours that come along with the role. There are always income considerations as well, and although employers try to buy loyalty with compensation packages, COVID-19 pandemic-era survey data suggest that work–life balance and other lifestyle issues are more important to many lawyers, at least during this challenging period and our transition out of it.

The extent to which you can be proactive in finding (or as an employer, promoting) a suitable balance in work and home life is highly dependent on the employment situation, the employer, and whether you have flexibility to design an arrangement that allows you to maximize your time and energy in both your work and home domains.

- On the individual level, it is important to be deliberate in your decisions. Having clarity about your values and goals can help you prioritize roles and responsibilities, and set important goals for work and home life. You will be more likely to be satisfied when making a deliberate decision to work long hours, or in a particular setting, rather than doing so by default. Once you begin this process of examining your work and home life goals, priorities, and level of involvement, it will be easier to stay on track.
- Periodically re-evaluate your values, goals, priorities, and degree to which your behavior reflects each, particularly in light of any changes in circumstances.
- Having carefully prioritized and set work and family-related goals, it is important to also develop a strategic plan for maintaining healthy habits and managing stress.
- Work to develop cognitive and behavioral flexibility, which can influence your ability to negotiate and carry out reasonable expectations at work while also allowing you to meet role expectations and needs at home.
- In addition to getting 7–8 hours of sleep, maintaining a healthy diet, and daily exercise, mindfulness activities can help lawyers be fully present in the moment and engaged in their role-related responsibilities.
- Vacations are essential for recharging our minds and bodies and reconnecting with loved ones and friends. Everyone needs a

vacation. And everyone should be able to take time off without a workplace implosion. There are a few ways to go about this, such as the traditional week or two vacation, taking periodic long weekends, and something that is increasing in popularity—organization-wide vacations via a one-week shutdown at the end of the calendar year and/or during the summer.

- Meditation and mindfulness have taken the legal profession by storm in recent years, and for good reason. These activities not only take you out of your head and bring you into the present moment, but they also promote acceptance and a recognition of what we can and cannot control.
- Work toward developing a more positive mindset, expecting the best while preparing for the worst.
- Pay attention to perfectionist tendencies and know when the work is "good enough" to pass muster, or when the benefits outweigh any risks to taking an expedited approach.
- Employers should similarly re-evaluate values, goals, priorities, and the degree to which policies reflect and promote each.
- The ability to proactively address workplace expectations and arrangements requires flexibility on the employer side as well, such as allowing for supervisor discretion in negotiating work arrangements with lawyers and staff based on individual circumstances, and re-negotiating as needed.
- Organizational policies and practices, such as supervisor discretion, which promote flexibility in hours and location of work, such as flextime, hybrid, and remote work options.
- Organizational policies and practices, such as supervisor discretion and role-modeling, which promote utilizing vacation time and taking family leave. Vacation times and lengths may be driven by workflow patterns.

See Chapter 4, Self-Care Strategies and Overcoming Barriers to Healthy Routines; Chapter 10, Creating Change; and the section on time management in Chapter 5, Understanding and Addressing Workplace Issues Which Impact Well-Being, for more information.

Note

1 Data was broken down into two categories, "Total married couple families," which includes same-sex married couples, and "Opposite-sex married couple families." Same-sex married couple families data was not separated out. In 2020, in both categories, the percentage of families with both parents employed was just under 60%. Notably, when looking at families in both categories with children under age 6, the percentage of families with both parents employed was 56%

in 2020 and just under 60% in 2021, potentially reflecting parents leaving the workforce to care for children when childcare options became scarce during the early phase of the COVID-19 pandemic.

Bibliography

Briscoe, F., & Kellogg, K. C. (2011). The initial assignment effect: Local employer practices and positive career outcomes for work–family program users. *American Sociological Review*, *76*(2), 291–319. https://doi.org/10.1177/0003122411401250

Carlson, D. S., & Frone, M. R. (2003). Relation of behavioral and psychological involvement to a new four-factor conceptualization of work–family interference. *Journal of Business and Psychology*, *17*(4), 515–535.

Carlson, D. S., Grzywacz, J. G., & Zivnuska, S. (2009). Is work—Family balance more than conflict and enrichment? *Human Relations*, *62*(10), 1459–1486. https://doi.org/10.1177/0018726709336500

Carlson, D. S., & Kacmar, K. M., & Williams, L. J. (2000). Construction and initial validation of a multidemensional measure of work–family conflict. *Journal of Vocational Behavior*, *56*(2), 249–276.

Chang, E. C. , Watkins, A. F., & Banks, K. H. (2004). How adaptive and maladaptive perfectionism relate to positive and negative psychological functioning. *Journal of Counseling Psychology*, *51*(1), 93–102.

Choroszewicz, M., & Kay, F. (2020). The use of mobile technologies for work-to-family boundary permeability: The case of Finnish and Canadian male lawyers. *Human Relations*, *73*(10), 1388–1414. https://doi.org/10.1177/0018726719865762

Christensen, K., & Schneider, B. (2011). Introduction: Making a case for workplace flexibility. *Annals of the American Academy of Political and Social Science*, *638*(1), 6–20. www.jstor.org/stable/41328576

Cipriano, T. A. (2007). Relationships among work–family interference, conflict, and health risk outcomes in attorneys: Moderation by dispositional optimism and perfectionism. Doctoral Dissertations, AAI3279270. https://opencommons.uconn.edu/dissertations/AAI3279270

Frone, M. R., Russell, M., & Cooper, M. L. (1992). Antecedents and outcomes of workfamily conflict: Testing a model of the work–family interface. *Journal of Applied Psychology*, *77*(1), 65–78.

Gianakos, I. (2002). Predictors of coping with work stress: The influences of sex, gender role, social desirability, and locus of control. *Sex Roles*, *46*(5–6), 149–158.

Greenhaus, J. H., & Beutell, N. J. (1985). Sources and conflict between work and family roles. *Academy of Management Review*, *10*(1), 76–88.

Greenhaus, J. H., & Powell, G. N. (2006). When work and family are allies: A theory of work–family enrichment. *Academy of Management Review*, *31*(1), 72–92. https://doi.org/10.2307/20159186

Grzegorek, J. L., Slaney, R. B., Franze, S., & Rice, K. G. (2004). Self-criticism, dependency, self-esteem, and grade point average satisfaction among clusters of perfectionists and nonperfectionists. *Journal of Counseling Psychology*, *51*(2), 192–200.

Grzywacz, J. G., & Carlson, D. S. (2007). Conceptualizing work–family balance: Implications for practice and research. *Advances in Developing Human Resources*, *9*(4), 455–471. www.proquest.com/scholarly-journals/conceptualizing-work–family-balance-implications/docview/221131201/se-2?accountid=15172

Hewlett, S. A. (2002, April). Executive women and the myth of having it all. *Harvard Business Review*. https://hbr.org/2002/04/executive-women-and-the-myth-of-having-it-all

Higgins, C. A., Duxbury, L. E., & Irving, R. H. (1992). Work–family conflict in the dualcareer family. *Organizational Behavior and Human Decision Processes*, *51*(1), 51–75.

Koch, A. R. & Binnewies, C. (2015). *Journal of Occupational Health Psychology, 20* (1), 82–92. doi: 10.1037/a0037890.

Kvande, E. (2009). Work–life balance for fathers in globalized knowledge work. Some insights from the Norwegian context. *Gender, Work and Organization*, *16*(1), 58–72. https://doi-org.yale.idm.oclc.org/10.1111/j.1468-0432.2008.00430.x

Mansour, S., & Tremblay, D. (2018). Work–family conflict/family–work conflict, job stress, burnout and intention to leave in the hotel industry in Quebec (Canada): Moderating role of need for family friendly practices as "resource passageways". *International Journal of Human Resource Management*, *29*(16), 2399–2430. https://doi.org/10.1080/09585192.2016.1239216

Mitchelson, J. K. (2009). Seeking the perfect balance: Perfectionism and work–family conflict. *Journal of Occupational and Organizational Psychology*, *82*(2), 349–367. https://doi.org/10.1348/096317908X314874

Murphy, L. D., Dasborough, M., Murphy, L. D., Thomas, C. L., & Cobb, H. R. (2021). A review of the LGBTQ work–family interface: What do we know and where do we go from here? *Journal of Organizational Behavior*, *42*(2), 139–161. https://doi.org/10.1002/job.2492

O'Driscoll, M. P., Ilgen, D. R., & Hildreth, K. (1992). Time devoted to job and off-job activities, interrole conflict, and affective experiences. *Journal of Applied Psychology*, *77*(3), 272–279.

Organisation for Economic Cooperation and Development (OECD). (2022, August 23). *Employment by education level (indicator)*. https://doi.org/10.1787/26f676c7-en

Parasuraman, S., & Greenhaus, J. H. (2002). Toward reducing some critical gaps in work–family research. *Human Resource Management Review, Special Issue: Changing Views of Work and Family Roles*, *2*(3), 299–312.

Parasuraman, S., Greenhaus, J. H., Rabinowitz, S., Bedeian, A. G., & Mossholder, K. W. (1989). Work and family variables as mediators of the relationship between wives' employment and husbands' wellbeing. *Academy of Management Journal*, *32*(1), 185–201.

Parker, K. (2015, October 1). Women more likely than men to adjust their careers for family life. Pew Research Center. www.pewresearch.org/fact-tank/2015/10/01/women-more-than-men-adjust-their-careers-for-family-life/

Poelmans, S., Odle-Dusseau, H., & Beham, B. (2009). Work–life balance: Individual and organizational strategies and practices. In S. Cartwright & C. L. Cooper

131

(Eds.), *The Oxford handbook of organizational well-being* (pp. 180–213). Oxford University Press. (reprinted 2014).

Rung, A. L., Oral, E., & Peters, E. S. (2020). Work–family spillover and depression: Are there racial differences among employed women? *SSM—Population Health, 13*, 100724. https://doi.org/10.1016/j.ssmph.2020.100724

Sandler, D. H., & Szembrot, N. (2020, June 16). Cost of motherhood on women's employment and earnings: New mothers experience temporary drop in earnings. *United States Census Bureau, American Counts*. www.census.gov/library/stories/2020/06/cost-of-motherhood-on-womens-employment-and-earnings.html

Stovell, C., Collinson, D., Gatrell, C., & Radcliffe, L. (2017). Rethinking work–life balance and wellbeing: The perspective of fathers. In C. L. Cooper & M. P. Leiter (Eds.), *The Routledge companion to wellbeing at work* (pp. 221–234). Routledge Companions.

US Bureau of Labor Statistics. (2022). *Families with own children: Employment status of parents by age of youngest child and family type, 2020–2021 annual averages*. Economic News Release. www.bls.gov/news.release/famee.t04.htm

CHAPTER 7

The Impact of Financial Resources on Well-Being

Financial Stress Is Prevalent and Harmful

A 2014 WellsFargo survey found that death, religion, politics, taxes, and health are all easier to talk about than personal finances. At the same time, a large percentage of the people responding also reported experiencing stress around personal finances. Similarly, the American Psychological Association Stress in America Survey consistently finds that financial worries are a top stressor for US families.

Financial well-being is an important component of overall well-being. If you are financially secure, you feel prepared for the inevitable curve-balls life throws your way. You feel financially prepared for the future, or at least on track. You have the flexibility to engage supporting services to help manage your household when needed. You can take a vacation to rest, restore, and recharge when needed. Financial well-being is related to your overall experience of life, as well as your psychological health, in terms of pleasure, meaning, and coping. While financial security provides a buffer when faced with other life stressors, conversely, financial distress exacerbates stresses arising from other aspects of your life.

If you are up at night worried about finances, whether it be an unexpected major household or healthcare expense, a new baby on the way, or having enough in retirement, your well-being and work can suffer. Your relationships may become strained. You may be less able to participate freely in entertainment experiences with friends and family. The physiological effects of financial stress are no different than stress derived from other circumstances, and your physical and mental health can suffer. You may have difficulty concentrating and getting your work done efficiently if you are not sleeping well and financial worries occupy your mind.

Our Relationship with Money Is Complicated

Most people have complicated relationships with money, which develop based on life experiences, and the values and beliefs instilled in us while we were growing up. How we think and feel about money, and our decision-making around it, are all strongly influenced by subjective social, cultural, and emotional values, which help define the related beliefs and meaning we place on money. When we think about money, we tap into unspoken meaning attributions and our implicit understanding of many cultural values, including how we define achievement, success, power, and status. We also tap into beliefs about the importance of being mindful and responsible with spending. Thoughts about money also stir up savings and financial security concerns, and financial literacy worries. It does not help matters that money is a taboo topic, often preventing transparent conversations and promoting avoidance due to not knowing how to discuss money matters with one's family or trusted peers.

Even though we may not talk about money directly, at the same time we continually receive subtle messages about financial and social status from society, the media, our peers, family, and entertainment. We also communicate about ourselves and our socioeconomic status through our behaviors.

Does Money Buy Happiness?

If you took a poll asking people whether a significant raise will make them happier, it is likely most people would say "yes." We learn early on that money is related to rewards and therefore we are driven to seek it. Western values, beliefs, behaviors, and satisfaction around money are each influenced by cultural norms and social learning. At a basic level, the financial "rat race" is founded on the underlying belief that increased wealth will bring increased happiness.

Past research suggests that up to a certain point, money can increase happiness, but the threshold is not as high as you might think. Once the necessities of living are covered, increased income tends to have a minimal impact on long-term happiness after perhaps a temporary, limited boost. There are thought to be at least three primary reasons for this: 1) where we stand in the financial hierarchy as compared to colleagues, friends, and neighbors has a greater influence on our perceptions than the monetary value itself; 2) our rapid adaption to a higher income threshold changes our perception of the new level and what it means to us; and, 3) the fact that salary is just one of many components of our work life, and money is just one component in our lives overall. All three can help explain why a high percentage of people who work in countries without strong labor laws, in low-paying jobs under abhorrent conditions, report moderate to high levels of happiness, whereas in higher income nations salary increases do little to boost happiness and well-being in the long term.

More recently, research suggests we obtain a happiness benefit from increasing income above subsistence level, though the benefit does decrease at higher income levels in the US. Additional 2018 research suggests that millionaires receive a happiness boost, as compared to other millionaires, when their wealth levels are above $8–10 million—and notably, it has been earned, instead of inherited.

Relative Standing in the Financial Hierarchy Appears to Influence Happiness More Than Income Level

The issue of whether relative standing and social comparison in relation to others influences any happiness benefit from increased income has been debated in the literature. One study involving over 33,000 adult employees in the US found a linear increase in subjective well-being as income increased, even above the previously identified $75,000 threshold. Despite this finding, other recent research from around the globe supports earlier findings that a social comparison effect does exist; when contemplating our financial standing, where we stand in comparison to others has a greater impact on our happiness than actual salary level. The social comparison effect varies depending on whether we are looking at our salary levels compared to colleagues versus our neighbors and friends. Salary as compared to that of colleagues reflects status within the organization.

- Lawyer salaries in Manhattan and San Francisco, as compared to average lawyer salaries across the US, tend to be on the higher end. Nonetheless, when taken in context of salaries of colleagues within the same organization, or others in one's peer group, neighborhood, or geographic location, the social comparison effect can diminish a relatively higher salary's perceived value, and thus any potential happiness boost when it falls lower in the financial hierarchy for one's work and social orbit (cost of living differences aside).

Movement into Higher Income Thresholds Changes Our Perceptions and Expectations

Similarly, when our financial situation changes, so do our expectations. What was once an acceptable lifestyle when at the high end of a pay-range may suddenly feel woefully inadequate upon entry into a new job-class where comparisons with colleagues highlight your position on a lower rung of the new food chain.

> "Look, I finally have a 'purple card'! All the other partners have one and until now I was the only one without one at dinners."

A dining companion once gleefully called my attention to their new "purple" credit card with a "$550 annual fee." Finally, they felt like they had a legitimate seat at the partnership table. At any business dinner, it is not unheard of to see "purple cards," "black cards," and other status cards subtly flashed, casually left on the table a little longer than necessary when it comes time to pay the bill, or in rarer instances explicitly mentioned. The displays are intended to show that one has "made it" professionally and financially; depending upon the others at the table, such displays are also a way of trying to establish pecking-order position. While some lawyers decide such cards are not worth the annual fee, many do find value, which may be status, convenience, service, or all three.

Higher Salaries Are Related to Lower Job Satisfaction, Relationship Satisfaction, and Health

And yet... higher salaries also tend to be related to lower satisfaction with one's job, relationships with loved ones, and health. This may be because higher salaries tend to be accompanied by increased work pressures and longer work hours, whereas a lower paying job in a different work setting might provide greater overall job satisfaction, as well as allow for time to build and maintain close relationships and focus on healthy behaviors. It may also reflect the cognitive adjustments mentioned earlier, leading to only a brief psychological boost from salary increases. Perhaps not suprisingly, there is only a weak relationship between salary and satisfaction with one's financial situation.

The Role of Salaries in Promoting Well-Being in the Legal Profession

In a 2021 survey by *Bloomberg Law*, lawyers were asked to rate the reasons why they were planning to leave their job—a higher salary came in at number 4, behind "better work–life balance," "reduce work stress," and "increase focus on personal life," respectively.

When thinking about all of this in the context of the legal profession, both lawyers and their employers tend to operate under the assumption that more money will bring happiness and contentment with one's job. We see the effects of this thinking with job-hopping for more money, and in the salary races particularly seen among large corporate law firms. Nevertheless, in surveys across countries which ask employees to rate the importance of salary as compared to other aspects of the workplace, salary usually ranks below many other factors, including feeling valued and respected, the work itself, relationships among colleagues, and work–life balance. Salary does not appear to increase happiness at work.

So, what does this mean for lawyers and their employers? Based on what we know about the relationship between money and well-being, a narrow focus on salary is misguided. While increasing income might be all that is needed for some lawyers, a strategy of increasing salary to the exclusion of all else will not be enough for many. A better approach might be to focus more on quality-of-life factors instead of straight salary numbers. If we know that once basic needs are met, as salary levels increase most people begin to prioritize work–life balance, job conditions and the ability to foster relationships and good health over salary, what can legal employers do to promote well-being beyond boosting salary? Income is certainly a vehicle that can help meet these other interests and needs, but it is not the only piece in the puzzle.

Money, Meaning, and Happiness. There is, however, some suggestion that although meaning in life is important for happiness, this connection is weaker in people with more financial resources. The reasons behind this recent research finding are unclear, although one theory posited is that people with fewer financial resources need to rely on internal processes for happiness, such as meaning, more than others who can seek happiness through more expensive routes, such as travel and entertainment activities. Before we ditch any efforts toward creating meaning in our lives for a more hedonistic approach, meaning still plays a role in happiness, even if that role varies for some based on income level.

Financial Security for Overall Well-Being

When discussing professional liability issues arising from lawyers who dip into client fund accounts, and how this relates to stress in the legal profession, an interesting and rarely discussed anecdotal angle was brought to my attention: Many lawyers are not very good at saving for retirement. Why is this? Many theories have been proposed as to why people procrastinate when it comes to saving for retirement, including a lack of financial planning education, a lack of appreciation for the importance of beginning to save for retirement when one enters the work force (and the long-term consequences of not doing so), and hedonism. Along these lines, many lawyers have not had exposure to coursework or training in financial management as a part of their education, and if financial management was not addressed by their family of origin, they may not be well-versed in handling personal or business finances. In addition, long work hours leave little time for the second job of managing your money. Without diligent planning, or the assistance of a financial planner, over-spending can result from an exceedingly optimistic view of future income status combined with a desire to live a lifestyle congruent with pre-existing idealizations about that of a successful lawyer.

More recently, additional thought processing explanations for retirement under-saving have arisen. Notably, retirement financial worries have been found to interfere with thought processing of information related to retirement planning. In other words, paradoxically, people who worry about saving enough for retirement also have more difficulty thinking about and processing the information needed to adequately plan for their retirement. In addition, if financial planning efforts have fallen short, anxiety and shame around this problem make it more difficult to seek assistance from a financial professional and can lead to avoidance.

Remember that 2014 WellsFargo survey mentioned earlier? People who considered their financial situation to be "poor" were twice as likely to update their Facebook profile than they were to take stock of their finances. Psychologists call this avoidance. If the general population is impacted in this way by financial worry and shame, what does this imply for the perfectionistic legal profession? Financial stress related to burgeoning debt takes a toll on mental and physical health. Worry about finances interferes with your ability to concentrate, problem-solve, and exercise good judgment.

Many law students enter *juris doctor* programs with visions of financial sugarplums dancing in their heads. It is not uncommon for fresh-out-of-law school lawyers to immediately begin living the lifestyle to which they aspired, without taking stock of their current financial situation. This translates into much less saving for retirement, or worse, can quickly lead to mounting debt. You have likely heard of what has been called the "Golden Handcuffs"; for the first time, many associates are making a good salary, and take on expenses or debt responsibilities that require them to continue working at a large firm, or in another high-pressure legal position, whether they like it or not, just to meet their existing financial obligations. This stance does not position you well in terms of promoting the many aspects of well-being.

Staggering Law School Debt

> An early-career associate at a larger firm once told me their office mate had asked for a not-insignificant loan. The associate was taken aback by this request, especially considering their salaries.

Recent data suggests the cost of legal education itself is problematic for many lawyers, with law school tuition fees skyrocketing. Ninety-five percent of the 20,000+ lawyers responding to the *2020 American Bar Association (ABA) Law Student Debt Report* indicated they had taken on debt to finance their law degree. The average student loan debt of the responding law school graduates was over $150,000, and the upper quartile had student loan debt between $200,000 and $385,000. At the same time, the National Association for Law Placement salary distribution curve for the law school class of 2021 shows that 51% of graduates earned a salary between $45,000 and $80,000. Add in cost-of-living increases, including rent or mortgage, and the numbers do not add up. Large percentages of lawyers reported that they have had to delay major life milestones such as having children (48%) or purchasing a home (55%).

Over a third reported taking a job for the money over one that better suited their interests or taking a position outside of the legal field that paid more. Vacations—seemingly a luxury but also an important component of well-being, allowing you to relax, recharge, and reconnect—also had to be delayed or skipped altogether according to close to 60% of lawyers responding.

Many aspiring lawyers take on law student debt with the belief they will be able to quickly pay it off with a high paying job, but the reality is that law school tuition and debt have risen much more rapidly than salaries. Even for the small percentage of graduates who end up in coveted Big Law positions, those salaries have also not increased at a rate consistent with the rise in law school tuition. This debt burden may seem insurmountable to many, especially if they do not want to remain in an unsatisfying or draining position, or if they are faced with additional unexpected major financial responsibilities. It can lead to physical or mental health challenges, burnout, work-quality or productivity issues, and for some, even desperation.

Professional Liability—Desperate Times, Desperate Measures, Desperate Outcomes

A penchant for thrill-seeking can make things worse, such as a lawyer engaging in financially risky investments, or gambling for entertainment. For some, gambling is a stress management strategy. (Gambling addiction is another taboo topic with very real and potentially dire consequences.) Over time, compounding faulty financial decisions, or a major unforeseen circumstance, may tip the balance. Losses accrued can potentially create a spiraling abyss of debt. For some lawyers, an overwhelming mound of debt can tempt "borrowing" from client accounts—with the intent of paying it all back, of course—often with dire professional consequences. Minor "dips" into client funds frequently soar out of control, leading to professional liability and criminal charges. Some desperate individuals, unable to manage their shame and other emotions, turn to substances, reckless behavior, or suicide.

What Are You Doing to Attend to Your Financial Well-Being?

If you are up at night worried about finances, whether it be an unexpected major household expense, a new baby on the way, or having enough in retirement, your well-being and work will suffer. As with all stressors, begin by focusing on where you have control. This may involve taking time to do a deep dive to better understand your financial situation, and learn more about financial planning. It may mean working with a financial planner, or if that is not feasible, possibly talking with a trusted family member or friend. Do not forget the self-care aspects as well, such as those discussed in Chapter 4, Self-Care Strategies and Overcoming Barriers to Healthy Routines.

This chapter is intended to help you recognize the relationships among financial health and your overall well-being. For advice on how to achieve and maintain financial health, consider working with a financial advisor.

In the meantime, there are a few questions you can ask yourself as you begin to take stock of your financial situation and consider your needs. When thinking about finances, you likely have both short-term and long-term financial needs, goals, and aspirations, even if they are not fully crystallized. What are they? Other issues to discuss with a financial advisor, once you have established your needs, goals, and aspirations, include what you are doing on a weekly and monthly basis to ensure you meet them. How are you managing competing expenses and goals? In addition to immediate budget planning and concerns, your plans for supporting yourself in retirement or if you should become unable to work, are equally important.

- Do you know by what age you want to retire?
- Do you know what kind of retirement lifestyle you would like to have or are envisioning?
- Do you know whether you will have the necessary finances to retire at that age, and maintain that envisioned lifestyle?
- Do you have a contingency plan, should you become ill or incapacitated, or have unexpected caregiver responsibilities?

What Is Your Firm Doing to Promote the Financial Well-Being of Lawyers and Staff?

Although we read frequently in the popular press how many young lawyers are not motivated solely by salary, a competitive salary and bonus are still important. Within the small segment of young lawyers who have scored a position at one of the largest law firms, considering the realities of working endless hours in a high-pressure, negative environment, at some point for many no amount of money will be enough to remain at their job. Smaller firms may grapple with retaining talent for the opposite reason—they are not paying what is considered a competitive lawyer salary or benefits.

We know that many lawyers struggle with law school debt. We know that many are trying to juggle work with burgeoning family responsibilities, in the form of both childcare and elder care. We know healthcare costs are high, and that mental health needs often go unmet because of inadequate insurance coverage. In addition to offering a competitive salary and bonus, there are other benefits your organization might offer to promote financial well-being. These include:

- Robust and comprehensive health insurance.
- 401k plan, with some level of employer contribution or match.

- Access to reliable, trustworthy, and competent childcare.
- Childcare and/or eldercare subsidies.
- Financial planning lunch and learn events.
- Other self-care benefits:
  - Health club membership discount or onsite fitness center.
  - Access to yoga or meditation classes.
  - Healthy meal planning events.
  - Access to a nutritionist.
  - Entertainment discounts.

Your firm may try to be more creative when thinking about benefits and resources. Additional resources might include employer benefits targeting the elimination of educational debt. Other compensation benefits might go toward housing expenses in high-cost areas or dependent child tuition costs. Smaller firms may have to get especially creative or make some difficult decisions when considering health insurance offerings.

No Easy Answers

Financial well-being is a complicated area. The individual and contextual influences on finances are vast and difficult to measure and control. The best you can do is be aware of the issues and address them as well as you can, focusing on that which you can control, whether it be through education, resources, or seeking assistance.

Bibliography

American Bar Association, Young Lawyers Division. *2020 law school student loan debt survey report*. www.americanbar.org/content/dam/aba/administrative/young_lawyers/2020-student-loan-survey.pdf

American Psychological Association. (2007–2022). *Stress in American survey*. Press Releases. www.apa.org/news/press/releases/stress.

Becchetti, L., Corrado, L., & Rossetti, F. (2011). The heterogeneous effects of income changes on happiness. *Social Indicators Research, 104*(3), 387–406. https://doi-org.yale.idm.oclc.org/10.1007/s11205-010-9750-0

Bijleveld, E., & Aarts, H. (Eds.). (2014). *The psychological science of money* (pp. 3–19). © Springer Science+Business Media. https://doi.org/10.1007/978-1-4939-0959-9_1

Bloomberg Law. (2021, September 29). *Analysis: Leaving? Money talks, but wekk-being now wants a word*. Bloomberg Law Analysis. https://news.bloomberglaw.com/bloomberg-law-analysis/analysis-leaving-money-talks-but-well-being-now-wants-a-word?context=article-related

Brickman, P., Coates, D., & Janoff-Bulman, R. (1978). Lottery winners and accident victims: Is happiness relative? *Journal of Personality and Social Psychology, 36*(8), 917–927. https://doi.org/10.1037/0022-3514.36.8.917

BusinessWire. (2014, February 20). *Conversations about personal finance more difficult than religion and politics, according to new Wells Fargo survey: A third of Americans say they are more worried about their financial health than their physical health.* www.businesswire.com/news/home/20140220005317/en /Conversations-About-Personal-Finance-More-Difficult-Than-Religion-and-Politics-According-to-New-Wells-Fargo-Survey

Catapano, R., Quoidbach, J., Mogilner, C., & Aaker, J. L. (2022). Financial resources impact the relationship between meaning and happiness. *Emotion.* https://doi.org/ 10.1037/emo0001090

Diener, E., Sandvik, E., Seidlitz, L., & Diener, M. (1993). The relationship between income and subjective well-being: Relative or absolute? *Social Indicators Research, 28*(3), 195–223. https://doi.org/10.1007/BF01079018

Donnelly, G. E., Zheng, T., Haisley, E., & Norton, M. I. (2018, May). The amount and source of millionaires' wealth (moderately) predicts their happiness. *Personality and Social Psychology Bulletin, 44*(5), 684–699. https://doi.org/10. 1177/0146167217744766

Gutierrez, H., & Hershey, D. (2013). Impact of retirement worry on information processing. *Journal of Neuroscience, Psychology, and Economics, 6*(4), 264–277. https://doi.org/10.1037/npe0000013

Hardyment, R. (2018). *Money, wages and wellbeing, in* The wellbeing purpose: How companies can make life better. (1st ed., Chapter 3, pp. 31–44). Routledge. https://www. taylorfrancis.com/chapters/mono/10.4324/9781351001045-3/money-richard-hardyment

Jebb, A. T., Tay, L., Deiner, E., & Oishi, S. (2018). Happiness, income satiation and turning points around the world. *Nature Human Behavior, 2*(1), 33–38.

Jennison, C. (2022, August 24). The student loan debt fire burning around us, American bar association, young lawyers division, after the bar. www.americanbar.org/ groups/young_lawyers/publications/after-the-bar/student-loans-and-finances/ student-loan-debt-fire-aba-young-lawyers/

Killingsworth, M. A. (2021). Experienced well-being rises with income, even above $75,000 per year. *Proceedings of the National Academy of Sciences of the United States of America, 118*(4), e2016976118. https://doi.org/10.1073/pnas.2016976118

Lakshmanasamy, T., & Maya, K. (2020). Is it income adaptation or social comparison? The effect of relative income on happiness and the Easterlin paradox in India. *Indian Economic Journal, 68*(4), 477–495. https://doi.org/10.1177/0019466220987025

Lay, A., & Furnham, A. (2019). A new money attitudes questionnaire. *European Journal of Psychological Assessment, 35*(6), 813–822. https://doi.org/10.1027 /1015-5759/a000474

National association of law placement, salary distribution curves, class of 2021. www. nalp.org/salarydistrib

Newcomb, S. C. (2016). *Loaded: money, psychology, and how to get ahead without leaving your values behind,* Chapter 1, *When it comes to money, we've all got issues,* and Chapter 2, *Money messages.* John Wiley & Sons, Inc. Retrieved from June 6, 2022. ISBN 9781119258339,1119258332, 9781119258346, 1119258340, 1119258324, 9781119258322, 9781119258322.

Satya, P., & Guilbert, D. (2013). Income—Happiness paradox in Australia: Testing the theories of adaptation and social comparison. *Economic Modelling, 30,* 900–910. https://doi.org/10.1016/j.econmod.2012.08.034

Yu, Z., & Chen, L. (2016). Income and well-being: Relative income and absolute income weaken negative emotion, but only relative income improves positive emotion. *Frontiers in Psychology, 7,* 2012. https://doi.org/10.3389/fpsyg.2016.02012

CHAPTER 8

The Essential Role of Personal Relationships and Social Supports in Well-Being

The Conundrum of Lawyer Traits, Demands of the Profession, and Relational Support

Relationships, or social supports, are the fabric of our lives. They are central to our overall well-being. Our need for relationships is primitive, rooted in protection and survival, with safety in numbers and the benefits of a group collectively working together to meet basic needs. Relationships influence our experience of our workplace and the degree to which we are impacted by work-related stress. In the face of stressful events, social support both within and outside the workplace can help protect us from the negative consequences of stress. In modern society, genuine connection to others, for most people, is vital for achieving a sense of life satisfaction.

Common Lawyer Traits Inhibit Relationship-Building and Accessing Social Support

Much has been written about lawyer traits and tendencies, and how some of these might influence the extent to which social supports are available to lawyers. Lawyers are often sociable, extroverted, and good communicators. Lawyers also tend to be persevering when the going gets tough. Many lawyers were highly academically focused throughout their schooling, and self-disciplined.

A Negative, Competitive, and Demanding Orientation. At the same time, the legal profession is defined by strong personalities with high levels of cynicism and skepticism, lower levels of empathy, and a disdain for negative feedback. Many lawyers have a high need for attention and approval, and have a tendency to respond with distrust, defensiveness, and argumentativeness when presented with a differing point of view. In general, lawyers tend to be competitive, aggressive, achievement-oriented, and perfectionistic, with a robust desire to be dominant and in control. The highly competitive, perfectionistic nature of lawyers can translate into correspondingly highly judgmental and critical behavior when relating to others outside of workplace tasks (or when evaluating one's own performance).

DOI: 10.4324/9781003285519-8   144

While many of these traits and tendencies—up to a certain point—can be viewed as promoting professional success, they do nothing to promote relationship-building and in fact can be quite damaging to personal relations. Traits that are initially adaptive for legal work can become heightened and excessive, interfering with relationships with clients and colleagues, as well as spouses and other family members or loved ones.

Avoidance. Overarching competitiveness, perfectionism, and the need to feel in control or dominant often inhibit lawyers from reaching out to others and seeking support during times of difficulty or crisis. Law students quickly learn in the first year of law school that emotions represent weakness and a lack of control. As a result, budding lawyers learn to suppress their emotions and hide how they are truly feeling, honing this avoidance as they enter the profession and advance their careers. A strategy of emotional avoidance may work if occasionally utilized during brief interactions, but chronic emotional suppression comes at significant personal and interpersonal costs.

Research suggests law students and lawyers are more likely to try to manage internal distress by isolating and turning to substances, rather than relying on a support network. While an external face of calm, secure competence is the norm, many lawyers experience internal distress. Efforts to manage conflicts between internal feelings of distress or vulnerability, and external presentation of competence and control, can be draining. Although many lawyers are sociable, at least when entering law school, over time lawyers may become more isolated and experience loneliness even if they continue to socialize.

Internal distress is thought to also lead to increased hostility, aggressiveness, and achievement-focus in law school and beyond. Hostility is a behavior which has been linked to a much greater likelihood of premature death due to cardiovascular disease or other health issues. For more on the relationships among stress, hostility, and health, see Chapter 3, Attention to Overall Physical and Mental Health.

Devaluation of Interpersonal Concerns and Collaboration. The logical, rational, objective, and efficiency focus of many lawyers, reinforced in law school through academic and social learning, further limits relationship-building opportunities. Lawyers tend to place less emphasis on, or are less interested in, interpersonal concerns, emotions, the feelings of others, and self-reflection. Judgmental, distrusting, and less emotionally attuned tendencies fostered by skepticism and low empathy further interfere with one's ability to connect with others on a personal level and thus develop close relationships.

Similarly, lawyers' strong need for autonomy and dominance can make collaboration difficult. In addition, law school reinforces decision-making that does not consider the social or emotional impact of one's decisions on others, disregarding another important element of relationship-building.

145

The Importance of Social Connection

Collaborative Problem-Solving

Many of the traits mentioned above can be helpful when thinking strategically about a case and dealing with opposing counsel. At the same time, they are a hindrance to relationship-building, which is an essential aspect of well-being, collaboration, and a healthy work environment. The importance of being able to collaborate with others and gain support during challenging times cannot be over-stated.

Personal Connection Can Enhance Business Development

A lawyer once said to me, "I don't see people as friends, I see them as opportunities to generate business." This was a striking statement. Yet, while most people are not as direct, many relationships are *quid pro quo* or represent potential business development. Instead of approaching interactions as opportunities in and of themselves, seeking out commonality for the sake of building a relationship, this approach focuses more on finding out what someone can do for you, how big and how powerful is their network, and what is their own influence and power. This approach is consistent with many of the lawyer traits and tendencies highlighted at the beginning of this chapter and is akin to those conversations with people you meet for the first time at social or networking events, where the questions asked within the first minute pull for you to recite your CV and family history for the last seven generations. It is certainly an efficient approach, though it is hardly a way to build a lasting personal connection. Case in point: When you get a bunch of lawyers together in a group, it is likely everyone scans the room, sizing each other up, determining where they fit in the pecking order. Boasting, or more subtle sharing about accomplishments and pedigree, is *de rigueur*. Granted, some of this behavior reflects rainmaking efforts, but it is not exclusive to rainmaking opportunities and at times is simply a reflection of embedded social norms borne out of well-worn traits, social learning, and a carryover of behaviors engaged when dealing with competitors and opposing counsel.

Importantly, for some others, the emphasis on the relationship itself is more primary, with the possibility of a business connection in the background, should someone need something. In fact, this latter approach is not only better for relationship-building; it is also thought to be better for business development. Building a solid relational foundation, based on liking and trust, is considered more effectual than some traditional marketing strategies.

Limiting Loneliness

As mentioned earlier, lawyers often experience loneliness. You can be surrounded by people, yet still feel alone. Loneliness reflects unmet needs for close and caring connections. Quality personal relationships—those that are healthy, close, and reciprocal—provide a sense of belonging and help prevent feeling isolated. While not everyone experiences a strong need to "belong," most people do benefit from personal, ongoing relationships with at least a few others. People who have an active social life involving multiple quality relationships tend to experience the greatest life satisfaction and happiness.

The Risks of Loneliness and a Lack of Supports. You can work hard and be top in your field, but what happens at the end of the day, when you eventually must go home? Many lawyers turn to alcohol in the evening, to help unwind and manage negative emotions. Another popular strategy for avoiding loneliness at home, if not working late into the night, is to fill the void at the end of the day at networking events and entertainment venues. Getting out and socializing is a good thing, but any social support benefits will be dependent upon the depth of relationships and frequency of interaction with the people you meet. Often these events involve alcohol, which can lead to a developing or worsening substance use problem, particularly if alcohol is used as a balm for loneliness or as a shield to ward off uncomfortable feelings.

When you are constantly on the go with no time to relax, reflect, or recharge, it can be challenging to build intimate relationships, which require energy, effort, personal reflection, empathy, and quality one-on-one time.

The Connection Between Relationships and Well-Being

Our relationships play an important role in our mental and physical health, which in turn contribute to our overall sense of well-being. Relationships with significant others, family, and friends provide companionship and genuine enthusiasm for your successes during the good times, and needed support and resources during challenging times. If you have a strong support network, you will likely be better able to cope in the face of difficulty.

Social support takes many different forms and may include any of the following:

1. *Companionship*, or sharing experiences, spending time together talking, meals together, and overall shared intimacy.
2. *Emotional support*, which involves communicating with empathy, care, concern, and trust.
3. *Informational support*, or helping with problem-solving, such as through advice-giving, suggestions or information.
4. *Instrumental support*, which involves providing material aid or service, and may be financial or task-driven.
5. *Appraisal support*, involving providing feedback or information which helps the recipient engage in more accurate self-evaluation, change, and growth.

Companionship. Our connections with others provide outlets when we simply need to relax and recharge, and they bring joy when celebrating life's small victories. Friendships and shared experiences help us feel connected to the world, to something bigger. As social beings, without close connections with others we begin to feel isolated and lonely, even if we are surrounded by people and not necessarily alone. Your sense of well-being increases with the number of close relations in your network—the number of people you can trust, confide in, and with whom you can discuss important issues or problems. On the other hand, an over-abundance of casual acquaintances or strangers in your social network can have the opposite effect.

Informational, Instrumental, and Appraisal Support. Importantly, having a strong support network can help with navigating any rough patches at work or at home. Supports can help problem-solve. They can help you reframe, so you can see stressful circumstances in a less negative light. Your close colleagues, friends, and loved ones can provide advice, information, or other resources to help you to better manage stressors, and ultimately lessen any detrimental impact.

Emotional Support. Our relationships provide us with emotional support when we need it during challenging times. Supports sometimes are most beneficial when they just listen and provide a caring sounding board. In fact, our perceptions alone of the strength of our relationships and the accompanying support they give can influence our thinking about the level of threat a challenge presents and our ability to manage it. Confiding in at least one close friend or loved one provides an important buffer to stressful events. The health benefits of self-disclosure are well known, affording an outlet for the release and processing of negative emotion which can otherwise foster poor mental and physical health.

Social Support Promotes Physical and Mental Health. A strong social network of close ties, with people you have known for a long time or see regularly, is related to happiness and a healthy immune response, as well as higher survival rates in cancer and heart disease. In addition to providing a sense of connection and promoting healthy coping strategies, social supports can also facilitate personal growth during challenging times. Our friends can also help keep us accountable to our exercise and healthy eating goals, and can provide a measure of good-natured competition to further motivate us.

Conversely, a lack of social relationships is associated with increased vulnerability to psychological distress and poor health, decreased immune response, as well as increased rates of illness and death following a major life stressor or loss. Similarly, unhealthy, dysfunctional relationships marred by conflict, or excess support or loyalty to a partner who does nothing to help themselves, further put well-being at risk. Paradoxically, friendships can also negatively affect well-being by encouraging unhealthy behaviors or inducing heightened concerns about belonging and acceptance. We need to pay attention to our relationships, nurture them, as well as periodically re-evaluate if any becomes more draining than boosting outside of the usual ups and downs of life.

When it comes to romantic relationships, research has found that people who are in a committed romantic relationship have lower emotional loneli-ness and higher satisfaction with life than do singles, or mingles (loosely committed), respectively. There are some notable gender differences: women need higher-commitment relationships to meet their relational needs and not feel lonely, as well as their needs for autonomy and competence; for men, these needs can be met in low commitment relationships.

Social Support Reflects Psychological Safety in the Workplace

Effective leadership and healthy, productive work environments are built on trust and relationships. And yet, trust and relationship-building tend not to be high on the priorities list for many lawyers. Building relation-ships, in the workplace or otherwise, takes time and effort. It requires emo-tional intelligence, an ability to self-reflect, recognize, and manage internal experiences. It requires empathy and the ability to focus one's attention on someone else, listen closely, and interpret both verbal and non-verbal cues. It requires some degree of vulnerability, and a willingness to "put your-self out there". Healthy relationships are balanced, founded upon mutual respect and equality. While you may not feel like you have the time, mak-ing an effort can lead to increased civility, greater productivity as a result of increased collaboration and decreased tension, and an overall healthier work environment.

There may be times when you experience a slip-up and do not manage your emotions as well as usual when addressing a challenge with an associate or staff member. While you cannot continually treat people poorly and then apologize, occasional leadership lapses can be addressed through corrective action and social support such as providing advice or assistance to improve performance, thus preventing lasting negative impacts on the psychological safety of individual lawyers or overall workplace culture. Taking interper-sonal risks—such as help-seeking, asking for feedback, or raising a differing perspective on a work-related issue—is facilitated by a belief that one has the support of others and can do so without negative repercussions. For more on psychological safety, please see Chapter 5, Workplace Issues.

Social Support Needs Vary

The COVID-19 pandemic highlighted differing relational needs at work within the legal community (and among workers in general), depending upon personal situation and preferences. While remote work provided significant welcomed flexibility to parents of young children, particularly women, others could not stand the social isolation. Young singles and extroverts of all ages (as well as those who perform best with structure and routine), could not wait to return to the office.

Workplace social support may simply involve a casual chat while you get your morning coffee, or a quick afternoon conversation in the hall, both of which help us to feel connected, valued, and give us a sense of belonging. Social support might also involve giving someone practical advice or information when they pop into your office with a question, or simply listening with empathy and caring when a colleague shares a difficult challenge. This last part, involving empathy, can be tricky for lawyers, potentially considered an inefficient use of time and unnecessary as a "soft" skill. Learning to slow down and tune in to the emotional needs of others can go a long way in creating psychological safety and building loyalty, important aspects of a healthy and productive workplace.

BOX 8.1 POP QUIZ

Yes or No:
Do you regularly take a lunch break with colleagues?

Many people feel they are too busy to take time for lunch away from their desk, but giving yourself permission and setting aside time to do so can have many benefits. Lunch with colleagues can help foster collaborative work relationships and a sense of community, in addition to giving yourself an important break to relax, refuel, and recharge. Try for at least once a week.

Social support in the workplace is not only directly related to reduced work stress, but may also help soften the impact of work stress when it does occur. Support from your supervisor has been found to provide the greatest benefit, followed by support from colleagues. Support from family and friends outside of the workplace tends to be the least beneficial when we experience work stress. This is likely because our colleagues and supervisors are in our work sphere, having inside knowledge of the pressures involved, as well as our needs in relation to those stressors, not to mention being available to provide immediate support during the workday (at least before the COVID-19 induced remote work explosion). Interestingly, research suggests the most helpful conversations with supervisors around work stress tend to be positive job-related discussions, followed by non-work-related discussions as second most beneficial. Conversations about a negative situation, or a "gripe session," have not been found to be helpful.

Toxic Positivity Can Undermine Social Support Efforts and Psychological Safety

Over the course of the COVID-19 pandemic, a backlash in the popular press has arisen in response to what is being called "toxic positivity." Toxic positivity is not a clinical term or an official organizational behavior term, but it is grounded in emotional suppression research. It reflects an unhealthy focus on the positive, including the detrimental ignoring of negative emotions in yourself or others.

The positive psychology movement changed the way we think about mental health and well-being. Instead of taking a negative, flaw-based approach to describing people, traits, and motivations, positive psychology brings a welcomed fresh perspective, focusing on strengths, the possibility of learning and growth from mistakes and losses, and the importance of mindset. A positive approach appeals to business leaders and is a pillar of thinking in executive coaching and leadership circles because of the benefits to person and organization. The focus on strengths, growth, reality-based hope and optimism, and positive mindsets is distinguished from toxic positivity, which ignores and denies underlying negative emotion.

Lawyers May Be at Risk for Toxic Positivity Because of Their Aversion to Negative Emotion

With the exception of anger, which feels empowering, most lawyers are averse to experiencing negative emotion. The answer, however, is not putting on your happy face. We cannot simply put a positive spin on something and ignore our negative emotions. When we try to do so, it can lead to harmful psychological, behavioral, and physiological reactions. We may think we are providing social support by telling people to "Tough it out," "Look on the bright side," or "Cheer up," but the reality is such statements tend to invalidate the experience of the person who is distressed and can lead to feeling worse instead of better. When we receive messaging like this, messaging which tells us directly or indirectly that our negative emotional experiences are not welcome or reflect character weakness, we are more likely to suppress them and put on a face of positivity. This imposed positivity and lack of recognition of undesirable emotions is known as "toxic positivity" because it prevents people from acknowledging and addressing negative feelings, either their own or someone else's. Responding to distress with a positive platitude may be a misguided attempt to provide hope or optimism, or it may be an effort to avoid the discomfort brought on by negative emotion. Either way, it leaves the person you are responding to feeling unheard, invalidated, invisible, and perhaps as though their negative emotion is in itself a problem.

Failure to acknowledge someone's negative emotions can also create distrust in the workplace. It can lead to distrust on the part of the person expressing their emotions, and their subsequently faking positivity. In addition, when someone is clearly in distress and yet faking positivity, the incongruous behavior can create distrust on the part of those who witness it. As this new cycle of distrust plays out, toxic positivity can negatively impact productivity and workplace culture by increasing internal distress, as well as distrust, and decreasing psychological safety and engagement.

Finding the positives in challenging situations is an important coping skill but doing so without first acknowledging negative emotions can lead to greater distress, and poorer well-being. Efforts to help someone in distress can backfire and leave the recipient of positive platitudes feeling unheard and demoralized if their negative emotions are not first recognized with empathy. For more information on the impact of toxic positivity on well-being, see Chapter 4, Self-Care Strategies and Overcoming Barriers to Healthy Routines. The importance of being attuned to the emotions of yourself and others in the workplace is addressed in the section on emotional intelligence in Chapter 5, Understanding and Addressing Workplace Issues Which Impact Well-Being.

How to Provide Support and Foster Relationships

Providing Support

Colleagues, friends, and family members in distress need genuine empathy, not simply words of encouragement, at least not initially. You can start by providing your full attention (no device in hand or visible!), listening carefully with concern, reflecting back what you hear. You can let the person know you understand what they are saying, and (if it does) that it makes sense, or simply let them know you see and appreciate they are upset and ask how you can help. You might ask if they would like you to help them find an appropriate person to talk with to address their concern, or if they would like you to help them in some other way, such as finding a solution.

Fostering Relationships

When meeting new people, it is helpful to look for something in common, any one thing, to find a place of connection. It also helps to look for at least one thing you like about a person or group of people. In this way, you are approaching these new interactions from a place of positivity and optimism. Building strong relationship bonds takes time and effort. Our relationships are like plants, we need to tend to them, nurture them, feed them. If we neglect them, there is a good chance they will fade away. Tending to relationships includes taking time to focus on the other person and their needs, asking questions, listening, responding appropriately—in a way that signals you are paying attention, appreciate their perspective, and are engaged in the conversation. This behavior reflects a supportive stance, not unlike the one described immediately above. You can further signal valuing and respect for another person by giving them the opportunity to initiate or take the reins if you are always the one directing in the relationship.

There is no "perfect" way to build relationships and doing so is not another structured task in your day, or a competition to become everyone's friend or acquire a certain number of friends; it is an organic process that begins to emerge with repeated interactions and common interests.

We can begin building relationships with others through shared interests, such as our work or hobbies. Over time, relationships may deepen and become more than a casual connection. We create meaningful, authentic relationships through openness and sharing our personal experience. Not just the faux-self-deprecating stories you tell the group at dinner to get a laugh, but also those thoughts and feelings that you keep hidden. It is through vulnerability that we build intimacy, both in friendship and romantic relationships. This is not to say that you should be a walking megaphone, sharing everything with everyone. Levels of intimacy will vary depending on context and other factors in your relationships—with your colleagues, your loved ones, your cooking class, your tennis foursome, your book club, and the people you invite to your home for dinner, to spend time just hanging out and talking. Instead of focusing on how many people you can surround yourself with, focus on identifying those people with whom you experience a natural sense of connection, those with whom interactions are a little more comfortable, and who seem interested in you as a person, ask you questions, and follow-up by checking in and reciprocating.

Building authentic relationships and relying on them for support are challenges which may seem increasingly foreign the further along you are in your legal career. But recognizing the need to work toward relationship-building is the first step. With time, effort, and self-compassion, you can find your way to fulfilling relationships, or at least a decreased sense of isolation.

Bibliography

Amati, V., Meggiolaro, S., Rivellini, G., & Zaccarin, S. (2018). Social relations and life satisfaction: The role of friends. *Genus, 74*(1), 7. https://doi.org/10.1186/s41118-018-0032-z

Barefoot, J. C., Dahlstrom, W. G., & Williams, R. B., Jr. (1983). Hostility, CHD incidence, and total mortality: A 25-year follow-up study of 255 physicians. *Psychosomatic Medicine, 45*(1), 59–63. https://doi.org/10.1097/00006842-198303000-00008

Beehr, T. A., & McGrath, J. E. (1992). Social support, occupational stress and anxiety. *Anxiety, Stress and Coping, 5*(1), 7–19. https://doi.org/10.1080/10615809208250484

Bernstein, E. (2021, November 2). Toxic positivity is very real, and very annoying. *Wall Street Journal*. www.wsj.com/articles/tired-of-being-told-cheer-up-the-problem-of-toxic-positivity-11635858001?reflink=desktopwebshare_permalink

Bucher, A., Neubauer, A. B., Voss, A., & Oetzbach, C. (2019). Together is better: Higher committed relationships increase life satisfaction and reduce loneliness. *Journal of Happiness Studies, 20*(8), 2445–2469. https://doi.org/10.1007/s10902-018-0057-1

Chapman, B. P., Fiscella, K., Kawachi, I., Duberstein, P., & Muennig, P. (2013). Emotion suppression and mortality risk over a 12-year follow-up. *Journal of Psychosomatic Research, 75*(4), 381–385. https://doi.org/10.1016/j.jpsychores.2013.07.014

Chiu, A. (2020, August 19). Time to ditch "toxic positivity" experts say: "It's okay not to be okay". *The Washington Post*. www.washingtonpost.com/lifestyle/wellness/toxic-positivity-mental-health-covid/2020/08/19/5dff8d16-e0c8-11ea-8181-606e603bb1c4_story.html

Cohen, S., & Wills, T. (1985). Stress, social support, and the buffering hypothesis. *Psychological Bulletin, 98*(2), 310–357. http://ovidsp.ovid.com/ovidweb.cgi?T=JS&PAGE=reference&D=ovfta&NEWS=N&AN=00006823-198509000-00006

Cranford, J. A. (2004). Stress-buffering or stress-exacerbation? Social support and social undermining as moderators of the relationship between perceived stress and depressive symptoms among married people. *Personal Relationships, 11*(1), 23–40. https://doi.org/10.1111/j.1475-6811.2004.00069.x

Daicoff, S. (1997, June). Lawyer, know thyself: A review of empirical research on attorney attributes bearing on professionalism. *American University Law Review, 46*(5), 1337–1427.

Edmondson, A. C. (1999). Psychological safety and learning behavior in work teams. *Administrative Science Quarterly, 44*(2), 350–383.

Edmondson, A. C., & Lei, Z. (2014). Psychological safety: The history, renaissance, and future of an interpersonal construct. *Annual Review of Organizational Psychology and Organizational Behavior, 1*, 23–43. https://doi.org/10.1146/annurev-orgpsych-031413-091305

Everson, S. A., Kauhanen, J., Kaplan, G. A., Goldberg, D. E., Julkunen, J., Tuomilehto, J., & Salonen, J. T. (1997). Hostility and increased risk of mortality and acute myocardial infarction: The mediating role of behavioral risk factors. *American Journal of Epidemiology, 146*(2), 142–152. https://doi.org/10.1093/oxfordjournals.aje.a009245

Fenlason, K. J., & Beehr, T. A. (1994). Social support and occupational stress: Effects of talking to others. *Journal of Organizational Behavior, 15*(2), 157–175. www.jstor.org/stable/2488497

Ford, B. Q., Lam, P., John, O. P., & Mauss, I. B. (2018). The psychological health benefits of accepting negative emotions and thoughts: Laboratory, diary, and longitudinal evidence. *Journal of Personality and Social Psychology, 115*(6), 1075–1092. https://doi.org/10.1037/pspp0000157

Gross, J. J., & Levenson, R. W. (1997). Hiding feelings: The acute effects of inhibiting negative and positive emotion. *Journal of Abnormal Psychology, 106*(1), 95–103. https://doi.org/10.1037/0021-843X.106.1.95

Heaney, C. A., & Isreal, B. A. Part three, chapter 9: Health behavior and health education: Theory, research and practice, on-line companion materials. *Social networks and social support*. www.med.upenn.edu/hbhe4/part3-ch9-key-constructs-social-support.shtml

Matthews, K. A., Gump, B. B., Harris, K. F., Haney, T. L., & Barefoot, J. C. (2004). Hostile behaviors predict cardiovascular mortality among men enrolled in the multiple risk factor intervention trial. *Circulation, 109*(1), 66–70. https://doi.org/10.1161/01.CIR.0000105766.33142.13

Mellor, D., Stokes, M., Firth, L., Hayashi, Y., & Cummins, R. (2008). Need for belonging, relationship satisfaction, loneliness, and life satisfaction. *Personality and Individual Differences, 45*(3), 213–218. https://doi.org/10.1016/j.paid.2008.03.020

Mor-Barak, M. E. (1988, October–December). Social support and coping with stress: Implications for the workplace. *Occupational Medicine, 3*(4), 663–676.

Myers, D. G. (2000). The funds, friends, and faith of happy people. *American Psychologist, 55*(1), 56–67. https://doi.org/10.1037/0003-066X.55.1.56

Nahum-Shani, I., Henderson, M. M., Lim, S., & Vinokur, A. D. (2014). Supervisor support: Does supervisor support buffer or exacerbate the adverse effects of supervisor undermining? *Journal of Applied Psychology, 99*(3), 484–503. https://doi.org/10.1037/a0035313

Perkins, H. W. (1991). Religious commitment, yuppie values, and well-being in post-collegiate life. *Review of Religious Research, 32*(3), 244–251. https://doi.org/10.2307/3511209

CHAPTER 9

Cultivating Meaning and Purpose for Well-Being

Meaning and purpose provide us with a sense of connection to our world, and a reason to continue to push forward and persevere during challenging times. We derive pleasure from activities that contribute to or promote our sense of meaning and purpose, but pleasure is only one aspect. Passions, or activities that tap into, and are consistent with, our personal identity—our beliefs about who we are, our place and role in the world—including contributing to something bigger than we are or the greater good, tend to be perceived as meaningful. These activities, in addition to providing a sense of purpose, also can have positive mood and health benefits.

Tunnel Vision and Fear of Being Left Behind/Fear of Missing Out

I recall meeting an attorney while on an on-campus interview during law school. I had studied abroad for a semester and had also taken a semester off to consider applying to graduate school for my doctorate in clinical psychology. Ultimately at the time, I chose to finish what I had started and try to make the most of it (perhaps some of my own Type-A tendencies were at work here). What struck me most during the interview was a discussion with my interviewer, a successful partner at a mid-to-large-sized law firm, about taking time off from law school. He asked about my time off, then shared that he had taken a year sabbatical during law school and has felt "behind" his peers ever since, in terms of professional advancement, status, and wealth accumulation. I was quite surprised by this disclosure, by an attorney who appeared to have done well for himself. While I did appreciate where this partner was coming from, I wondered whether this time off really made much of a difference in the grand scheme of his career and financial goals. I was left with the impression of constant striving and perpetually unmet non-material needs.

As I reflect on this experience today, I also wonder whether perhaps he was more successful than he would have been otherwise, after taking that time off and conceivably learning more about himself, his beliefs, values, and goals, and his passions. And yet, there was that sense of emptiness, of unmet needs.

Although money is usually the first thing most people think about when asked why they work, upon further reflection there is often a realization that a strong underlying goal is to engage in something fulfilling, either at work, or with the money earned. At one time, going to work was meaningful,

DOI: 10.4324/9781003285519-9   156

when people had more time to spend on their work, and to develop workplace relationships, when people worked at one job for the long-haul, trusted their employer and felt committed to the organization. Working itself was meaningful.

Issues of corporate responsibility can also come into play when thinking about meaningful work. Are you proud of the way your organization (or the client organizations you represent), accesses and utilizes resources of all kinds? Are you proud of how people are treated, not just within the organization but those possibly impacted when carrying out the organizational mission?

When lawyers report a lack of motivation and feelings of emptiness, both can be related to a lack of meaning at work. An auto-pilot laser-focus on status-related goals and keeping up with the perceived successes of colleagues and peers can leave little if any room for thinking about your values and beliefs, and those of your workplace, never mind pursuing a more meaningful course.

Balancing Achievement with Life Meaning

It is not uncommon for lawyers to find themselves on a treadmill, constantly striving for more as each goal is met, never quite feeling the contentment or satisfaction desired. The intense and at times all-consuming achievement focus of lawyers can come at the expense of life meaning and purpose. A strong emphasis on achievement, power and wealth in our culture is not limited to the legal profession, but it certainly plays a pervasive role, leading some to believe they will feel satisfied only if and once they attain certain achievements. For some, there is also an unrealistic expectation of an immediate financial windfall upon graduation from law school, as though a switch has been flipped, and a tendency toward favoring external measures of (financial) "success." The desire to prove financial success, particularly after a perceived setback, may create a risk for tenuous financial decisions. For more on the financial aspect of well-being, see Chapter 7, The Impact of Financial Resources on Well-Being.

Lawyers' competitive nature can lead to tunnel vision and an all-consuming drive to become a partner, or achieve other professional, monetary, or status goals. Some experience extreme difficulty with losing, or simply not achieving *all* of their goals. For many lawyers, the drive to make money is paramount, to the detriment of work satisfaction and engaging in meaningful activities, or even mere interest in the subject matter or content of their work. These tendencies can leave you feeling empty and unsatisfied and can lead to malaise or depression, as well as potentially unhealthy coping through the use of drugs or alcohol. It can further lead to other escapist activities which involve spending large sums of money, such as shopping or making large purchases, travel, gambling, or non-stop entertainment activities. These large expenditures then require more work, with less time for self-reflection and engagement in meaningful activities, and thus the cycle continues.

> I recall an experience during my first year of law school. After class, a group of us stood around for a bit talking and the conversation shifted to our career goals. Most people were hoping to reap strong financial rewards. One or two people wanted to feel good about their work. I recall stating it would be great to both feel good about my work while also making a decent living. Everyone quickly burst out in laughter: You cannot feel good about what you do *and* earn a decent living! It is one or the other—you need to pick one.

This thinking seemed very limited to me. I thought there had to be a third option. Yes, there were the obvious extremes of Wall Street law firms and small non-profits, but why couldn't there be something in between these two extremes? Admittedly, my desire to find work that both provided a sense of purpose and paid the bills added a layer of complication to the process, but it also appeared the competitive drive of some of my classmates could lead them to feel dissatisfied if they were not reaping the greatest financial rewards possible.

The Role of Meaning and Purpose in Life

What Is Meaning?

Psychologists and philosophers have long been interested in meaning in life and how to define it. Perspectives on finding meaning in life vary. Assorted definitions can be found in the psychological literature, ranging from the subjective experience of having an impact on a purpose greater than oneself, or having a coherent sense of one's life, to the more concrete aspects of being goal-directed and purposeful in one's decisions and actions. In 2006, Steger and colleagues proposed a new definition of meaning which encompasses the varying perspectives: "'meaning in life' [is] the sense made of, and significance felt regarding, the nature of one's being and existence."

Meaning, and purpose, or adding value to the world, are important motivators. If your goals, beliefs, and values do not align with solely making as much money as possible, to the exclusion of all else, then striving for the position that pays the most regardless of content and working conditions will likely lead to dissatisfaction, stress, and possibly distress. Even if wealth accumulation is your top priority, long hours in a high demand and adversarial position can still lead to dissatisfaction or distress. Money as a motivator only goes so far and after a certain point does not bring increased happiness.

Impact of Meaning on Health and Well-Being

Meaning in life is related to effective emotion regulation and coping strategies, and less substance use. Life meaning has been found to be inversely related to psychological distress, including depression, anxiety, post-traumatic stress disorder (PTSD), and levels of suicidal ideation. The greater the sense of meaning one has in life, the lower the levels experienced in each of these areas, and vice versa. Meaning in life has also been found to be related to living longer, less risk of disability, less later-life cognitive decline, and overall reports of more positive health. Of note, while meaning is generally considered a stress buffer, one study in the United States involving a sample of African Americans found meaning to be related to a reduction in depressive symptoms but not stress.

Mood benefits associated with meaningful and purposeful activities tend to be longer term, as compared to those derived from passive entertainment activities (such as going to a movie, theater, concert, or a party) or other hedonic pleasures, which tend to be associated with short-lived benefits. Interestingly, people who report the lowest levels of meaning in life have also been found to engage in the highest number of hedonic behaviors.

Research suggests that meaning-based intrinsic goals such as growth, relationships, community giving, and health are associated with increased well-being. In contrast, externally focused goals, such as wealth, fame, and beauty, are negatively associated with well-being. While men and women have been found to be equally motivated by meaning stemming from working autonomously, a sense of making an impact, and the sense of competence that develops through performance of job responsibilities, women tend to be more motivated by meaning arising out of a sense of social value or usefulness related to their job mission.

Finding Meaning

People who report experiencing a sense of meaning in their life tend to be less depressed, and experience greater life satisfaction, self-esteem, and optimism. But how do we find it?

When you are working long hours and barely have time to meet your basic needs, such as sleep, exercise, a healthy diet, and maintaining healthy relationships, it is difficult to think about cultivating meaningful experiences. And when you have developed an external focus, one that derives pleasure (or at least provides comfort) from cultivating external symbols of success, those which are expected of someone at your level of success—actual or aspired to—there is little room to consider your internal values, beliefs, wants, and needs.

We create a sense of meaning and purpose through growth- and goal-directed activities which are engaged in service to something that is much bigger than us as an individual, or our own individual needs. Comprehensive definitions of meaning reflect: 1) being attuned to your beliefs, values, and goals, including who you are as a person, how you view the world, as well as your role in the world; 2) how you make sense of all these things; and 3) engaging in autonomous goal-directed behavior consistent with your beliefs, goals, and values. This process is thought to involve a self-reinforcing feedback loop which can foster personal growth and feelings of accomplishment.

Your work itself may be meaningful, you may feel good about the clients you are helping, or your contribution to an area of practice or a segment of the population. If you are lucky, you have found a way to connect your work to your values. Perhaps the challenges and opportunities to learn and grow as a legal practitioner provide a sense of meaning. If you are not so fortunate, you may need to look outside of your work to derive a sense of meaning. This may be through legal pro bono work, or volunteering for a meaningful-to-you non-profit, or your role in the lives of loved ones.

If you are not clear on your goals, beliefs, and values, it may help to engage in self-exploration work. But first, there are theoretical perspectives related to happiness, pleasure-seeking, and self-actualization that help us to think more deeply about meaning and fulfillment and the ways we go about finding both.

Hedonia, Eudaimonia, and Meaning and Purpose

The concepts of hedonia and eudaimonia date back to Aristotle and are frequently addressed in the psychological happiness and well-being literature, in the quest to conceptualize optimal functioning. Whereas *hedonia* has been defined as pleasure-based happiness, a more self-focused, in-the-moment, temporary pleasure, or an overall goal of simply maximizing pleasure and minimizing pain, the concept of *eudaimonia* has been described as involving more "virtue-driven" intentional behavior geared toward self-improvement, self-actualization, and meaningfulness.

Descriptions of eudaimonia and hedonia vary in the psychological literature, with some placing more emphasis on virtue, dignity, and promoting the greater good, while others focus more on challenging oneself and immersing oneself in an effortful task which elicits feelings of competence and accomplishment. Alan Waterman (1993), describing his research findings, related the two as follows:

> [F]eelings of personal expressiveness [eudaimonia] were more strongly associated with the perception of activities as affording opportunities for the development of one's best potentials... [F]eelings of personal expressiveness [eudaimonia] were [also] more strongly associated with feeling challenged, feeling competent, investing a great deal of effort, having a high level of concentration, feeling assertive, having clear goals, and knowing how well one is doing, whereas hedonic enjoyment was more strongly associated with feeling relaxed, excited, content, happy losing track of time, and forgetting one's personal problems. Feelings of personal expressiveness [eudaimonia] were also found to be more strongly associated with the level of challenges afforded by an activity and

the level of skills brought to it. With respect to the rated importance of activities, a stronger association was found with feelings of personal expressiveness [eudaimonia] than with hedonic enjoyment.

Various studies have explored the connection between both concepts and happiness, and most recognize there may be an overlap between the two, with hedonia at times considered a component of eudaimonia, depending upon the context. In 1989, Carol Ryff identified several areas important to happiness which had not been adequately addressed in prior research, namely: self-acceptance, positive relations with others, autonomy, environmental mastery, purpose in life, and personal growth. Each of these concepts goes beyond simple pleasure-based happiness—as might be experienced with a good meal, or going to a movie, concert, theatrical performance, theme park, etc., or through behaviors traditionally considered vices such as recreational drug use and masturbation—and reflect meaning-based happiness.

Well-being and happiness derived through eudaimonia is thought to reflect more intrinsically motivated, intentional, and purposeful living with mindfulness and awareness, and a focus on fostering healthy, quality relationships. While hedonic pursuits are defined by their immediate self-gratification, unrestrained self-expression, and lack of reflection, eudaimonic pursuits tend to be more goal- or growth-directed.

What Is the Important Takeaway Here?

Bottom line, while both may have positive associations with well-being, hedonia by itself is thought to convey temporary well-being benefits, whereas eudaimonia (including overlapping hedonia) has been found to lead to longer-term benefits.

The fact that there are no definitive definitions of eudaimonia and meaning makes sense. Just as we are all unique individuals, with differing values, beliefs and goals, our derivation of meaning in our lives will also vary. For some, virtue and promoting the greater good are paramount, for others pursuing challenges and personal growth is most satisfying, and for still others it may be a combination of these or other things. The key is knowing what motivates you, what provides you with the greatest sense of meaning and purpose, and then seeking those types of experiences either in work or life outside of work.

Values, Beliefs, and Morals Are the Basis of Meaning in Life

We derive meaning from behavior that is consistent with our values, beliefs, and morals. On the other hand, our values, beliefs, and morals can guide us to behaviors and ways of being that provide a sense of meaning and purpose. They help us to feel connected to others and our world, a part of something greater than us, and often are at the root of our passions.

161

Amorality Is a Potential Barrier to Experiencing Meaning in Work and Life

Amorality in Lawyers. An amoral approach is another example of legal profession circumstances which can lead to suppression of, or at least a lack of reflection upon, internal values, beliefs, and morals. "Amoral" is defined by the *New Oxford American Dictionary* as "unconcerned with the rightness or wrongness of something." A lot has been written about the amorality of lawyers, which is distinguished from being immoral. Some of this writing includes questions about whether lawyers tend to fall within a certain stage of moral development, or just think differently about morality, in a more neutral, unemotional fashion. Often theorists are considering morals, morality, and amorality in the context of legal ethics and professional responsibility. The issues of ethics and professional responsibility go beyond the purposes here, but the debate itself is telling; moral questions are an important part of legal representation, though like many subjective matters, each lawyer approaches moral dilemmas differently. Dilemmas can arise when deciding whether to represent a client, as well as whether to disclose to clients, or withhold from others, certain information about the law or its enforcement. Examples include whether or not to share enforcement information with a client in regulatory cases in which the law specifies certain requirements for good reason, but enforcement may be minimal, or whether to engage in legal representation that falls within the bounds of the law but the lawyer deems as promoting immoral behavior.

Law School Fosters Amorality. Teaching law students to "think like lawyers," including teaching them to ignore internal emotional and physical cues, has also been criticized for its role in suppressing budding lawyers' moral compass (never mind the negative well-being implications). Learning experiences requiring the ability to take a strong stance on whatever position is thrown at you, and not getting caught up on "soft" issues related to the social needs of clients, moral concerns, or compassion, promote an amoral stance.

The Benefits of Amorality. Although this approach to teaching is criticized, there are valid reasons why an amoral approach is fostered in law school. Amorality in lawyers can be adaptive for legal practice, allowing lawyers to represent clients without being influenced or deterred by moral judgment. In practical terms, if you are constrained by morals, beliefs, or values which conflict with those of the client or case at hand, it will be difficult to provide "zealous" representation. If you simply refuse to represent anyone whose case circumstances or personal values conflict with your own, this will greatly limit your client pool. More importantly, on an access to justice level, to deny legal representation to someone whose case conflicts with your own beliefs, values, or morals can have negative human rights implications.

A refusal of representation based on the lawyer's morals also serves to impose those morals on the client. Considering the important role lawyers play in the protection of rights and freedoms, and the specialized knowledge and power they possess, this lack of access to legal representation would limit individual rights and be contrary to individual autonomy, diversity, and equality.

The Risks of Amorality. Over time, you may develop a true amoral stance, learning to think about issues without tapping into your morals or values. There are at least two related risks here. For one, there is a risk of completely losing touch with your moral compass, which may lead to behaviors contrary to the law and professional responsibility. Second, if you remain attuned to your moral compass, efforts to take a neutral or amoral stance despite your own conflicting values may lead you to ignore or suppress those values to represent clients whose behavior is discordant with them. While it may in some ways be psychologically "adaptive" to not be attuned to underlying conflicting views—it would be very difficult to represent a client while feeling disgust, guilt, or shame—a lack of self-reflection and dismissal of closely held beliefs and important values can be detrimental to your health and well-being. For more on how emotional avoidance impacts well-being and relationships, see Chapter 4, Self-Care Strategies and Overcoming Barriers to Healthy Routines, and Chapter 8, The Essential Role of Personal Relationships and Social Supports in Well-Being.

Finally, an amoral stance is by definition one that does not include values, morals, and beliefs about right and wrong. If your work each day requires you to not be attuned to your values, or to actively tune them out, it can be very difficult to derive a sense of meaning from your work.

Cultivating Well-Being Through Meaning and Purpose

When was the last time you asked yourself, "What do I believe in?" or "What do I most value in life?" Knowing your core values and beliefs is essential to finding meaning and achieving a sense of fulfillment. Values, goals, hopes, and dreams are different for everyone, so the focus needs to be on you, not what your colleague, friend, neighbor, spouse, or kids think. As you ponder about this further, consider these questions: What are you passionate about? What gets you fired up? What activities make you lose a sense of time? We are not talking about watching television, scrolling through social media, playing video games, or surfing the internet, all of which are what I will call here "passivities" (passive ways to pass the time). Perhaps think back to those definitions of eudaimonia and hedonia mentioned earlier.

Self-reflection and self-exploration can be mentally and emotionally challenging. Yet, if we neglect to do this, and continue to ignore or suppress the unique person in each of us, it can lead to feelings of dissatisfaction and emptiness, and even depression and anxiety. This is particularly true if we are living our lives in ways that not only do not reflect our values and beliefs, but are also inconsistent with them. Behaving in ways that are inconsistent with our internal sense of who we are leads to what is known as "cognitive dissonance," a sense of discomfort that can vary in intensity depending on the degree of inconsistency in our behaviors, beliefs, and values, and the significance of the behavior. If you feel powerless to change your behavior for one reason or another, you may try to suppress your discomfort, or "self-medicate" with alcohol or drugs, which over time can lead to a multitude of serious mental health, physical health, relationship, professional liability, and other legal consequences, or even death.

Instead of continuing to charge ahead, advancing yourself professionally and financially, it is important to ask yourself whether you are living your life in a way that reflects *all* your top priorities, including family, relationships, and health. When making decisions about whether to take something on, or continue with some activity (or relationship for that matter), think about the balance, and ask yourself:

- How well does this match my priorities?
- Is it personally fulfilling in some way?
- At what cost?
- What would I be giving up?
- How might I better use my time?

You might also reflect on activities which gave you the greatest sense of fulfillment in the past, including in childhood. You may not be able to replicate these activities in your work or pro bono activities, but they can help you begin to build a framework around activities and interests that spark your passion and provide a sense of purpose, fulfillment, and perhaps meaning.

An activity which helps us shift our thinking to a positive focus on what we are grateful for, our goals and priorities, as well as proactively trying to live consistently with them, is a great way to begin.

Gratitude Exercises Can Help Promote a Sense of Meaning. Research shows that experiencing and expressing gratitude for the positives in our lives, no matter how small, has numerous benefits, including, mood, behavior, health, relationships, and life satisfaction. Gratitude is thought to reflect the recognition or acknowledgement that you attained a gift or benefit, material or non-material, conferred without necessarily being earned or deserved, and with the cause or source of that outcome being external to you. This recognition and appreciation of another person or external force may further engender empathy, which involves looking outside oneself and appreciating the altruism of the giver, gift, or positive outcome. The benefits of gratitude, in terms of positive emotional states, selflessness, and appreciation of others, in turn serve to promote and strengthen relationships, which are important sources of social support during difficult times. Another, more spiritual, definition of gratitude reflects a recognition of our small place in the larger universe and the interconnectedness among all of us.

By recognizing what we are grateful for, we can tap into our core beliefs and values, those things which are most important to us and which give our lives meaning. Engaging in brief gratitude exercises also helps shift our focus away from negative thoughts and ruminations, by focusing our attention, thoughts, and perceptions on something positive. This shift in thinking, and transition away from more negative thought processes, can lead to positive mood benefits and increased optimism. In addition, the positive mood benefits further enhance our thinking and problem-solving abilities by promoting broader, more flexible, and creative thinking.

Daily or even weekly gratitude exercises have been shown to have positive benefits. Gratitude exercises can involve thinking about something for which you are grateful, sharing an expression of gratitude, or writing/journaling.

Gratitude Journaling. When it comes to gratitude journaling, while the benefits are more robust with daily journaling, weekly journaling is still worthwhile. Similar to other journaling exercises, gratitude journaling helps create meaning through organizing thoughts, integration of thoughts and emotions, and eventual appreciation of the broader context of your experience. Expressions of gratitude do not have to be grand and can reflect something small in your daily experience. See Chapter 4, Self-Care Strategies and Overcoming Barriers to Healthy Routines for more on the positive benefits of gratitude and brief exercises.

Journaling about Stressors. One journaling strategy involves writing for 15 to 30 minutes per day. Psychologist James Pennebaker has done extensive research on the value of journaling to deal with both traumatic events and more common stressors. Journaling, or simply writing, about salient life events or experiences using emotion-laden language helps to organize your thoughts, and how you think about a stressful event. The resulting cohesive narrative, which integrates your thoughts and feelings, can then be easily summarized and filed away in memory, decreasing it's cognitive and emotional load. The best journaling results involve use of a combination of many positive emotion words and a moderate amount of negative emotion words, reflecting reality-based optimism. In addition, writing over the course of several days which reflects building an understanding over time (through increasing use of causal words, words showing insight, and words reflecting recognition of connections), and ultimately creating a story or narrative, is most related to positive benefits.

Remarkably, this type of reflective journaling has both mental health, physical health, and performance benefits across contexts. While it may lead to decreased positive affect in the hours after writing, in the ensuing weeks psychological health tends to improve.[1] Journaling is thought to provide a sense of control and predictability to the writer and helps create a sense of resolution as thoughts and emotions are integrated into a coherent narrative. Rumination tends to decrease. Creating a narrative through writing also benefits immune function, decreases pain, decreases depression, and improves performance. The meaning derived here is related to making sense of the stressor or loss and integrating it into your existing belief and value structures.

Journaling to Deal with Stigma. Significantly, journaling about group membership has been found to benefit self-esteem in under-represented or stigmatized individuals, with caveats depending upon whether one's under-represented or stigmatized group membership status is visible or known to others in the community at large.

- If you have a "visible stigmatized identity" (e.g., race, ethnicity, weight), journaling about being a member of the broader community, and areas of potential connection or commonality, is thought to be more beneficial than focusing on difference. This makes sense, as focusing on areas where you might find ways to connect with others provides hope and room for positive ways to manage the situation. It may be that since the stigmatized trait is visible to all, the best way to deal with it is to come to accept it and find ways to connect with others who are accepting of differences.
- On the other hand, if you have a "non-visible identity" (e.g., LGBTQ+ status, religious affiliation), research suggests you might see more benefit from writing about your experiences as a member of a stigmatized group(s). This finding also makes sense. When you hold these secrets of difference, it can lead to feelings of isolation. Sharing with others helps promote intimacy and connection. But depending upon the risks involved, you may not feel comfortable sharing certain details about yourself with others. Journaling is a way to express your thoughts and feelings, make sense of your situation, and consider your options going forward. It may be that once you have constructed your narrative, you no longer feel isolated or a need to share with others. On the other hand, the process of developing your narrative may lead you to take proactive steps to change your situation in one way or another.

Meaning through Religion or Spirituality. Many people derive a sense of meaning and purpose through religious practice. Religious faith is associated with well-being and happiness, and decreased susceptibility to depression. It is also associated with decreased negative impact and shorter duration of such after a major negative life event or loss. It is thought that the social support and community provided by active religious faith as well as the sense of meaning and purpose derived from one's faith, not to mention hope, may help explain the relationship between religiosity and well-being. Notably, one study of 860 college-educated adults found that those with low religious commitment and high "yuppie orientation" (defined as being self-oriented and valuing financial and occupational success over family and close relationships), were much less happy. Many people describe themselves as spiritual though not religious, perhaps recognizing their small role in a large universe, and an interconnectedness between humans and the rest of the natural world. Experiences related to spirituality can similarly create meaning.

Self-Exploration Can Take Many Forms. Journaling is just one effective way to make sense of the world, your experiences in it, your values and beliefs, and your vision of your role in the bigger picture. It is an effective tool for connecting thoughts and emotions into a coherent story, your story, making sense of incongruous pieces, and developing an appreciation for how it relates to the rest of the world. By creating a narrative through journaling, you can frame your life story, digest and process various circumstances and events in your life, and explore how they impacted you in the moment and going forward, how they connect and integrate with your beliefs and values, and ultimately create meaning. Importantly, when engaging in self-exploration, especially if you have a difficult or traumatic past, it is a good idea to connect with a professional who can guide you through the process and help you learn and practice strategies for managing any distress that may arise.

Making Meaning After a Traumatic Loss or Experience

As a graduate student research assistant, I helped run a study involving the process of meaning-making. Sometimes, we are forced to confront our beliefs, values, and sense of meaning in life. Shocking events can bring people out of the whirlwind of their daily lives and the collective rat race, and into the present moment. In the search for meaning after a traumatic experience or loss, people will try to make sense of what happened, which involves reconciling their beliefs and views of the world with an intensely inconsistent event. Such an experience could be a large-scale event or national tragedy, such as a natural disaster, a terrorist attack, or an act of war. Or it could be a personal near-death-experience or event, such as a life-threatening accident, a major health event or diagnosis, or relationship loss. Larger-scale events, such as the September 11, 2001 terrorist attacks, can temporarily eliminate communication barriers, opening doors to frank conversations and connections across diverse perspectives and backgrounds as people try to make sense of what happened and reconcile their beliefs of a fair and just world.

As a lawyer, disturbing images, videos, and stories involving abuse and maltreatment, or what you consider a highly unjust outcome involving human rights and freedoms, can induce a search for meaning. For more on vicarious trauma and how to manage it, see Chapter 5, Understanding and Addressing

Workplace Issues Which Impact Well-Being, and Chapter 4, Self-Care Strategies and Overcoming Barriers to Healthy Routines. Finding yourself in an ethical quagmire or another professional responsibility crisis, and wondering how you got there, can also invoke a personal meaning quest.

Post tragedy, as part of the meaning-making process, people often report that the event caused them to re-evaluate and appreciate life in a way they never had before, enabling them to connect with others and live in the moment, bringing unexpected happiness while simultaneously facing their mortality. Because it can be difficult to sit in this uncomfortable existential space, after a traumatic event many people return to their pre-event way of being over time but depending upon the scope of the tragedy and the level of personal connection, many do not. You may be familiar with cancer patients saying a cancer diagnosis was "the best thing that ever happened" to them. These statements may sound strange and difficult to believe at face value. What people are usually saying is the event led them to re-evaluate their life, goals, values, priorities, and actions, to find meaning.

It is unfortunate that often life is not fully appreciated or meaning sought until one is staring death in the face or about to lose everything after a lapse in professional judgment. I recall an article in the *New York Times* in early 2018 about a new app called *WeCroak*. The app pinged users at random five times a day with a reminder of their mortality, to help users contemplate death in the hopes of helping people live in the moment and enjoy life, knowing they could "croak" at any moment. The app never seemed to take off, at least in my circles (I did not hear of it before or after reading the *New York Times* article).

Not until we are actually forced to contemplate death can we truly begin to appreciate, at our core, what it means to die. While I understood the premise behind the app—that we need to be faced with our mortality before we can make the most out of life—it was misguided in that it took a negative approach, focusing on death, when most of us go through life, arguably by necessity, with a more hopeful and positive stance. In fact, hope and optimism are important traits related to extending life. We do not want to be thinking about our mortality several times a day, even if death is impending. And once we do, it often takes a lot of hard work to come to terms with that finality and pursue or reinvent our lives in a meaningful way. In the end, we are resilient and hopeful beings by nature, adjusting and adapting as needed, finding meaning and the positive in our losses, whatever they may be.

Pandemic-Induced Re-Evaluation of Meaning, Purpose, Career, and Life Trajectories

Although not necessarily traumatic for all, the deadly COVID-19 pandemic and its major negative impact on societal functioning prompted many people to re-evaluate their goals and priorities. If you are someone who has been working long hours and in a less deliberate manner, finding yourself frequently ill with various respiratory illnesses or other infections, perhaps you too have been rethinking your goals for the present and future.

Amid the pandemic, many lawyers began to reflect on their long hours in stressful environments and ask themselves, "Why?" and "To what end?" Spurred by circumstances related to the pandemic, including additional downtime before vaccines became widely available, many people took stock of where they were in their work and lives and whether these were consistent with their overarching values, beliefs, and goals. The Great Resignation was a result of the many people who decided the cons of their jobs outweighed the pros, and their values, beliefs, and goals could be better addressed elsewhere.

Meaning at Work Promotes Engagement and Well-Being

Finally, meaning at work is important from an organizational perspective because it influences engagement and well-being. A sense of meaning at work is created when people believe they are making a valuable contribution with their work, when they are involved in activities which promote their own learning, growth, and development, and when their activities support the people or causes most important to them.

When people are engaged with their work, they are energized, dedicated, absorbed with, and connected to their work. Engaged lawyers and staff are not workaholics, driven by an inner compulsion to work excessively, yet not enjoying their work, and constantly thinking about work even when not working; rather, engaged lawyers and staff are immersed in and derive pleasure from their work, and also have outside interests. One might say they experience eudaimonia. Underlying motivators, as well as work-related emotions, are thought to be more positive for engaged workers and more negative for workaholics. In addition, and importantly, research suggests engaged workers are less likely to experience burnout.

- Supervisors can enhance engagement and a sense of meaning by involving lawyers and staff in project-related discussions, seeking input, providing opportunities for professional growth and development, giving constructive feedback, and acknowledging a job well done.

While the connection between meaning and engagement applies across practice areas and settings, many lawyers derive a deep sense of meaning and purpose from their work in areas of perceived social impact. Some of these areas of practice, such as criminal law, including child protection or domestic violence, as well as immigration or asylum law, and family law, can put lawyers at increased risk for burnout or vicarious trauma resulting from narrative or imagery exposure, especially for lawyers high in empathy. Vicarious trauma involves an experiencing of traumatic stress reactions by a lawyer or other professional who is exposed to material which is deeply disturbing or challenges one's world view. As mentioned above, dealing with vicarious trauma is addressed in Chapter 4. It is important for leaders and supervisors to recognize the risks and signs, as well as provide training and resources to help prevent and mitigate any psychological impact.

Note

1 Notably, journaling may not be effective—or worse, may create more emotional distress—for people dealing with severe depression or PTSD.

Bibliography

Bradshaw, E. L., Conigrave, J. H., Steward, B. A., Ferber, K. A., Parker, P. D., & Ryan, R. M. (2022). A meta-analysis of the dark side of the American dream. *Journal of Personality and Social Psychology.* https://doi.org/10.1037/pspp0000431

Burbano, V., Padilla, N., & Meier, S. (2020, March 4). *Gender differences in preferences for meaning at work gender differences in preferences for meaning at work.* www.columbia.edu/~np2506/papers/burbano_gender_job_preferences _Mar2020.pdf

Chalofsky, N. E. (2010). *Meaningful workplaces : Reframing how and where we work.* Jossey-Bass. https://search.library.yale.edu/catalog/14817984.

Chalofsky, N., & Cavallaro, L. (2013). A good living versus a good life: Meaning, purpose, and HRD. *Advances in Developing Human Resources, 15*(4), 331–340. https://doi-org.yale.idm.oclc.org/10.1177/1523422313498560

Clark, M. A. (2016, April 1). Workaholism: It's not just long hours on the job. *Psychological Science Agenda.* https://www.apa.org/science/about/psa/2016/04/ workaholism

Deci, E. L., & Ryan, R. M. (2008). Hedonia, eudaimonia, and well-being: An introduction. *Journal of Happiness Studies, 9*(1), 1–11. https://doi.org/10.1007/ s10902-006-9018-1

Emmons, R. A., & Stern, R. (2013). Gratitude as a psychotherapeutic intervention. *Journal of Clinical Psychology, 69*(8), 846–855. https://doi-org.yale.idm.oclc.org /10.1002/jclp.22020

Emmons, R., & McCullough, M. E. (2003). Counting blessings versus burdens: An experimental investigation of gratitude and subjective well-being in daily life. *Journal of Personality and Social Psychology, 84*(2), 377–389. https://doi.org/10. 1037/0022-3514.84.2.377

Fredericks, S. A. (2006). The irresponsible lawyer: Why we have an amoral profession. *Texas Review of Law and Politics, 11*(1), 133–156.

Kaufman, A. L. (1986). A commentary on Pepper's "the lawyer's Amoral ethical role". *American Bar Foundation Research Journal, 11*(4), 651–655. www.jstor.org/ stable/828289

La Ferla, R. (2018). Think you'll live forever? This app dashes all hope. *The New York times*, New York Edition. Style Section, p. 4.

Moran, R. J., & Asquith, N. L. (2020). Understanding the vicarious trauma and emotional labour of criminological research. *Methodological Innovations, 13*(2). https://doi.org/10.1177/2059799120926085

Myers, D. G. (2000). The funds, friends, and faith of happy people. *American Psychologist, 55*(1), 56–67. https://doi.org/10.1037/0003-066X.55.1.56

Park, C., Clark, E. M., R Williams, B., Schulz, E., Williams, R. M., & Holt, C. L. (2018). Meaning predicts declines in depressive symptoms but doesn't buffer stress in a national sample of African Americans. *Innovation in Aging, 2*(Suppl 1), 433. https://doi.org/10.1093/geroni/igy023.1621

Parker, K., & Horwitz, J. M. (2022, March 9). *Majority of workers who quit a job in 2021 cite low pay, no opportunities for advancement, feeling disrespected.* Pew Research Center. www.pewresearch.org/fact-tank/2022/03/09/majority-of -workers-who-quit-a-job-in-2021-cite-low-pay-no-opportunities-for-advancement -feeling-disrespected/

Pennebaker, J. W., & Seagal, J. D. (1999). Forming a story: The health benefits of narrative. *Journal of Clinical Psychology, 55*(10), 1243–1254.

Pepper, S. L. (1986). The Lawyer's amoral ethical role: A defense, a problem, and some possibilities. *American Bar Foundation Research Journal, 11*(4), 613–635. www.jstor.org/stable/828287

Perkins, H. W. (1991). Religious commitment, yuppie values, and well-being in post-collegiate life. *Review of Religious Research, 32*(3), 244–251. https://doi.org/10. 2307/3511209

Ryff, C. D. (1989). Happiness is everything, or is it? Explorations on the meaning of psychological well-being. *Journal of Personality and Social Psychology, 57*(6), 1069–1081. https://doi.org/10.1037/0022-3514.57.6.1069

Schaufeli, W. B., Taris, T. W., & van Rhenen, W. (2008). Workaholism, burnout, and work engagement: Three of a kind or three different kinds of employee well-being? *Applied Psychology, 57*(2), 173–203. https://doi.org/10.1111/j.1464-0597. 2007.00285.x

Shuck, B., & Rose, K. (2013). Reframing employee engagement within the context of meaning and purpose: Implications for HRD. *Advances in Developing Human Resources, 15*(4), 341–355. https://doi-org.yale.idm.oclc.org/10.1177/1523422313503235

Steger, M. F., Frazier, P., Oishi, S., & Kaler, M. (2006). The meaning in life questionnaire. *Journal of Counseling Psychology, 53*(1), 80–93.

Steger, M. F., Shin, Y. J., Shim, Y., & Fitch-Martin, A. (2013). Is meaning in life a flagship indicator of well-being? In A. S. Waterman (Ed.), *The best within us: Positive psychology perspectives on eudaemonia* (pp. 159–179). Ch. 8. American Psychological Association.

Sullivan, W. M., Colby, A., Wegner, J. W., Bond, L., & Shulman, L. S. (2007). *Summary: Educating lawyers: Preparation for the profession of law.* The Carnegie Foundation for the Advancement of Teaching. http://archive.carnegiefoundation. org/publications/pdfs/elibrary/elibrary_pdf_632.pdf

Van Tongeren, D. R., Hill, P. C., Krause, N., et al. (2017). The mediating role of meaning in the association between stress and health. *Annals of Behavioral Medicine, 51*, 775–781. https://doi-org.yale.idm.oclc.org/10.1007/s12160-017-9899-8

Waterman, A. S. (1993). Two conceptions of happiness: Contrasts of personal expressiveness (eudaimonia) and hedonic enjoyment. *Journal of Personality and Social Psychology, 64*(4), 678–691, 689. https://doi.org/10.1037/0022-3514.64.4. 678

Waterman, A. S. (2013). Eudaimonia: Contrasting two conceptions of happiness: Hedonia and eudaimonia. In J. J. Froh & A. C. Parks (Eds.), *Activities for teaching positive psychology: A guide for instructors* (pp. 29–34). American Psychological Association. https://doi.org/10.1037/14042-005

CHAPTER 10

Creating Change

Recognizing a Problem Exists and Weighing the Challenges and Benefits of Addressing It

Change is slow and complicated. First, we need to recognize there is a problem which needs to be addressed. Once we acknowledge a problem, however, we are not yet out of the woods. We may still question whether anything needs to be done about it. What is involved and is it worth the inevitable hassle? Do we want to put in all the effort?

For a long time, many lawyers and legal employers did not recognize that lawyer dissatisfaction, stress, and burnout were problems which needed to be addressed. The thinking went (and still goes for many), "Law is stressful. Lawyers work long hours. Just tough it out." In the early 2000s, my presentations primarily focused on raising awareness that there even was a problem in the legal profession in terms of stress and work–life balance. Many young lawyers appreciated this, but many in the older generations did not.

There are economic reasons for promoting well-being and a healthy work environment, also known as "the business case" for lawyer well-being. These include the acknowledgement that a stressed-out, sleep-deprived, unhealthy, and potentially addicted workforce creates risks for decreased productivity and performance, increased healthcare costs, difficulties with recruitment and retention, not to mention potential professional liability risks.

Over the years, with each graduating class and newly minted lawyers, awareness of the importance of well-being increases. Generation Z in particular does not want to experience what the Japanese call "*karoshi*," or death by over-work, and they are voting with their feet. Gallop survey results in 2021 found that the number one thing Gen Z wants from their employer is concern for their well-being. Similarly, a 2021 Bloomberg Law survey found the top three reasons why lawyers were leaving their jobs were: 1) "Better work–life balance"; 2) "Reduce work stress"; and 3) "Increase focus on personal life."

During the 2010s, awareness of the economic importance of promoting well-being steadily increased. Large law firms began hiring directors of well-being, and other firms set up wellness committees. The American Bar Association and state bar associations set up well-being task forces and

    DOI: 10.4324/9781003285519-10

committees, dedicated to raising awareness, providing education, and sharing resources.

When the COVID-19 pandemic hit in early 2020, the stress, uncertainty, and disruption only served to reinforce the need for greater focus on lawyer and staff well-being. Even prior to the US pandemic-related shutdown in March 2020, many lawyers were struggling with anxiety and depression. The results of an American Lawyer Media survey, published in February 2020, revealed that 64% of respondents reported anxiety, 31% reported feelings of depression, and 13% thought they had an alcohol or drug problem. Recognizing the mental health and well-being of the legal profession was at risk—as a result of existing universal stressors across the profession combined with the upheaval resulting from the COVID-19 pandemic—BloombergLaw.com implemented its quarterly Attorney Workload and Hours Survey. The survey's quarterly results revealed anxiety, depression, and a difficulty disconnecting from work. Many other surveys of lawyers across the globe have found high rates of anxiety, depression, and substance use (some of which are referenced in Chapter 1).

Many legal employers may finally be reaching the point at which the perceived benefits of promoting well-being and healthy work environments outweigh the challenges involved in doing so.

The Formula for Making a Change

The basic formula for change is the same, but interventions will vary depending on your needs and resources, and any contextual factors:

1. Identify a moderately challenging situation which you think you can successfully address.
2. Choose and commit to an intervention.
3. Implement the intervention.
4. Review and identify impediments to the consistent implementation of the intervention.
5. Modify the intervention to help overcome the impediment(s).
6. Commit to practicing the strategy and recording the outcome on a consistent basis.
7. Re-evaluate regularly and tweak as necessary.

This approach applies to the self-care strategies highlighted in Chapter 4, Self-Care Strategies and Overcoming Barriers to Healthy Routines, as well as other change strategies mentioned throughout this book.

Make a Commitment

Whenever you want to make a change, it is essential to make a commitment, first and foremost; in the absence of a commitment, your goals are more likely to get lost in the daily grind.

Pledging Your Commitment to Change as an Organization

The legal profession's acknowledgement that well-being-related change is needed, while an important first step, in and of itself is insufficient. (As with goals on the individual level, a commitment is necessary for staying on track, signaling a level of priority and importance, and intentionality.) Intentionality is a key component of change...making plans and taking steps with an intention of creating change within a set time frame is essential. By setting these structural deadlines for ourselves, we make a commitment and create a framework for accountability. But before we can set deadlines for ourselves and our organizations, we need to know what changes we plan to make. Having concrete questions and potential goals in mind can help facilitate conversation.[1]

Creating or Adopting a Well-Being Pledge Is One Way to Start the Change Conversation

A well-being pledge (see Appendix III for a template) is one way to start the conversation around areas that could be improved, to begin thinking about what changes need to be made, and how to go about making these changes. Creation of a well-being pledge is a good vehicle to help stimulate discussion while also leaving organizations in the driver's seat regarding the specifics of time frame and degree of well-being-related changes.

Signing Onto a Pledge Is Just the Beginning

It is important to recognize that a well-being pledge is not an end in itself. Signing on to a well-being pledge is a starting point; it is a tool to stimulate thoughts and conversations about change within legal culture and cannot possibly address all aspects of well-being. It is also a great way to create a sense of accountability, particularly if everyone in the organization has the opportunity to (anonymously) weigh in at the end of the pledge year. A lot can be learned from anonymous feedback from lawyers and staff who share their perspective on how much progress was made toward pledged goals, and whether any goals were fully met. Importantly, if goals are met, try to acknowledge the achievement in some small way that includes the entire organization.

Commitments Which Reflect Well-Being, Broadly Defined

Well-being as a *Way of Being* requires a broad conceptualization, encompassing both individual and organizational aspects needed to promote self-care and a healthy work environment. Self-care resources and strategies are key, such as in-house resources (e.g., a meditation room, a lactation room, healthy eating resources, and/or a weekly yoga class) and educational opportunities addressing well-being, mental health, and substance use. At the same time, overall organizational culture is paramount. For instance, if you designate a "meditation room" in your workplace, but attorneys and staff are not supported in taking the time to utilize it (or worse, stigmatized), this meditation room simply serves as a well-being mirage. Alternatively, if the meditation room (or another resource or policy) is embraced by your firm, attorneys may freely utilize it, but if they must be accessible nearly 24/7, or the firm work culture is toxic, these negative workplace forces will likely eventually lead to burnout despite a person's best efforts at self-care. Key issues to consider are identified later in this chapter, and in the Lawyer Well-Being Pledge Commitment Template found in Appendix III.

Set Realistic Goals

In the pledge commitment template found in Appendix III, once your organization is ready to make a commitment, you are asked to commit to only those changes you reasonably believe you can achieve, instead of just checking all the boxes and hoping something sticks. By picking a few (or even one or two) areas of realistic change, you are being more thoughtful and intentional in your commitment, and are more likely to succeed.

How Will You Meet Your Pledge Goals, and What Are the Potential Barriers?

To further increase the likelihood of success, you can task yourself with listing two to three objectives (see Appendix III), statements explaining how you plan to make the pledged changes. By engaging in this strategic thought exercise, you can think more deeply about your priorities, begin to anticipate any challenges that may arise along the way to achieving your goal, and develop an action plan.

Set a Pledge Date

One of the goals for each year thereafter is for your organization to evaluate progress made and re-commit to the pledge, either with the same items, or ideally, adding one or two more commitments.

Review and Rate Your Progress

Fostering accountability is an important yet often neglected step. At the end of each pledge year, it helps to self-rate your progress toward your pledged goals by completing a pledge progress form (for an example, see Appendix

III). This self-rating exercise can be used to rate your progress for each goal, on a scale of 1–10. Doing so allows you to track progress toward your goals and may also help promote accountability depending on who else sees the results. In the sample form, you are also asked to write down any barriers to achieving your goals. This additional writing exercise is designed to help you further think through and evaluate your progress, ideally addressing what went well, what didn't go so well, and identifying any barriers, and how those barriers can be addressed.

Anonymous Feedback Helps Promote Accountability and Employee Voice

In addition, an important part of the exercise is to have lawyers and staff separately and *anonymously* complete pledge progress forms. This evaluation is important for a few reasons. Not only do you get important feedback, but it also helps to create an additional, external sense of accountability on the part of leadership. Similar to an exercise buddy—that person with whom you commit to meeting at a certain time for a workout, making it more difficult for you to skip the workout even if you don't feel like you have the time or energy—the knowledge that lawyers and staff will be evaluating organizational progress on pledge commitments serves as an accountability measure to help your organization stay motivated and on track to achieving those commitments. Equally important, it gives everyone in the organization a voice, with an opportunity to both be heard and possibly help shape the transformation process.

Key Issues

Key issues that might be addressed in a pledge include:

- What are the expectations around electronic communications outside of "normal" business hours?
- Do attorneys and staff utilize their vacation time? Are vacations encouraged?
- What do typical interactions among attorneys and staff look like?
- Are help-seeking and self-care consistently promoted and encouraged by your firm?
- What is your organizational culture around substance use? Is alcohol a "must have" for all extracurricular team-building activities?
- Is your work environment psychologically safe for lawyers and staff, representing diverse race, ethnicity, culture, and identity backgrounds?
- Do health insurance policy offerings include quality mental and physical health benefits and access to a robust provider network?

- Is there flexibility in terms of hours worked, hybrid and/or remote work options?
- Are attorneys and staff encouraged to make suggestions for initiatives and policies which promote well-being and a healthy work environment?
- Is attendance required at all, or a percentage of, organization-wide well-being-related educational programs and events?
- What in-house well-being resources do you offer?

These are a few of the questions your firm leaders might consider asking as you embark on workplace well-being culture transformation.

Among other things, promoting self-care, psychological safety, and access to quality mental healthcare with a robust provider network should be top priorities on every law firm's list of goals.

Leadership Challenges

As a leader, you have a lot to juggle. What are you doing to ensure that your workplace is productive, profitable, and a healthy environment that draws and retains high-quality talent? What are you doing to support your team? Are the lines of communication open and healthy? Do people experience psychological safety? What are you doing to promote and role-model a healthy workplace? What are you doing to help people manage work–life balance, or issues at home?

⇒ *Thought Exercise.* What do you want your "Legal Legacy" to be? If you could do or change one thing to improve lawyer well-being at your office, or in the legal profession as a whole, what would it be?

How are you managing your own stress and work–life balance issues? This includes engaging in self-care, adaptive stress management strategies, and skillful emotion regulation. You want to figure out how to navigate that line where you are available to your team and are helping to build a healthy workplace, but also setting boundaries, protecting your own time, and making time for strategic thinking toward the future, self-reflection, and self-care. Throughout this book, an effort has been made to help you understand the underlying issues and begin to address them, both individually and organizationally.

Harnessing Lawyers' Competitive Spirit to Promote Healthy Habits

There is nothing like a friendly competition to motivate and promote healthy habits among colleagues and friends. Lawyers in particular tend to embrace competitive activities. You can harness this competitive drive by committing to a friendly competitive "challenge" with a colleague, or by setting up a firm-wide or department-wide competition, offering a "prize" for the winner at the end of the month.

Workplace Challenge—Annually, Semi-Annually, Bi-Monthly, or Monthly

You can easily set up a workplace challenge with self-care strategies and a calendar. The challenge can be anywhere from annually to semi-annually to monthly. A holiday challenge can be a great reminder to take care of yourself during months typically filled with holiday activities and end-of-year deadlines. (See Appendix IV, Office Challenge Template.)

Creating Change at the Individual Level

Commit to adopting and implementing a strategy—one which meets your needs, priorities, interests, and abilities—consistently over time. You can do this on your own, or, even better, pick a well-being partner or partners to work with and hold you accountable, your Accountability Buddy or Buddies.

Start small. It is important to commit to something which you believe you can achieve without too much difficulty. You do not want to set yourself up for failure before you even begin. A reasonable goal is one that will take some effort but is quite doable. Success from a small goal will be reinforcing and energizing, helping you to continue to move forward with incrementally more challenging goals. For instance, as a simple example, if you know you need to drink more water each day, a reasonable commitment might be to do just that: drink more water every day.

Think about How You Will Achieve Your Goal

Think of one to three objectives, things you can do to help ensure you will achieve your goal. By engaging in this exercise, you are not only problem-solving, but also becoming more invested in achieving the goal. In the water bottle example above, this may include: 1) buying a 24-oz water bottle; 2) bringing it with you to work each day; 3) planning to refill at three separate times during the day.

Think about What Might Get in the Way of Achieving Your Goal and How to Overcome These Obstacles

Continuing with the water bottle example, what are 1-3 things which might get in the way of achieving this goal? (This step should be easy; you are simply thinking like a lawyer.) 1) forgetting your water bottle; 2) forgetting to refill it during the day; or, 3) needing to take a break at an inconvenient time.

Now consider what you might do to overcome these obstacles. For instance, 1) the night before, put the water bottle in your car if you drive to work, or near your keys or another essential item you routinely bring with you; 2) add refill reminders to your calendar at convenient times; or, 3) adjust your refill schedule to accommodate for times when break options will be more limited.

Decide When You Will Begin

When establishing a new behavior, it helps to be structured about it. Pick a date (and time if applicable) in the near future when you will begin to take steps toward achieving your goal. You want to get started while you are still inspired and motivated. Most people have had the experience of attending a conference or other event which creates excitement around creating new goals, only to return home and fall back into old routines and patterns unless those ideas were quickly put into action.

Evaluate Your Progress and Modify Your Strategy as Needed

You will want to regularly evaluate progress on any goals, identify any barriers to implementation, and adjust as needed. How frequently you assess progress will depend upon the type and complexity of your goals. Again, the water bottle: In this low-complexity example, the best approach initially would be to evaluate your progress at the end of each day, but as you successfully build this new routine, you can review less frequently.

Build on Your Progress

Over time, you can add and implement new goals, progressively more challenging. As you move toward well-being as a *Way of Being*, you may want to gradually modify or change several behaviors (healthy habits) or thought processes (mindset). You may want to develop more adaptive ways of relating to others, and perhaps prune relationships which do not nourish you, or worse, are draining and detrimental to your well-being. You may want to focus on engaging more in meaningful activities, at work or outside of work, or finding your passions. You may want to revisit your relationship with money and what it means to you, or do more to reduce financial stress and promote your financial well-being through budgeting and planning ahead. You may want to engage in better time management, boundary setting or self-advocacy at work, develop better communication skills, or engage in more professional development activities.

180

Keep Moving Forward

The strategies above are just a few options for beginning to promote self-care and a healthy work environment. The best approaches will be targeted, identifying and addressing the unique constellation of factors at play in any given situation related to the people involved and the work and workplace contexts. As you embark on your well-being journey, remember change is slow, and sometimes we take two steps forward and one step back. Practice self-compassion, evaluate and reflect on what is working and what isn't, make any necessary course corrections, and keep moving forward!

Note

1 An example of such a conversation starter is a well-being pledge, such as the one I helped the Connecticut Bar Association Lawyer Well-Being Committee to develop in 2020–2021.

Bibliography

Church, A. H., & Dawson, L. M. (2018). Agile feedback drives accountability and sustained behavior change. *Strategic HR Review*, *17*(6), 295–302. https://doi.org/10.1108/SHR-07-2018-0063

Connecticut bar association well-being pledge, pledge commitment form. www.surveymonkey.com/r/9MJ9FPW

McLellan, L. (2020). *Lawyers reveal true depth of mental health struggles*. Law.com (February 19, 2020). Retrieved from www.law.com/2020/02/19/lawyers-reveal-true-depth-of-the-mental-health-struggles/

Miller-Kuwana, K. (2021, September 29). *Analysis: Leaving? Money talks, but well-being now wants a word*. Referencing *Bloomberg Law's Q2 2021 attorney workload and hours survey*. https://news.bloomberglaw.com/bloomberg-law-analysis/analysis-leaving-money-talks-but-well-being-now-wants-a-word?context=article-related

Nielsen, K., Nielsen, M. B., Ogbonnaya, C., Känsälä, M., Saari, E., & Isaksson, K. (2017). Workplace resources to improve both employee well-being and performance: A systematic review and meta-analysis. *Work & Stress*, *31*(2), 101–120. https://doi-org.yale.idm.oclc.org/10.1080/02678373.2017.1304463

Nishiyama, K., & Johnson, J. V. (1997). Karoshi—Death from overwork: Occupational health consequences of Japanese production management. *International Journal of Health Services*, *27*(4), 625–641. https://doi.org/10.2190/1JPC-679V-DYNT-HJ6G

O'Boyle, E. (2021, March 30). *4 things Gen Z and millennials expect from their workplace*. Gallup. www.gallup.com/workplace/336275/things-gen-millennials-expect-workplace.aspx?version=print

Prochaska, J. O., Redding, C., & Evers, K. E. (2008). The transtheoretical model and stages of change. In K. Glanz, B. K. Rimer, & K. Viswanath (Eds.), *Health behavior and health education: Theory, research and practice, 4ᵗʰ ed* (pp.97–121). Jossey-Bass.

Prochaska, J. O., & Velicer, W. F. (1997). The transtheoretical model of health behavior change. *American journal of health promotion: AJHP, 12*(1), 38–48. https://doi.org/10.4278/0890-1171-12.1.38

Ryan, R. M., & Deci, E. L. (2000). Self-determination theory and the facilitation of intrinsic motivation, social development, and well-being. *American Psychologist, 55*(1), 68–78.

Simmons, C. (2018). *Law firms face malpractice risk over substance use, poor mental health.* NU property casualty 360. Retrieved December 4, 2018, from www. propertycasualty360.com/2018/12/04/another-hazard-of-poor-attorney-mental-health-malp/?slreturn=20211012113822. Original article published in New York Law Journal. Retrieved November 28, 2018, from www.law.com/newyorklawjournal/ 2018/11/28/another-hazard-of-poor-attorney-mental-health-malpractice-risk/

Appendix I: Self-Care Strategies and Exercises

21 Brief In-the-Moment "Resets" to Decrease Stress and Improve Focus

Find the brief healthy activities (on this list or on your own) which most easily help you "get out of your head," live in the moment for a few minutes, and recharge. Try experimenting with different items. Everyone has their own preferences and finding yours will lead to the best results. Think of some others not listed here!

1. Stretch and engage in deep, "belly" breathing for 1–2 minutes.
2. Take a 5-minute walk around the office, or up and down some stairs.
3. Take a 15-minute walk outside.
4. Massage your forehead and scalp.
5. Get up and have a light conversation with a nearby colleague.
6. Talk with someone you trust.
7. Smile or laugh (muscles send signals to the brain which release tension).
8. Find the humor in stressful situations.
9. Seek out humor (i.e., podcast, humor book, family photo).
10. Drink a glass of water or milk.
11. If you are hungry, eat a healthy snack—slowly.
12. Turn off your mobile phone for 15 minutes.
13. Take a 20-minute power nap (set an alarm).
14. Think of three things you are grateful for in your life, no matter how small. Even better, express gratitude.
15. Listen to soothing music.
16. Write down your thoughts or anxieties (in a journal, on a piece of paper, in your personal phone "notes").
17. Color in a mindfulness coloring book.
18. Engage in a 1–2 minute mindfulness exercise.
19. Engage in 1–2 minutes of progressive muscle relaxation.
20. Meditate for 5 minutes.
21. Pay someone a genuine compliment, particularly that annoying person.

Self-Care Basics: Tip Sheet

The basics of self-care (some of which can be combined!), take time and planning:

- Sleeping 7–8 hours each night.
- Daily exercise.
- Eating a healthy diet, low in fats and sugars and high in raw fruits and vegetables.
- Limiting, or abstaining from, alcohol.
- Limiting caffeine.
- Making time for social connection with family, loved ones, and friends.
- Making time for a favorite activity or hobby (at least weekly or monthly).
- Giving yourself permission to take a few days off, or a longer vacation.
- Set boundaries around electronic devices—no devices in the bedroom, one hour before bed, or at dinner.
- Learn to manage your time more effectively.
- Set realistic goals and maintain realistic expectations at work and at home.

You have control over your own behavior—such as creating a structured work schedule, recognizing your need for breaks and taking them, getting regular exercise, engaging in healthy eating, healthy sleep habits, adaptive communication, socializing and connecting with others, deep breathing, mindfulness, yoga and meditation, and… having fun. Develop a routine that works best for you, based on your needs, preferences, and schedule.

DIY Stress Management Exercises

1) *Your Stress*

Stress often manifests itself in muscle tension and headaches. Most often, tension is felt in the neck, shoulders, and back. You might notice your jaw is clenched, or your brow furrowed. You might feel short of breath.

2) *Your Stress Management Tools*

A few different types of stress management exercises are included here:

- Deep breathing
- Box breathing
- Guided imagery

- Mindfulness
- Progressive muscle relaxation (brief overview only)

Each of these exercises can be done almost anywhere, such as sitting, lying on your back, or standing. Each of these exercises can lower blood pressure, heart rate, and respiration rate. In addition, progressive muscle relaxation has the further benefit of targeting and relaxing your tense muscles.

3) *Your Commitment*

- Experiment with deep breathing, imagery, mindfulness, and progressive muscle relaxation exercises. See which you prefer.
- For a few minutes each day, practice one of the exercises.
- Tell some of the important people in your life (e.g., family, close co-workers) about your commitment and that you are going somewhere (or closing your door) to "practice" for a few minutes.

Deep Breathing Exercise

Sit up straight. (Do not arch your back.) If sitting in a chair, place both feet flat on the floor. If sitting on the floor, sit cross-legged. Exhale completely through your mouth. Feel the tension leaving your body.

- Place your hands on your stomach, just above your waist.
- Try breathing in slowly for three seconds until you have a full breath and hold that for three seconds. Notice the air filling your lungs and abdomen.
    (Note that this is the opposite of the suck-in-your-gut on the beach or at the pool breathing you may have done as a teenager.)
- Slowly and steadily breathe out through your mouth, feeling your stomach contract, until most of the air is out. Exhalation should take a little longer than inhalation.
- Feel the tension leaving your shoulders, your neck, your jaw, your forehead, your back. Feel the support of the chair you are sitting on, or other surface if lying down. Allow yourself to sink into the chair or other surface.

Once you are comfortable with the exercise and more attuned to your body, you don't need to use your hands to check your breathing. You can practice deep breathing in various settings and positions.

- Experiment with breathing in for longer or holding it for longer and see what works for you.

185

- You might try it while lying down on your back. Deep breathing exercises can help you to relax before you go to sleep for the night, or fall back asleep if you awaken in the middle of the night.
- You can also practice deep breathing exercises standing—such as when you are standing in a long line at the grocery store or somewhere else.
- And of course, deep breathing is a great strategy when you are sitting in the car, stuck in traffic.
- At times when you are especially tense, your chest will tighten and it might feel as though you are holding your breath or can't quite catch your breath; simply concentrate on slowly breathing in and out.

Box Breathing

Box breathing exercises provide further structure to breathing practice, through counting and holding breaths, which can create a sense of control. Box breathing is used by members of the US Military.

Start by exhaling through your mouth, *releasing all air from your lungs*, then complete the box by following these four steps:

1) Inhale slowly through your nose for a count of 4: "1… 2… 3… 4…"
2) Hold for a count of 4.
3) Exhale through your mouth for a count of 4.
4) Hold for a count of 4.

Repeat in order three times, or until you feel relaxed. Importantly, be sure to *expand* your abdomen and lungs when inhaling, allowing them to fill with air.

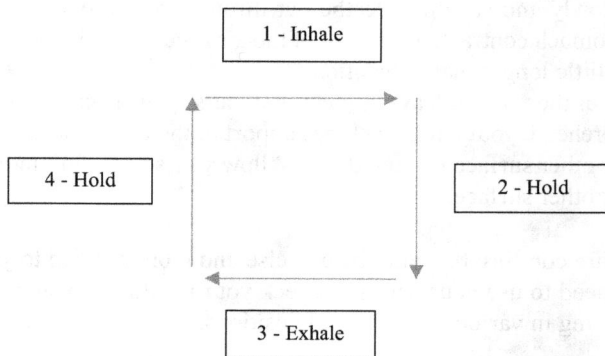

```
                    ┌─────────────┐
                    │ 1 - Inhale  │
                    └─────────────┘

   ┌───────────┐                      ┌───────────┐
   │ 4 - Hold  │                      │ 2 - Hold  │
   └───────────┘                      └───────────┘

                    ┌─────────────┐
                    │ 3 - Exhale  │
                    └─────────────┘
```

Imagery Relaxation Exercise

Ask yourself:

"What's the first place that comes into my mind when I think of a time when I felt truly relaxed?"

Often, this question will evoke a vacation location, or a place that you deliberately seek out when you want to relax. Pick a place. It could be a garden, a waterfall, a beach, a mountain, a room, or anywhere else. Just pick a peaceful place where you feel comfortable and safe.

Engage:

Close your eyes and transport yourself to that favorite place. Do it in the following steps, focusing on as many details as you can:

1. Create a visual picture of what you would see at that place. It can help to imagine the place on a big IMAX movie screen.
2. Create a soundtrack in your mind, listening for what you might hear: wind, birds, water, silence, etc.
3. Try to feel what you might feel tactually, sand between your toes, a breeze on your face or wind blowing your hair, the warmth of the sun or a fire on your face and body, etc.
4. Spend some time here, imagine how you feel in this place, relax.

Remember these sensations; they are the sensations of your peaceful place. A place where you can relax. Say to yourself, "I am relaxed, my body feels warm and heavy, I am safe here." Enjoy the feeling of deep relaxation.

Brief Mindfulness Exercise

Mindfulness exercises are a quick and effective way to relieve stress by bringing you out of your worries and into the moment, giving your brain and your body a rest from the otherwise endless cycle of stress.

Sight

Look around you. What do you see?

- Name all the different colors you see.
- Count how many windows, plants, lights, chairs, pictures on the wall, etc., you see.
- If you are near a window, observe the weather outside. Is it sunny? Cloudy? Foggy? Snowing? Raining? Nightime?

187

Touch

What are your tactile sensations?

- Place your right hand on your chair seat. Is it hard or soft? Smooth or textured? Cool or warm?
- Place your left hand on your desk or table. Is it harder or softer than the chair? More smooth or more textured? Cooler or warmer?

Sound

Listen. What do you hear?

- People talking? Is it muffled or clear?
- An air vent? Is it smooth or rattling?
- Street noise? Muted or loud? Sirens? Car horns? Construction?
- Music? Loud or soft? What kind?

Progressive Muscle Relaxation Overview

Progressive muscle relaxation simply involves the tensing and then relaxing of different muscle groups within the body, one group at a time, often in combination with deep breathing. The tension should be intense, without straining your muscles. If you feel sharp pain with a particular muscle group, stop immediately, consider consulting with a physician, and move on to the next muscle group.

This technique is simple, but it may take several practice efforts before you feel comfortable with it and begin to see quick results. You can find audio exercises to listen to in apps and on the internet. You can also work with a therapist or properly trained coach.

Bibliography

Goldfried, M. R., & Davison, G. C. (1994). Relaxation training. In *Clinical behavior therapy* (Exp. ed., Ch. 5, pp. 81–111). John Wiley & Sons.

Craske, M. G., Barlow, D. H., & O'Leary, T. A. (1992). Direct worry control. In *Mastery of your anxiety and worry: Client workbook* (Ch. 8, p. 92). Harcourt Brace & Company.

Ma, X., Yue, Z. Q., Gong, Z.-Q., Zhang, H., Duan, N.-Y., Shi, Y.-T., Wei, G.-X., & Li, Y.-F. (2017). The effect of diaphragmatic breathing on attention, negative affect and stress in healthy adults. *Frontiers in Psychology*, *8*, 874. https://doi.org/10. 3389/fpsyg.2017.00874

Najavits, L. M. (2002). *Seeking safety: A treatment manual for PTSD and substance abuse*. New York: Guilford Press.

Röttger, S., Theobald, D. A., Abendroth, J., & Jacobsen, T. (2021). The effectiveness of combat tactical breathing as compared with prolonged exhalation. *Applied Psychophysiology and Biofeedback*, *46*(1), 19–28. https://doi.org/10.1007/s10484 -020-09485-w

Appendix II: Setting Boundaries

As an associate, you can do any of the following to set boundaries and protect your time (but leadership support is needed for any one of these strategies to be truly effective):

- Set aside time in your calendar to work on specific projects.
- Block off time for meetings, professional development events, or other engagements.
- Silence your devices so you are unavailable for an hour or two while working on a document or in a meeting or workshop.
- Set aside times to check email and messages, depending on your workflow and the importance of email to your immediate tasks. It could be every two hours, or two to three times a day.
- Set expectations at the outset, by letting clients and supervisors know when they can expect a response from you, or a completed work product.
- Ask partners and supervisors assigning competing projects to clarify which assignment is top priority, and share their expectations around prioritization of other assignments.
- If you are really swamped, you can say "no," recognizing the risks that may be involved depending on levels of leadership support. It may also be time to have a conversation with supervisors or a senior ally about workload expectations and supports.
- One approach to managing multiple competing assignments and deadlines is to tell the assigning partner, "I am working on a pressing assignment for Partner(s) X and will not be able to get to this before next week. If you need it sooner, please talk with Partner(s) X, so I know where to focus my time."

SUPPORT MATERIAL

Appendix III: Lawyer Well-Being
Pledge Commitment Template

In recognition of the value and importance of promoting well-being and a healthy workplace, in the coming year (beginning date—end date), _____, Firm/Organization _____ will make every effort to:

1. Actively and consistently promote and encourage self-care and help-seeking as core values of our organization.
2. Implement flexible work-schedule policies, including remote-work options.
3. Ensure access to addiction and mental health treatment by providing quality mental health insurance coverage and/or EAP resources.
4. Foster and role model psychologically safe and healthy workplace interactions among colleagues.
5. Implement workplace electronic communication policies, limiting the need to respond to electronic communications and phone calls to certain hours of the day, with limited exceptions.
6. Strongly encourage vacation time off (i.e., through role-modeling by firm leaders, vacation/paid time off requirements, or an organization-wide end-of-year shutdown).
7. Invite and encourage attorneys and staff to make suggestions for initiatives and organizational policies which promote well-being and a healthy work environment.
8. Provide educational opportunities to attorneys and staff on topics related to well-being, mental health, and substance use disorders.
9. Require attendance at ___ percentage of organization-wide well-being related educational programs and events.
10. Offer an in-house yoga class, a meditation room, and/or a lactation room.

Please describe two to three objectives (or more) that your firm will focus on in the coming year to enhance the goals outlined by this framework.

1. _____
   _____
   _____
   _____
   _____
   _____
   _____

2. _____
   _____
   _____
   _____
   _____
   _____
   _____

3. _____
   _____
   _____
   _____
   _____
   _____
   _____

Name: _____

Signature: _____

Title: _____

Date: _____

192

SUPPORT MATERIAL

Well-Being Pledge Progress Form Template

In recognition of the value and importance of promoting well-being and a healthy workplace, in the coming year (beginning date— end date), _____, *Firm/Organization* _____ *will make every effort to:*

   OR

In the past year (beginning date—end date), _____ *has successfully:*

1. Actively and consistently promote and encourage self-care and help-seeking as core values of our organization.

0	1	2	3	4	5	6	7	8	9	10
Not at all										To the greatest extent

2. Implement flexible work-schedule policies, including remote-work options.

0	1	2	3	4	5	6	7	8	9	10
Not at all										To the greatest extent

3. Ensure access to addiction and mental health treatment by providing quality mental health insurance coverage and/or EAP resources.

0	1	2	3	4	5	6	7	8	9	10
Not at all										To the greatest extent

4. Foster and role model psychologically safe and healthy workplace inter-actions among colleagues.

0	1	2	3	4	5	6	7	8	9	10
Not at all										To the greatest extent

5. Implement workplace electronic communication policies, limiting the need to respond to electronic communications and phone calls to certain hours of the day, with limited exceptions.

0	1	2	3	4	5	6	7	8	9	10
Not at all										To the greatest extent

6. Strongly encourage vacation time off (i.e., through role-modeling by firm leaders, vacation/paid time off requirements, or an organization-wide end-of-year shutdown).

0	1	2	3	4	5	6	7	8	9	10
Not at all										To the greatest extent

7. Invite and encourage attorneys and staff to make suggestions for initia-tives and organizational policies which promote well-being and a healthy work environment.

0	1	2	3	4	5	6	7	8	9	10
Not at all										To the greatest extent

8. Provide educational opportunities to attorneys and staff on topics related to well-being, mental health, and substance use disorders.

0	1	2	3	4	5	6	7	8	9	10
Not at all										To the greatest extent

9. Require attendance at ___ percentage of organization-wide well-being related educational programs and events.

0	1	2	3	4	5	6	7	8	9	10
Not at all										To the greatest extent

10. Provide free, in-house resources, such as (but not limited to) a weekly 30-minute yoga class, a meditation room, or a lactation room.

0	1	2	3	4	5	6	7	8	9	10
Not at all										To the greatest extent

Please describe any barriers to meeting the objectives that your firm focused on in the past year to enhance the goals outlined by this framework, or any other relevant information. Feel free to use as much space as necessary, including adding a new page(s).

1. _____

_____

_____

_____

_____

_____

_____

195

2. _____
   _____
   _____
   _____
   _____
   _____
   _____
   _____

3. _____
   _____
   _____
   _____
   _____
   _____
   _____
   _____

Name: _____

Signature: _____

Title: _____

Date: _____

Appendix IV: Office Challenge Template

Create a friendly competitive "challenge," with a "prize" for the winner at the end of the month.

Participants are asked to make a commitment by picking a few of the following healthy habits to engage in daily, and recording progress made. Participants are instructed to challenge themselves, but also commit to what they think is reasonably achievable. This list is not exclusive, so feel free to add other health-promoting behaviors. At the end of the month, consider extending the challenge for another month (or longer), suggesting participants build upon those behaviors which have been mastered.

1. Get at least 20 minutes of exercise each day.
2. Drink several glasses of water each day.
3. Get at least seven hours of sleep at night.
4. Check the news only twice a day.
5. Turn off your mobile phone for 15 minutes.
6. Do something for someone else.
7. Thank someone else for something they did that made things easier or made your day brighter.
8. Engage in a restorative healthy activity.
9. Replace that second cup of coffee with decaf, tea, or water.
10. Substitute a soothing cup of decaf tea for that glass of wine or cocktail.
11. Reach for a healthy raw food snack instead of processed foods.
12. Practice compassion, for yourself and others. Recognize others are carrying burdens you cannot see and let the little things go.

	Monday	Tuesday	Wednesday	Thursday	Friday	Saturday	Sunday
Exercise 20 mins							
Water (8 glasses)							
Sleep 7+ hours							
News 2× max							
Phone off							
Altruism							
Gratitude							
Healthy "escape"							
Limit coffee							
Limit alcohol							
Healthy snack							
Compassion							

INDEX

Note: Page numbers in **bold**, *italics* and followed by 'n' refer to tables, figures and notes

For Product Safety Concerns and Information please contact our EU
representative GPSR@taylorandfrancis.com
Taylor & Francis Verlag GmbH, Kaufingerstraße 24, 80331 München, Germany

www.ingramcontent.com/pod-product-compliance
Lightning Source LLC
Chambersburg PA
CBHW070326270326
41926CB00017B/3779

9 781032 258959